MW01104678

Strategies in Academic Discourse

Studies in Corpus Linguistics

SCL focuses on the use of corpora throughout language study, the development of a quantitative approach to linguistics, the design and use of new tools for processing language texts, and the theoretical implications of a data-rich discipline.

Volume 19

Strategies in Academic Discourse
Edited by Elena Tognini-Bonelli and Gabriella Del Lungo Camiciotti

Strategies in Academic Discourse

Edited by

Elena Tognini-Bonelli
University of Siena

Gabriella Del Lungo Camiciotti
University of Florence

John Benjamins Publishing Company
Amsterdam/Philadelphia

™ The paper used in this publication meets the minimum requirements
of American National Standard for Information Sciences – Permanence
of Paper for Printed Library Materials, ANSI z39.48-1984.

Cover illustration from original painting *Random Order*
by Lorenzo Pezzatini, Florence, 1996.

Library of Congress Cataloging-in-Publication Data

Strategies in Academic Discourse / edited by Elena Tognini-Bonelli and
    Gabriella Del Lungo Camiciotti.
        p.   cm. (Studies in Corpus Linguistics, ISSN 1388–0373 ; v. 19)
    Includes bibliographical references and indexes.
        1. Discourse analysis--Congresses. 2. Academic writing--Congresses.

    P302.18.S77 2005
401/.41--dc22   2005055473
ISBN 90 272 2290 8 (Hb; alk. paper)

John Benjamins Publishing Co. · P.O. Box 36224 · 1020 ME Amsterdam · The Netherlands
John Benjamins North America · P.O. Box 27519 · Philadelphia PA 19118-0519 · USA

Table of contents

Introduction

Elena Tognini Bonelli
University of Siena

The papers in this volume were selected from the contributions made at a small but remarkably productive conference in June 2003 at the Certosa di Pontignano, Siena. The conference, hosted by the organising committee of a research project co-financed by the Italian Ministry and a consortium of Italian Universities (Modena, Florence, Siena and Lecce), had as its topic "Evaluation in Academic Discourse". Two books were commissioned after the conference, allowing the editors to focus on particular aspects of evaluation in text. The first, published by Peter Lang (Del Lungo & Tognini Bonelli 2004), features papers specifically focusing on evaluation.

This second volume focuses on theoretical and descriptive issues and techniques in the study of text and discourse. The thirteen papers interlock with each other along several dimensions, and instead of the volume being divided into several sections, the papers are arranged so as to lead from one to another coherently, and to emphasise the common ground which they share. We will first draw attention to the various links among them, and then introduce each of them in the sequence in which they appear in the volume.

Quite a few papers describe academic language, concentrating on biology (Okamura), literature (Suarez), philosophy (Poudat and Loiseau), economics (Oakey) and agriculture (Thompson); some even turn language study in on itself and use linguistics texts as their data (Römer, Freddi and, partly, Poudat and Loiseau focus on linguistics, and Hunston on applied linguistics). Bamford alone draws our attention to spoken language corpora, using lectures from the Ann Arbor corpus of academic English (MICASE).

More general corpora are used by Aijmer and Ädel, both also using corpora of Swedish and English. Aijmer uses a parallel corpus of fiction and non-fiction, while Ädel compares native speakers with Swedish learners. These are two of the contrastive studies; the others are Okamura, who compares the usage of Japanese and English writers of English, Römer, who considers gender differences, and Poudat and Loiseau, who compare academic texts in linguistics and philosophy.

The texts studied by Hunston, Poudat and Loiseau, Oakey and Okamura are collections of published research papers, while Thompson has gathered a number of unpublished theses. Suarez and Römer found academic book reviews a rich source of evaluative language; Freddi opted for textbooks and Ädel for student essays.

Two papers deal with general matters and do not relate to any particular body of text material; Teubert places evaluation in the context of the social meaning of text, and Sinclair contributes a short note on the concept of "meta-" in language description.

We have chosen to order the papers according to the aspects of language that they principally discuss. We begin with papers concerning the author, the reader and the language community, starting with Hunston, who describes some ways in which academic writers express conflict and consensus. Hunston makes lively use of some of the published exchanges in recent years in *Applied Linguistics*, where scholars explicitly set out to argue with one another. Thirteen selected papers comprise her 'conflict corpus', which is compared with a larger corpus of academic articles, all from the journal *Applied Linguistics*. The papers which "construe conflict" rather than reporting it set up specific value systems and use attribution to manage the conflict. Hunston also points out that the same papers construe consensus, using similar strategies.

Bamford also studies the way in which academics express their position in argumentation, and looks at expressions of certainty and uncertainty in lectures. She distinguishes between when a speaker makes an objective prediction on the basis of scientific evidence, and when they use a more subjective assessment. Bamford selects two words with evaluative significance, the adjective *likely* and the adverb *probably*, and shows, using the MICASE corpus, that *likely* expresses likelihood when the prevailing semantic prosody is objective and scientific, while *probably* expresses a similar meaning in more interactive discourse, where there are largely subjective semantic prosodies.

Authorial stance is the focus of Thompson's paper, but his concern is with the distinction between averral and attribution – determining who is assigned responsibility for a piece of information or a point of view. He stresses that among the key skills in academic writing are the establishment of authorial control and the maintenance of a steady position; these require the skilful management of averral and attribution. An academic paper has its authority enhanced by rhetorical strategies such as the inclusion of intertextual references that demonstrate command of the field in which they work.

After Thompson we turn to Poudat and Loiseau, who study the styles of authorial presence in linguistic and philosophical writings, and Okamura, who is interested in Japanese writers of academic papers in English and the problems they encounter in presenting their findings effectively.

Both Poudat/Loiseau and Okamura select particular words and phrases to concentrate on. Poudat/Loiseau confine themselves to the personal pronouns in French which are regularly used to indicate the first person, while Okamura starts with the *we* pronoun and links it to the kind of verbs that are used by writers from different language backgrounds.

Poudat and Loiseau contrast academic texts in philosophy and linguistics, showing that philosophical papers prefer a universalist stance, while linguistic papers choose less formal styles of self-reference, giving a personal or neutral flavour to the writing. This paper shows how a sensitive analysis of a few pronominal choices can reveal genre differences that would be difficult to explain without the evidence.

Okamura's study also focuses on the pronouns that authors use for themselves, and reveals some of the subtlety of academic writing. It contrasts the pragmatic function of the use of *we* in native English and Japanese academic authors. The more flexibile tactical deployment shown by the native speakers is pointed out in a study of the verbs used with the pronoun.

Two other papers also nominate particular words and phrases as the objects of their study. Aijmer studies pragmatic markers in English and Swedish, and Römer details the way in which book reviewers express negative evaluations of their chosen texts.

Aijmer presents the various uses of *really* in modern English, using its various translations derived from a bidirectional parallel Swedish/English corpus. Although the meanings are not always tidily distinct, the intuitions of the translators make a satisfying tripartite classification into a 'reality' use, a hedging use and a conclusion from a number of alternatives.

Römer's study considers the ways in which academic book reviewers make negative evaluations, and in particular she examines whether there are systematic differences between male and female reviewers. She focuses on their use of adjectives such as *surprising* and *disappointing*, and concludes that our stereotypes of language and gender relations are not entirely reliable. Her corpus of book reviews in linguistics shows how a scholar can acquire a very useful specialised corpus nowadays without vast expenditure of time or money.

Suarez, like Römer, uses a personally-assembled corpus of academic book reviews. She considers the reviews *in toto* and approaches the question of how evaluation is related to the structure of the review. Working with a Move Analysis set up by Motta-Roth, she analyses a collection of academic papers on literature, half of which are in Spanish and half in English. Her findings show considerable consistency in the two languages with respect to the occurrence and the expression of evaluations, but with some rather different attitudes from the underlying cultures.

Also concerned with the overall structure of texts and the role of evaluation within them is Freddi, who uses a quantitative approach to show the way in which expressions of evaluation function as argumentative strategy. Concentrating on the introductory chapters of ten textbooks of linguistics – using, like Suarez and Römer, material which is fairly accessible – she posits a 'lexicogrammar of argumentation' and investigates a broad range of phenomena.

On a slightly more specialised note than Freddi, Ädel argues for a distinction between evaluation and metadiscourse, using a comparable corpus of student essays in English and Swedish. While 'evaluation' is often used as a cover term for a wide variety of discourse moves, 'metadiscourse' specifically foregrounds relations between the writer and the target reader; Ädel suggests that 'evaluation' could be kept for the relations between the participants and the subject-matter.

Sinclair's contribution is not a full paper, but a terminological note which refers to metadiscourse and so is placed at this point. He argues that discourse is linear, not only in the obvious, physical sense but also structurally; the idea that speakers and writers move 'up' to another level in order to comment on the discourse itself is, for Sinclair, a misleading notion – the discourse cannot go 'up', it can only go on. He does not question the existence or the importance of the phenomena that have attracted the term "*metadiscourse*", but he warns that using inappropriate terminology may divert a researcher's attention away from valuable observations.

Oakey's paper falls firmly into a 'meta' category because he studies the use of the word *evaluation* rather than the descriptive category of evaluation. From his experience with students of economics, Oakey picks out the word to show that the atomistic approach to meaning taken by vocabulary researchers can obscure some lexico-grammatical aspects of academic discourse, making the understanding of the texts more problematic than is strictly necessary. For Oakey the difficulties are more with unfamiliar combinations of familiar words than just "difficult words". The pedagogical implications of the study are that phraseological information needs presenting alongside more traditional vocabulary items.

Finally, Teubert rounds off this rich collection with a wide-ranging argument about the contrasts between language as a mental phenomenon and language as a social phenomenon. He argues that corpus linguistics cannot investigate the relations between speakers and hearers, but only relations between texts; there is no privileged access to discourse-external reality. The role of corpus study should be to analyse intertextual features, attribution etc., which several of the papers have shown leads to penetrating results.

References

Del Lungo Camiciotti, G. & Tognini Bonelli, E. (Eds). (2004). *Academic discourse – New insights into evaluation*. Bern: Peter Lang.

Conflict and consensus

Construing opposition in Applied Linguistics

Susan Hunston
University of Birmingham, U.K.

This paper discusses what is argued to be a distinct genre of academic discourse: the 'conflict article', where a writer explicitly opposes a named other writer or paper. Unlike other academic research articles, the writers of such articles often attack individuals rather than outcomes of research. The paper focuses on the ways that attribution is carried out in conflict articles, arguing that some phraseologies are specific to these articles and that they are implicitly insulting, and that in general ways of attributing are selected which prioritise interpretation of the reported utterances. It is also suggested that where conflict is realised, consensus is realised also, and that some distinctive features of the conflict articles have a consensual function. The paper raises issues of using corpus techniques to investigate discourse features such as evaluation.

Introduction

Most academic research articles construe opposition with other researchers, even if only in passing. To test and possibly refute the theories of others is one of the accepted justifications for writing such an article. Such opposition is normally construed within the constraints of research article conventions, including principles of politeness (e.g. Myers 1989). For example, where the article reports empirical research, the findings of the research may be presented as opposing other findings or theories, as in examples (1) and (2) (quoted from Hunston 1993: 121):

(1) *The present **results** can also be used to address Piaget's **claims**. Piaget **argued** that children under the age of seven years, especially between the ages of three and five years, find it difficult to accommodate the perspectives of their listeners. The **results** of the present study, however, **indicate** that children between*

> the ages of 3 and 4 years do adapt to differences in listener status and say
> 'thank you' more frequently to adults than to peers.   [emphasis added]

(2) Greif and Gleason also **found** that preschool-aged boys and girls **were** equally
     likely to say 'thank you' spontaneously. The present **results indicate** that
     preschool-aged girls say 'thank you' spontaneously more frequently than boys.
                                                               [emphasis added]

In these examples, responsibility for the opposition is devolved to the *results*.
This is polite, in that it construes opposition between research outcomes as opposed to construing an argument between researchers, but it is also persuasive,
in that the argument is presented in a way that appears to be 'objective' rather
than personal. The argument is weighted in subtle ways (Hunston 1993), balancing speculative *claims* and *argument* against factual *results* and time-specific
results (*found... were*) against general truths (*indicate... say*).

There is, however, a type of research paper which obeys a very different set
of conventions. These articles declare their purpose to be specifically to counter
the opinions expressed in previously-published articles. They do not present
new research but engage in an argument that is more overt and personal than
that found in typical research articles. For convenience, I shall call these articles
'conflict articles'. They are identified as those whose titles and/or opening para-
graphs explicitly set themselves in opposition to a previously published paper
or papers, as in example (3).

(3) Title: A **Response** to Block's (1996) Paper 'Not so fast...'
     Block (1996) raises a number of issues related to the current state of af-
     fairs in SLA... **This response** will focus purely on his treatment of 'accepted
     findings'...

Conflict articles are by definition responses to what I will call initiating articles: initiation and response comprise a 'conflict exchange'. Any article might
retrospectively be cast as the initial element in a conflict exchange, although
articles so identified do themselves often take a contentious stance and might
be said to be deliberately controversial. Unlike exchanges in spoken dialogue,
the conflict exchange has no defined end; any number of articles may respond
to each other, though in practice the maximum number of moves seems to be
three. There may, however, be two (or more) responding moves, produced by
different writers. A recent conflict exchange in *Applied Linguistics*, for example, consisted of an initiating paper (by Widdowson), independent responses
by de Beaugrande and by Stubbs, and separate responses to each of those by
Widdowson. This is summarised in Table 1.

Table 1.

I		WIDDOWSON	
R	DE BEAUGRANDE		STUBBS
R	WIDDOWSON		WIDDOWSON

The tone of conflict articles varies from the fairly measured to the outright antagonistic. Example (4) is a short illustration of the more extreme kind.

(4) *We are puzzled by Block's statement that being scientific 'will come' with rigor. Evidently the field has not yet met Block's criteria for rigor, although we are at a loss to imagine what these criteria are, or what sort of research he would characterize as 'quality research'. This puzzlement turns to disbelief when he tells us (74) that controlling for extraneous variables in SLA research is 'probably not even desirable'. Block acknowledges that this is 'a major philosophical difference between my stance and that of many authors' (74); for 'many', we would substitute 'all rational'. Do we actually need to point out the disastrous consequences of Block's 'stance' for SLA, or indeed for any intellectual inquiry?*
     Yes, it seems we do; after all, Block's paper got past three referees and into a journal. So let us apologize to those many readers who will feel that their intelligence is being insulted, and consider a couple of examples.

There are a number of points to be made about this extract. Firstly, it self-evidently construes, rather than reports, conflict. We are left in no doubt that we are expected to believe Block to be wrong and the writers to be right. At the same time, however, it construes consensus between writer and reader, especially those 'intelligent' readers who might regard what the writers say as obvious. Secondly, there are a large number of negatives, in this extract largely lexical (*we are at a loss to imagine*), though grammatical negatives are also frequent in this type of article (e.g. *Beaugrande does not demonstrate*). A list of keywords[1] includes *not, no, any, cannot, fails, anything, nothing, never.* Thirdly, interaction with the reader is explicit and includes a 'rhetorical' question (*Do we actually need to point out...?*) as well as overt reference to the writers themselves (*we, us*) and their feelings (AFFECT in Martin and White's model, see Martin 2000; Martin & White 2005), and a contrastive adverb (*actually*). These features combine to make the register both explicitly interactive and relatively informal.

Finally, like the other articles of this type, this extract is 'about' what other writers, in this case Block, have said and done. There are many statements attributed to other writers and many words relating to the process of research and argumentation. Of the top 100 keywords, over 30 are what might be called metalanguage: names of subjects such as *SLA* or *critical discourse analysis*, general research nouns such as *theory, evidence, argument* and *interpretation*, and words relating to more specific research activity such as *relativism* or *empirical*. Also among the keywords are verbs of attribution such as *cite, claim, criticise, say, argue, wonder, doubt, reject* and *accuse*.

In this paper, I shall examine aspects of both conflict and consensus in 13 articles from *Applied Linguistics*, compared with a 2 million-word corpus of general applied linguistics articles from a range of journals. I will refer to these two corpora below as the 'conflict corpus' and the 'research corpus' respectively.[2] The paper deals mainly with aspects of evaluation and of attribution in the articles using a mixture of methodologies, including commentary on individual text extracts and interpretation of evidence derived from the corpora, with *Wordsmith Tools* (Scott 1999) being used as the corpus investigation software. Evidence is taken from wordlists, concordance lines and lists of keywords.

Value in conflict articles

Evaluation both exploits and construes a value system belonging to the relevant community; members of the community recognise that certain qualities have a positive value while others have a negative one. This knowledge may not be immediately available to people outside the community, but the texts belonging to the community will contain linguistic cues to valuation, so that the value system of the community may be inferred from its texts, even by a non-member. Indeed it is through these linguistic cues that the value system of the community is maintained.

'Value' itself is a term used by Hunston (1989, 1993, 2000) to refer to that aspect of evaluation in which the values 'good' and 'bad' are ascribed to an entity. Value is assigned by a text, either explicitly ('inscribed' in Martin and White's terms) or by indicating the grounds upon which value may be assigned ('evoked' in Martin and White's terms). What counts as good or bad depends on the bases for value-assignment available to a given discourse community. Martin and White (2005) systematise these bases as resources divided broadly into JUDGEMENT (which evaluates the actions of a rational being) and APPRECIATION (which evaluates the qualities of 'things'). In this paper as in earlier work, however, I treat the bases as discourse-specific (or corpus-specific) rather than as language-specific.

Table 2.

Basis for value	Value	Example (grounds)
Clarity	Negative	Actually, just what is distinctive about Beaugrande's program remains something of a mystery. [W] Block's charge...is not at all clear. [G]
Understanding demonstrated	Negative	[Beaugrande concludes that] in my text 'the entire discipline gets subsumed under one dominant orthodoxy'. But I was not talking about the 'venerable traditions of research' that he refers to... [W] Why does Beaugrande not try to understand what I am trying to say... [W] ...it now appears necessary to go over some of the issues that have been so strangely and profoundly misunderstood. [G] Block...fails to understand the point of Kuhn's argument, and ... misrepresents Long's and Beretta's arguments. [G]
Competence in research and argument	Negative	...Beaugrande does not demonstrate what kind of analysis [his program] yields, [or] how it contributes to the interpreting of my discourse. [W] But such a scholarly procedure is very different from just taking peevish pot shots. [W] Having failed to provide any evidence to support his contention... [G] But Block does no digging at all, and no demonstrating. [G]
Reasonableness	Negative	But how many readers of this journal, I wonder, would recognize the Beaugrande characterization of applied linguistics as corresponding with what they do? [W] Block acknowledges that this is 'a major philosophical difference between my stance and that of many authors'; for 'many', we would substitute 'all rational'. [G]

Two of the conflict articles (Gregg et al. 1997 and Widdowson 2001b) have been examined for instances of value, and the bases for that value are identified in Table 2.

Although the same bases are used in 'ordinary' research articles, they are less frequently given negative value as they are in these articles. Arguments are more usually evaluated negatively by being shown not to fit with experimental results, or to be 'unreasonable' in that they do not accord with current thinking in a particular discipline (Hunston 1989, 1993). Even when negative value is accorded, it is more likely to be attached to the outcomes of research (APPRECIATION in Martin and White's terms) than to the researchers themselves (JUDGEMENT in Martin and White's terms).

Table 3.

[Widdowson says that...]	Beaugrande says that...	Widdowson says that...	formalist linguistics is good.
[Widdowson says that...]	Beaugrande says that...	Widdowson does not talk about...	linguists who did deal with such experience.
[Widdowson says that...]	Beaugrande gives		a roll call of distinguished names.
[Widdowson says that...]	Beaugrande says that...		Widdowson is wrong.
[Widdowson says that...]	Beaugrande says that...		if you accept any degree of abstraction ...then you are a formalist of the deepest dye.

Attribution in conflict articles

One set of intuitive observations about the conflict articles concerns attribution. There seems to be a large amount of attribution, which is not surprising, as the topic of these articles is 'what someone else has said'. The attribution is frequently multi-layered and writers seem to use a wide variety of methods of attributing, including those that involve interpretation and judgement, rather than 'straight' reporting. Example (5) is an illustration of these points:

(5) *Beaugrande inteprets [my comments] as an espousal of formalist linguistics of a Chomskyan kind and accuses me of ignoring work of linguists who did deal with such experience and provides a resounding roll call of distinguished names. But this is vain gesturing. My point is simply that the making of a linguistic statement at all must involve some degree of abstraction from particulars, some distancing from immediate experience. Beaugrande will have none of this: if you accept any degree of abstraction as a necessary condition for linguistic enquiry of any kind, then you are a formalist of the deepest dye.*

Table 3 is a representation of who says what in example (5) (with some paraphrasing).[3]

There are several ways in which attribution (in a rather broad sense) is done in example (5), namely:

a. *interpret* something *as* something (i.e. the **V n** *as* **n** pattern);
b. *an espousal of* something (i.e. the **N** *of* **n** pattern), attributing a belief to someone;
c. *accuse* someone *of* something (i.e. the **V n** *of* **n** pattern);

d. *provides* something (i.e. the **V n** pattern), that is, does a speech act;
e. *will have none of this*, attributing rejection of Widdowson's ideas to Beaugrande;
f. *if you accept any degree of abstraction*. . . imitation of Beaugrande's position.

There is little of what might be called direct reporting here (as in *Beaugrande says that*); rather, Beaugrande's words are summarised, interpreted and even parodied, sometimes in what Leech and Short (1981) might call narrative report of speech act and even free direct speech.

Although it is easy to exemplify such features, they are difficult to quantify. Put briefly, attribution cannot be identified and counted in a corpus automatically. If an argument is to be made for the uniqueness of conflict articles, however, some quantification is necessary. There are several pieces of evidence, other than observation of individual texts, that indicate that attribution is more

Table 4.

Verb	Research articles		Verb	Conflict articles		Diff.
	Frequency	Normalised		Frequency	Normalised	
(a)						
ARGUE	312	1.56	ARGUE	39	5.82	4.26+
SAY	238	1.19	SAY	28	4.17	2.98+
THINK	102	0.51	THINK	16	2.38	1.87+
CLAIM	134	0.67	CLAIM	17	2.53	1.86+
CONCLUDE	84	0.42	CONCLUDE	15	2.23	1.81+
ASSUME	98	0.49	ASSUME	10	1.49	1+
SUGGEST	592	2.96	SUGGEST	25	3.73	0.77+
BELIEVE	145	0.73	BELIEVE	9	1.34	0.61+
NOTE	260	1.30	NOTE	6	0.89	0.41−
FIND	265	1.32	FIND	7	1.04	0.28−
SHOW	443	2.22	SHOW	16	2.38	0.16+
(b)						
INDICATE	287	1.43	POINT OUT	19	2.83	n.a.
REVEAL	121	0.60	IMPLY	7	1.04	n.a.
FEEL	107	0.53	DEMONSTRATE	5	0.74	n.a.
REPORT	91	0.46	RECOGNIZE	5	0.74	n.a.

* The raw frequency for the most frequent report verbs followed by *that* is given for each corpus, followed by the normalised figure of the number of occurrences per 10,000 words. The final column shows the difference between the two normalised figures (+ means the lemma is more frequent in the conflict corpus, − means it is more frequent in the research corpus). Part (a) of the table comprises those words exhibiting the greatest difference between the corpora, in decreasing order; part (b) shows lemmas which occur in one corpus only.

Table 5.

Only in research articles	Only in conflict articles
INDICATE	POINT OUT
REVEAL	IMPLY
FEEL	DEMONSTRATE
REPORT	RECOGNIZE
	More in conflict articles (≥ 1)
	ARGUE (4.26)
	SAY (2.98)
	THNK (1.87)
	CLAIM (1.86)
	CONCLUDE (1.81)
	ASSUME (1)
About the same (< 1)	
SUGGEST	
SHOW	
BELIEVE	
FIND	
NOTE	

frequent in the conflict corpus than in the research corpus. As mentioned above, several report verbs occur in the keyword list drawn from a comparison of the two corpora. Some report verbs can be identified because they are followed by *that*-clauses. As is shown in Tables 4 and 5, of the most frequent 15 lemmas of such verbs in each corpus, most occur more frequently in the conflict corpus than in the research corpus.

Furthermore, it has been argued that the attributions in the conflict articles make greater use of report verbs which interpret and evaluate as well as report. Again, the keywords list bears this out, as it includes verbs such as *CRITICISE, ACCUSE* and *REJECT.* Table 5 also shows that, of the six verbs that are maximally different between the corpora, five are verbs of this type: *ARGUE, THINK, CLAIM, CONCLUDE* and *ASSUME.*

A corpus can, however, be used to validate qualitative as well as quantitative observations. The phrases *we are told that* and *someone tells us (that)* are used extensively (eight times) by Widdowson, though by no other writer in this corpus. The eight uses are shown as concordance lines in example (6).

(6)

```
these two opposed views. We are then told that one reality is carried by
re not assigned keyness.  Thus we are told that the lemma argue occurs 25
 first paragraph  of his paper we are told that the keyword uncertainty is
 applied, for which he has previously told us he sees no compelling motive
therwise. The 'functional grammar' he tells us 'merely assumes that lingui
, 21/1) by  analysing my text, and he tells us that he has a corpus progra
  contextually modified. And this, he tells us, is Halliday's position too
 The ideological stance is given', he tells us. So there is no question of
```

On an intuitive reading, the phrase in each case implies a negative judgement of the proposition indicated by the *that*-clause. This might be demonstrated by quoting some of the concordance examples at greater length (examples (7) and (8)).

(7) *Thus **we are told** that the lemma <u>argue</u> occurs 25 times, and <u>assume</u> 22 times in my text. So what? Does this make them keywords? We are not told.*

(8) *The 'functional grammar . .' **he tells us** 'merely assumes that linguistic usage and grammar can serve to represent the world where the co-text and context are appropriate'. ... Agreed. But the central difficulty, of course (as we have seen), is in deciding what is appropriate and what is not. And if functional grammar really does 'merely' assume this, then how, one wonders, is it different from any other?*

In the research corpus there are 85 instances of the phrases combined, but they mostly do not occur in the context of attribution to another researcher. Examples include *experience... had told us that* and *the teachers were told that* (describing part of a report of experimental procedure). There is one exception, quoted here as example (9), which, like the Widdowson examples, attributes information to a supposed authority and which, as in the Widdowson article, implies a criticism of that authority:

(9) *Not all scientific developments are an unalloyed good, and we should acknowledge the wisdom of developing a community of people skilled in critiquing them. In the area of animal reproduction, for example, **we are told that** recently a sheep was successfully cloned in the UK. It is already possible to clone horses and cows, whose reproductive cycles, as we saw, were a focus of the Year 11 agricultural science lesson. Is this a desirable development?*

This phrase, then, is unusual in an academic context and it at least potentially implies scepticism or disapproval. In addition, however, it introduces *we/us* the readers into the discourse, so neatly construing consensus as well as conflict. In a single phrase, Widdowson positions his readers in alliance with himself and against de Beaugrande.

As another similar example I shall investigate a rather more widespread attributing phrase: *seems to think*. *SEEM to* in the conflict corpus occurs 93 times, of which 29 are used in attribution, across 10 texts. The most frequent verbs following *seems to* are: *be saying* and *think*. Examination of each instance confirms that scorn is generally implied. The *seems to* conveys incredulity, paraphrasable as 'the evidence suggests that the writer holds this opinion, although given the stupidity of the opinion this is scarcely credible so we can only suggest that he *seems* to do so'. Examples (10) and (11) illustrate this.

(10)   *In point of fact, replication is not such a common or automatic procedure in the hard sciences as Block* **would seem to think**.

(11)   *My paper is centrally concerned with such a motive. Beaugrande may not think it compelling, but then why not? Where are his arguments? He* **seems to think** *that he is under no obligation to provide any. He makes his ex cathedra pronouncement and that's that.*

In the research corpus, in contrast, *SEEM* in the context of attribution is extremely rare. There are only 12 instances (from an overall frequency of *SEEM* of 913). Most are of the type 'Most researchers seem to agree/disagree that'. Only one is of the 'scornful' type (example (12)).

(12)   *Ivani and Camps seem to acknowledge the looseness of their taxonomy in such statements on their research participants' efforts. . .*

In summary, *SEEM* when used with a verbal or mental process is a particular kind of interpersonal modification that implies (a) an interpretation rather than a straight report and (b) disapproval of the reported thought-processes or research methodology. It is a strong criticism, rare in ordinary research articles but relatively frequent in the conflict articles. Again, this attributive phrase arguably construes consensus as well as conflict (though in the absence of a signal such as *we* this is more difficult to prove), as the reader is invited to share the writer's incredulity.

Finally, the corpus can be interrogated, albeit indirectly, for instances of the pattern **V n** *as* **n/-ing**. This pattern is chosen because it has been demonstrated (Hunston 2004) to be associated with interpretation and evaluation as part of the attribution process. The complement of the preposition *as* is an interpretation of someone's position rather than a (direct or indirect) report of it. In addition, many of the verbs used in this pattern, such as *dismiss*, can be shown to indicate that the reported speaker's ideas are mistaken, in texts which construe conflict. Example (13) illustrates this.

(13)   *Psychology is radically different from physics and neurophysiology. The natural sciences have no way of saying that individual people see the world
differently, that one person's actions differ from another's because they have
different political beliefs, personal priorities or cultural backgrounds. Questions about such human matters therefore cannot be asked or answered using
the vocabulary of natural science. This is why people committed to a scientific
world-view often ignore them, or **dismiss them as** woolly minded sentimen-
talities. . . .*
*Yet thinking of the mind as a computational system leaves room for the view
that our beliefs and values are psychologically crucial.*

This example construes a conflict between a psychological view of the mind
and one inspired by natural science. The views of natural scientists are paraphrased as 'Questions about such human matters . . . are woolly minded sen-
timentalities', a form of words which probably no natural scientist would
be happy to use publicly. The negative view of psychology is then rebutted.
Hunston (2004) demonstrates that such a pattern of evaluation is typically used
with the verb *DISMISS*.

It might therefore be expected that this pattern would occur more frequently in the conflict corpus than in the research corpus. This is indeed the
case, though perhaps not as definitively as might be expected. A calculation of
24 lemmas occurring with this pattern shows that the occurrences per 10,000
words are over 12 in the conflict corpus (12.8) and just over 10 in the research
corpus (10.02). Table 6 shows the twelve most frequent verbs in each corpus
with this pattern.

Table 6.

Conflict corpus	Research corpus
SEE	SEE
INTERPRET	VIEW
VIEW	DEFINE
DEFINE	REGARD
PRESENT	DESCRIBE
IDENTIFY	REFER
DESCRIBE	PERCEIVE
DISMISS	IDENTIFY
TAKE	PRESENT
EXPLAIN	INTERPRET
UNDERSTAND	CONSIDER
REFER	UNDERSTAND

The lists are similar except for the presence of *DISMISS, TAKE* and *EX-PLAIN* in the first list and not in the second. There is some evidence, though, that in the research corpus this pattern is often used to indicate a general consensus of interpretation, and is therefore used in the passive, whereas this is less frequent in the conflict corpus. For example, nearly half the instances of *interpret... as* in the research corpus (48%) are passive, whereas only a quarter of the instances in the conflict corpus (25%) are. Example (14) below gives an active example from the conflict corpus; example (15) gives a passive one from the research corpus.

(14) *I submit that what he actually does is to simply pick on whatever textual bits are 'appropriate' to his purpose, and thereby **interprets my discourse as** an unwarranted attack on these approaches to linguistic description per se, rather than an attempt to delimit what is distinctive...*

(15) *However, on viewing our data in the light of the criteria discussed, we decided that the continuum needed to be extended further to the "left" to include bodily movements that, while not intended to communicate, **are normally interpreted as** meaningful by other members of the culture and oriented to, where necessary, in order to coordinate joint activity.*

On the whole, then, although it is difficult to quantify patterns, there is some support for the contention that this pattern is more frequent in the conflict corpus, and that it is more frequently used in that corpus than in the research one in a form that construes disagreement.

Conclusion

I have argued here that a group of articles called 'conflict articles' have features which differentiate them from ordinary research articles. Two sets of features have been discussed in this paper. The conflict articles draw on, and make very visible, a specific value system, often criticising previous researchers rather than previous research in a way that is unusual in academic discourse. They use attribution in a distinctive way. Some of the attributive devices they use (such as *seems to think*) are peculiar to conflict articles and are subtly insulting to the cited person. Others (such as *dismiss... as*) are not specific to them, but there is some evidence that the reporting patterns and lexis they use are differently weighted in the two corpora in terms of frequency.

These articles, which construe conflict, also construe consensus. This is evident to a certain extent in some of the attribution patterns, especially the idiosyncratic *we are told that*. Other indicators of consensus construal, such as personal pronouns and the adverbs *indeed, presumably* and *surely* appear high on the list of keywords.

This study has raised the question as to how qualitative features of discourse, such as aspects of evaluation, may be investigated in a large-scale corpus. On the one hand, as Martin (2003) notes, features such as these cannot be reduced to simple word frequency. On the other hand, for an argument to be made that certain features are typical of a type of discourse, or that certain features are associated with a particular kind of meaning, quantitative data must be obtainable. The method of working in this paper has gone from text to corpus and back again. Observation of individual texts has led to the formation of hypotheses, which are then checked in the corpus as a whole. For example, it was noted that the evaluation of the writer is often carried out in clauses that are lexically or grammatically negative. This does not mean that every instance of a negative will indicate evaluation or that evaluation can be quantified by counting negatives. On the other hand, the presence of negative words (*not, fail* and so on) significantly more frequently in the conflict corpus than in the research corpus is an indication that evaluation is likely to be more frequent in the former than in the latter.

Notes

1. Keywords are identified using the Keywords program in *Wordsmith Tools* (Scott 1999).

2. I would like to thank the editors of *Applied Linguistics* for permission to store and use texts from the journal, and Nicholas Groom for assistance in compiling the corpora.

3. It is indicative of the complexity of the attribution that paraphrase is necessary in order to distinguish the layers.

References

Hunston, S. (1989). Evaluation in experimental research articles. Unpublished Ph.D. thesis, University Of Birmingham.

Hunston, S. (1993). Professional conflict: Disagreement in academic discourse. In M. Baker, G. Francis, & E. Tognini Bonelli (Eds.), *Text and Technology: In honour of John Sinclair* (pp. 115–134). Amsterdam & Philadelphia: John Benjamins.

Hunston, S. (2000). Evaluation and the planes of discourse: Status and value in persuasive texts. In Hunston & Thompson (Eds.), 176–206.

Hunston, S. (2004). It has rightly been pointed out: Attribution, consensus and conflict in academic discourse. In M. Bondi, L. Gavioli, & M. Silver (Eds.), *Academic Discourse: Genre and Small Corpora* (pp. 15–34). Rome: Officina Edizioni.

Hunston, S. & Thompson, G. (Eds.). (2000). *Evaluation in Text: Authorial stance and the construction of discourse*. Oxford: Oxford University Press.

Leech, G. N. & Short, M. H. (1981). *Style in fiction: A Linguistic Introduction to English Fictional Prose*. London: Longman.

Martin, J. R. (2000). Beyond exchange: APPRAISAL systems in English. In Hunston & Thompson (Eds.), 142–175.

Martin, J. R. (2003). Introduction. *Text, 23*, 171–181.

Martin, J. R. & White, P. (2005 forthcoming). *The Language of Evaluation: The APPRAISAL framework*. Basingstoke: Palgrave.

Myers, G. (1989). The pragmatics of politeness in scientific articles. *Applied Linguistics, 10*, 1–35.

Scott, M. (1999). *Wordsmith Tools*, version 3.0. Oxford: Oxford University Press.

The conflict corpus

Bialystok, E. (1990). The dangers of dichotomy: A reply to Hulstijn. *Applied Linguistics, 11*, 46–52.

Block, D. (1996). Not so fast! Some thoughts on theory culling, relativism, accepted findings, and the heart and soul of SLA. *Applied Linguistics, 17*, 63–83.

Chappelle, C. (1992). Dembedding 'Disembedded figures in the landscape': An appraisal of Griffiths and Sheen's 'Reappraisal of L2 research on field dependence/independence'. *Applied Linguistics, 13*, 375–384.

de Beaugrande, R. (2001). Interpreting the discourse of H. G. Widdowson: A corpus-based critical discourse analysis. *Applied Linguistics, 22*, 104–120.

Gregg, K., Long, M., Jordan, G., & Beretta, A. (1997). Rationality and its discontents in SLA. *Applied Linguistics, 18*, 538–558.

Patkowski, M. (1990). Age and accent in a second language: A reply to James Emil Flege. *Applied Linguistics, 11*, 73–89.

Prabhu, N. S. (1990). Comments on Alan Beretta's paper: 'Implementation of the Bangalore Project'. *Applied Linguistics, 11*, 338–340.

Sheen, R. (1993). A rebuttal to Chapelle's response to Griffiths and Sheen. *Applied Linguistics, 14*, 98–100.

Sheen, R. (1999). A response to Block's (1996) paper, 'Not so fast! Some thoughts on theory culling, relativism, accepted findings, and the heart and soul of SLA'. *Applied Linguistics, 20*, 368–377.

Stubbs, M. (2001). Texts, corpora, and the problems of interpretation: A response to Widdowson. *Applied Linguistics, 22*, 149–172.

Tarone, E. (1990). On variation in interlanguage: A response to Gregg. *Applied Linguistics, 11*, 392–400.

Widdowson, H. (2001a). Interpretations and correlations: A reply to Stubbs. *Applied Linguistics, 22*, 531–538.
Widdowson, H. (2001b). Scoring points by critical analysis: A reaction to Beaugrande. *Applied Linguistics, 22*, 266–272.

Subjective or objective evaluation?

Prediction in academic lectures

Julia Bamford
University of Rome 'La Sapienza'

This paper considers the way in which academics express their position in argumentation and looks at expressions of certainty and uncertainty in lectures. A distinction is made between when a speaker makes an objective prediction on the basis of scientific evidence, and when they use a more subjective assessment. Two words with evaluative significance are selected, the adjective *likely* and the adverb *probably*, and investigated using the MICASE corpus. The analysis shows that *likely* expresses likelihood when the prevailing semantic prosody is objective and scientific, while *probably* expresses a similar meaning in more interactive discourse, where there are largely subjective semantic prosodies.

Introduction

There has been a surge of interest over the past few years in how speakers and writers convey their attitude towards the propositional content of their utterances and texts. Although those who have studied the phenomenon do not all use the same terminology – evaluation (Hunston & Thompson 2000), affect (Martin 2000), evidentiality (Chafe & Nichols 1986), hedging (Hyland 1996), epistemic modality (Nuyts 2000) and stance (Conrad & Biber 2000) – they all stress its fundamental role in various textual, interactive and experiential aspects of discourse. While many of these studies have examined evaluation in written texts emphasising subjectivity and opinion, in this paper I will look at spoken discourse and examine both objective and subjective evaluation. Evaluation in academic discourse is commonly thought to be "scientific" and "objective", although these notions have been challenged by sociologists of science (e.g. Gilbert & Mulkay 1984); consequently it is interesting to see how evaluation is achieved in lectures and if and how both subjective and objective evaluation is marked.

Conrad & Biber (2000:57) in their study of evaluation as 'stance' see this as being classified into three main types:

1. epistemic stance, commenting on the certainty (or doubt), reliability, or limitations of a proposition, including comments on the source of information;
2. attitudinal stance, conveying the speaker's attitudes, feelings or value judgements;
3. style stance, describing the manner in which the information is being presented.

In this paper I will be looking at the first of these and try to examine the interplay in lectures in scientific subjects between subjective and objective evaluation or how the lecturer comments on the degree of certainty of his propositions. The lectures examined in this paper are in disciplines which privilege the scientific method, thus making the relation between subjectivity and objectivity of particular significance in the analysis.

Academic lectures

Academic lectures have often been cited in the literature on oral/written differences as an oral genre with many of the characteristics of written texts. However, more recent research shows that lectures have many of the characteristics typical of conversation (Swales & Malczewski 2001) and provide evidence of wide variation following academic disciplines (Simpson 2001). It seems therefore, that empirical evidence and particularly corpus evidence indicates a much more complex and multi-faceted situation as regards oral academic discourse than was once supposed.

The availability of the Michigan Corpus of Academic Spoken English (MICASE) (Simpson et al. 1999) has permitted a wide range of academic disciplines in various spoken genres to be examined. This corpus is in continual expansion and has by now almost reached the two million-word stage; furthermore it has the advantage of allowing the user to select the type of academic spoken language to be analysed. The instances analysed in this paper are all lectures (as opposed to seminars, tutorials, office hours, etc.). The lectures were audio recorded at the University of Michigan and include a wide variety of academic disciplines in the arts, sciences, social sciences and humanities. For comparative purposes I have also drawn extensively on the work of Leech et al. (2001) who use the entire BNC as their reference corpus.

As mentioned above, evaluation, in particular that aspect regarding the likelihood of a state of affairs, has also been discussed under the heading of epistemic modality. For Nuyts (2000: 21–22), epistemic modality "concerns an estimation of the likelihood that (some aspect of) a certain state of affairs is/has been/will be true (or false) in the context of the possible world under consideration". Nuyts (2001) following Lyons (1977) has distinguished between subjective and objective epistemic modality (although he prefers the term 'intersubjectivity' for the latter). In this paper I will be looking at both of these categories and will distinguish between when the speaker speaks about the likelihood of a state of affairs, i.e. makes an objective prediction on the basis of scientific evidence, often generally accepted by the particular discourse community to which he belongs, and when he uses a predictive lexical item but with a much vaguer, interactive connotation that can be termed subjective. I will look in particular at the behaviour of two evaluative items, the adjective *likely* and the adverb *probably* and show how, while in the MICASE the former prefers an objective semantic prosody, the second has a more subjective semantic prosody.

Lecturers seem to distinguish between when they make a prediction which is objective, based on solid impartial evidence, and when they talk about likelihood interactively in a more subjective frame. Although the evidence is hardly ever rendered explicit in lectures, it is clear that it has been defined and subjected to empirical tests by the discourse community. This is paralleled by the contrast between the research article and the textbook (Hyland 2000): in the former, all but the most widely accepted evidence is attributed to a specific source, for example, through citation, while in textbooks it is presented as a fact. Lectures which have much in common with textbooks, in particular their common pedagogic purpose, tend to be unspecific about the evidence which supports predictions introduced by *likely*, except perhaps the evidence which directly relates to the topic.

Frequencies

As an indication of the relative frequencies of evaluative words in academic lectures I looked at selected evaluative adverbs and adjectives or epistemic modal adverbs and adjectives expressing varying degrees of certainty, namely *likely, probable, probably, certain, certainly, possible, possibly*. Using Leech et al.'s (2001)

Table 1. Occurrences per 1 million words in the BNC

word	spoken component	written component
likely	91	244
probable*	12	
probably	585	237
certainly	299	173
certain	169	226
possible	147	364
possibly*	73	

* This figure is for the whole corpus, i.e. both spoken and written components (adapted from Leech et al. 2001).

Table 2. Occurrences in MICASE lectures (611,275 words)

	raw numbers	normalised to 1 million
likely	140	229
probable	8	13
probably	341	558
certainly	115	188
certain	200	327
possible	132	216
possibly	22	36

computations of word frequencies in the spoken and written components of the BNC as a rough comparison to give an idea of the behaviour of these words in general discourse, I calculated the same frequencies for lectures in the much smaller MICASE corpus. In order to make the MICASE lecture corpus comparable to the BNC word frequencies which are expressed per one million words, the raw numbers were normalised to one million words.

As can be seen from Tables 1 and 2, there are some similarities and some differences in the relative frequencies of words evaluating a prediction. These involve similarities and differences between the MICASE and the BNC spoken component i.e. between a very small specialised corpus and a large general corpus, and also between these and the written component of the BNC. *Likely* shows, perhaps, the most marked difference since it is more than twice as frequent in the written component of the BNC as compared to the spoken, while in the MICASE it is almost as frequent as in the written part of the BNC. It is difficult to say anything significant about *probable* since Leech et al. only looked in detail at those words with more than 100 instances per million words; however we can see that in the MICASE it is already more frequent than in the written and spoken BNC combined. *Probably* on the other hand mirrors the spoken component of the BNC, while *certainly* is more common in the spoken part of the BNC, and *certain* more frequent in MICASE than in either the spoken or written BNC. *Possible* is used more frequently in MICASE than in the spoken BNC, but less than the written. As regards *possibly,* due to its low frequency, it is not possible to make a significant comparison since Leech at al. do not distinguish between its spoken and written occurrences.

Although for reasons of space this paper will concentrate exclusively on two of these evaluators – *likely* and *probably* – it should be mentioned that *probable,* while relatively infrequent, is always used in the MICASE corpus in a predictive sequence which is based on scientific evidence. In the following extract we can see that the speaker uses three different, but semantically related, evaluators of probability all expressing a scientifically tested evaluation.

```
you have to at least have the binding energy of the
electron. so, above the binding energy of electron
there's always some finite probability, you can have
photoelectric effect. it's more probable at lower
incident photon energies, but you have to be above the
binding energy of the atomic electron. it's more
likely in high atomic number materials, although it
does occur in low atomic                          (MICASE)
```

An examination of the corpus shows some evidence that the three evaluative words used in the extract – *probability, probable* and *likely* – express a cline of scientific objectivity with *probability* being more objective and *likely* less objective, but this claim needs more evidence before it can be asserted unequivocally. *Likely* and *probably,* while belonging to different grammatical classes, seem on the face of it to have semantic connections.[1] In fact the OED gives *probable* as a synonym of *likely* and, interestingly, as we shall see, *probable* and *probably* collocate in quite different semantic fields.

Apart from differences in relative frequencies of the evaluators chosen, the corpus analysis so far carried out also shows a marked difference in types of usage. There are two interesting aspects of these evaluators that seem worth exploring. Since the idea of degrees of certainty in scientific discourse is closely tied with the statistical notion of probability, which is a measurable phenomenon and thus considered to be objective, it is interesting to see if this 'statistical' semantic field is marked linguistically. To do this, simple explorations of the concordances of *likely* and *probably* were run and show quite marked and interesting differences in both collocation and patterning. The patterns which were observed, however, apply to a small specialised corpus, and thus any generalisations must refer to the specific genre of academic lectures. Obviously, since the corpus consists largely of lectures in disciplines which respect the norms of the scientific method, we must take into consideration the relation between statistical probability and the expression of degrees of certainty. While this statistical aspect is rarely rendered explicit in the corpus, it is obvious that it is implied in many of the propositions the speakers utter. This is illustrated in example (1) below where *likely* is chosen to indicate the statistical probability of an event taking place.

(1)   we assume randomized storage remember every point is
      equally likely to be selected, on the average where're
      you gonna go?

Likely

Likely in the corpus is in fact often, but not exclusively, used where a statistical probability is implied as the examples in Table 3 illustrate. The collocations show what I have hinted at above, that is, an 'objective' semantic prosody (Louw 1993). By this I extend the normal understanding of the term, which is usually taken to be either 'good', or 'bad' to include subjectivity and objectivity. Louw claims that words that are found in consistently negative contexts will take on a negative semantic prosody so much so that when they are used in a positive context they will be perceived as ironic. In the case of *likely*, as is evidenced in this corpus, academics tend to prefer using it when they talk about a predicted event whose degree of certainty or probability has been calculated statistically or at least estimated using objective criteria approved by the disciplinary community. In this context when a word is selected repeatedly it begins to take on an aura of meaning from the words that are found in its immediate environment and, as Sinclair (1996:87) states, semantic prosodies are "attitudinal and on the pragmatic side of the semantics-pragmatics continuum". Thus the marked tendency to use *likely* to express probability has given the word this objective aura. *Likely* seems to carry neither a particularly positive nor negative semantic prosody but an objective one in lectures, because its habitual collocates are scientifically proven facts. One of the advantages of using a small specialised corpus is that it enables us to point out how, within a genre, the lexico-grammar may be used in different ways or at least in one particular way to the exclusion of others, while a more general corpus will show a wider variety of usages. In the case of *likely*, which is a common word in general

Table 3. Concordance *likely*

```
         and sell them commercially, we're likely to, have available to
       the category of responses it's likely to be and therefore, know what
                  grow, and it's very likely that we'll have at
            of propaganda, um, the more likely they are to realize
             this kind of weather, is likely to be, hard, on
       example. where are those cells likely to metastasize to? well
   hard, on plants. it's, especially likely to be hard on
              well the thing is, how likely is it, suppose France
      are, are sexist boys, less likely to have friends? and
            that will make it, more likely that we get, away
   especially a cold winter, that's likely to have, a few
         population is not equally likely to mate with any
     interactions that the person is likely to be using the system for
       the incident photon the more likely the photoelectron is to
like with antibiotics, you're more likely to develop resistance i
```

Table 4. Concordance *likely to*

```
            trout. what temperatures are likely to kill a trout if a
              solid weeks, then you're likely to go crazy and you won't
       the category of responses it's likely to be and therefore, know what
something that interrupts metabolism, likely to have its greatest effect, when
       the uh, pollution effects are likely to be realized, so that um
           abstract noun. what am i likely to have based on what the
           it's abstract, it's not likely to be plural so, okay, good
              are they more likely to take steps if the press
          is yes they would be likely to retire earlier. but of course
   sense that desperate is it likely to be giving ten percent wage
   subsidy, this year, are they likely to offer me the big bucks
           life at the firm are likely to be like if i stay
     uh you're much more than likely to uh get no answer from
sequence of sediments, what you're likely to find, as a package, is
   cancers, the first place they're likely to to get hung up, is
```

usage, the corpus shows how it is used by speakers in lectures almost exclusively to express an objective prediction.

One of the most common grammatical patterns in which *likely* is to be found in this corpus is [verb to be + likely + to]; in fact all but 7 instances in the corpus showed this pattern and of these 3 occurred with ellipsis of the verb *to be*. *Likely* is, in fact, often found in the pattern *to be + likely* not only in lectures but in discourse in general, both written and oral. In fact Quirk et al. (1985) call 'be likely to' a semi-auxiliary or verb idiom, i.e. in the same category as 'be bound to', 'be able to', 'be about to', already indicating its fixed nature. Table 4 shows a selection of the instances to be found in the corpus.

Table 5. Colligation *likely* + question

```
         trout. what temperatures are likely  to kill a trout if a
    example. where are those cells likely  to metastasize to? Well
        are, are sexist boys, less likely  to have friends? And
      sense that desperate is it likely  to be giving ten
       or her landscape? is that likely? mm. likely. so when
          i gonna assay? what is likely  to go wrong? can
        well the thing is, how likely  is it, suppose France
   um when is genetic drift likely? we have problems again
   vein, of a mouse, what's likely  to happen? well from
       what is it people are likely,  to be motivated to
```

One clear advantage of corpus data over intuitive data is that such collocates can be extensively documented. Collocates which occur as verbs to the right of the node *likely to* include:

> *be, have, go, take, get, give, find, stay, see, offer, carry, realize, select, happen, occur, affect, visit, develop, follow, fail, comply, benefit, believe, approve, assume, cure, survive, warm up, kill*

Lemmas of the verb *to be* are by far the most frequent, while the others follow in order of frequency.

Several typical discourse patterns surrounding *likely* can be extracted from the corpus, in addition to the pattern [verb to be + likely to + verb]. One of these is the colligational pattern showing a prevalence of questions around the node word *likely*. Lexical patterns and grammatical patterns often go together, in fact as Tognini Bonelli (2001) states, grammatical patterns are systematically accompanied by or realised in connection with a lexical constellation. Questions are one of the distinctive characteristics of lectures where they serve the purpose of creating an interaction with the listener, and at the same time signal the discourse importance of the answer (Bamford 2000). Table 5 illustrates some of the instances of question sequences surrounding *likely* showing the speaker's attempt to project the listener's attention towards the answer.

In addition, if one looks to the left of the node word, i.e. if one does vertical scans at different positions in the concordance line, *likely* is found in colligations with gradability. The presence of gradability is hardly surprising in academic discourse where this form of comparative evaluation constitutes a major scientific/argumentative tool. For example, events can be deemed more likely to happen than others, or people to do things rather than others, as can be seen from the concordances in Table 6. Comparisons create textual cohesion in discourse by linking two or more parts of the text. In this corpus *more,*

Table 6. Concordance *more likely*

```
            greed. these things are more likely on the basis of their
                        are they more likely to take steps if the
      men who read pornography are more likely to commit rape. she's making
              eating disorders are, more likely to occur in teens, particularly
       um limits. and so they're more likely to be, sites for early
       with antibiotics, you're more likely to develop resistance if you're
     so, children in poverty are more likely to uh, have favorable attitudes
    of the atomic electron. it's more likely in high atomic number materials
  of the incident photon the more likely in high atomic number materials
      target has to change, the more likely of course the target is
greater the fear induced, the more likely the target to resist
       begin with, threats are more likely to be used. of course
    those conditions, you were more likely to get threats because, then
               um, the U-S is more likely to be successful with Russia
     that are less likely uh more likely to be used for commercial
```

less, most, least, equally, just as, are all found to collocate with *likely* although of these *more* is by far the most frequent.[2]

Additionally the argumentational nature of the corpus leads to the presence of several examples of the string *the more ...... the more likely*. By doing a horizontal search, first of all to the left of the node for *the more* and subsequently extending the search, several examples of this pattern were found.

(2) **the more**, fearful you make the target of yourself, **the more** resistance you're likely to encounter. mkay?

(3) the greater the fear induced, **the more** likely the target is to resist. and **the more** likely it is also ultimately to absorb, to absorb damage.

(4) **the more** educated the better educated usually people are, and the **more**, aware they are, of of the variety of information, and especially information that contradicts, kind of the the the snake oil kind of propaganda, um, **the more** likely they are to realize that that propaganda is is is based, totally on distorted information is wrong.

Finally if we look at the left co-text of the pattern [to be + likely+ to] we find other co-selected features such as subjects expressed as concrete nouns which either could be subsumed under the semantic field of humans (*women, men, boys, females, person, people, population, children, craftsman, group*) or NPs characteristic of technical discourse (*genetic drift, pollution effects, atomic electron, eating disorders, cancer cells, blood vessel*).

Table 7. Concordance *probably*

```
             here. the, third one you're   probably   most concerned with at the
               two more that you guys   probably   want to have
         setting it up this afternoon   probably   early... and it will be
                   um and i think he's   probably   right that in general, metabolic
    experience has been, that you   probably   need to think a little
               so, some of these are,   probably   you need to consider more
             store was_ we think was   probably   went out of business, in
            feather in your, hat, you,   probably   are not, um going to
   Chicken populations. the states   probably   you know within my lifetime
                  my guess is they were   probably   overharvested, early in the century
               it you know it's it's   probably   something that, uh some people
          and that's cuz you just   probably   don't have enough, data (there's
   think the majority of Americans   probably   it's not like their top
       enough to understand that we   probably   oughta go through it, uh
       later, uh, probably not today,   probably   tomorrow. now let's say we
```

Probably

Conversely, with respect to *likely*, the adverb *probably* displays a subjective, interpersonal, semantic prosody. Adverbs in general tend to be involved in subjective evaluations (Nuyts 2001), and, as we have seen, the adverb *probably* shows a much higher frequency in the spoken part of the BNC compared to the written; in addition it occurs more often in the conversational sections of the BNC with respect to task oriented speech, thus indicating its use in interactive situations (Leech et al. 2001). Lectures are more conversational than was once supposed: although there is often little or no overt interaction between speakers and listeners, the speaker always tries to engage the listener in a disciplinary conversation (see McCloskey 1985 for a discussion of a disciplinary conversation in economics). This engagement is essential for the creation of intersubjectivity between teachers and students, which can be defined as the explicit attention of the speaker to the 'self' of the listener, anticipating what his possible reaction to the content of what is being said might be, and at the same time paying attention to his 'face' needs.

The selection of concordances with *probably* in Table 7 can be seen to occur in interactive sequences of discourse where the speaker is addressing the audience directly, using metadiscourse, commenting on discourse, or commenting on the content. Lecturers make a special effort to ensure what conversation analysts call 'recipient design' where the speakers tailor their talk to the needs of the student listeners. Moreover they make efforts to be as conversational as possible trying to involve the listeners. Many of the instances of *probably* have a personal pronoun or name in the immediate vicinity.

Table 8. Concordance *you probably*

```
              in thirty-three. and um you probably know that he's most famous
     Marxism. okay...? okay, most of you probably know the term Marxism, as
        amino acid of similar size you probably or maybe, maybe won't get
         they've got, wiry gray hair, you probably put them, maybe above sixty
        anything in class today that you probably didn't say it. wanted to
     okay. truncation. now some of you probably would have said and wanted
  saying what the heck's that? <L> you probably don't even know what the
              in fact Kathy, you probably saw something this morning that
           to read to you um, you probably don't know the story and
if you're taking Willis's course you probably are, <L> doing things that
        evaluate the model. um as you probably discovered from just, earlier
              well, d- i mean uh you probably shouldn't be saying oops you're
         gull feather in your, hat, you probably are not, um going to
  my experience has been, that you probably need to think a little
          in thirty-three. and um, you probably know that he's most famous
```

Extending the collocational profile to look at *you probably*, it is evident that this is a frequent concordance; other collocations include *we, he, they, I*, or such strings as [you know + probably], [I think + probably], [I mean + probably], or prefaced by a hedge such as:

(5) that's kind of probably, an obvious, an obvious point

Table 8 provides a series of concordances of *you probably* which is the most frequent pattern, followed by *we probably*. Both of these indicate the highly interactive usage of *probably* in the corpus.

Conclusions

In this brief examination of two evaluators *likely* and *probably*, I have argued that the former is prevalently used in objective evaluations while the latter is used in subjective evaluations. *Likely* is used typically when scientific probability is involved while *probably* is used in interactive stretches of discourse when people (usually the student listeners) are being addressed. However I will make no attempt to claim that the two evaluative words can be directly compared due to their different grammatical function. At the same time the grammatical equivalent and synonym of *likely*, i.e. *probable*, while being used even more markedly in objective contexts, is so infrequent in the corpus as to make it difficult to make generalisations.

Notes

1. *Likely* can be used as an adverb as in the following:

```
but said hey, this likely means that, my remaining
```

I will not be taking this usage into consideration because of its low incidence in the corpus (1.7% of occurrences of *likely*).

2. Interestingly, *likely* with an emphasiser like *very* was relatively uncommon in the corpus (only 4 instances), compared to 46 occurrences of *more likely,* showing once again how specific genres, while using the same lexis as general discourse, do so with very different relative frequencies.

References

Bamford, Julia (2000). Question/Answer sequencing in academic lectures. In M. Coulthard, J. Cotterill, & F. Rock (Eds.), *Working with Dialogue* (pp. 159–170). Tübingen: Max Niemeyer Verlag.

Chafe, Wallace & Nichols, Joanna (Eds.). (1986). *Evidentiality.* Norwood: Ablex.

Conrad, Susan & Biber, Douglas (2000). Adverbial marking of stance in speech and writing. A corpus-based account of evaluative adverbials in three registers of English. In Hunston & Thompson (Eds.), 56–73.

Gilbert, N. Nigel & Mulkay, Michael (1984). *Opening Pandora's Box. A Sociological Analysis of Scientists' Discourse.* Cambridge: Cambridge University Press.

Hunston, Susan & Thompson, Geoff (Eds.). (2000). *Evaluation in Text: Authorial Stance and the Construction of Discourse.* Oxford: Oxford University Press.

Hyland, Ken (1996). Writing without conviction? Hedging in science research articles. *Applied Linguistics, 17* (4), 445–454.

Hyland, Ken (2000). *Disciplinary Discourses. Social Interactions in Academic Writing.* London: Longman.

Johansson, Stig (1993). "Sweetly oblivious". Some aspects of adverb-adjective combinations in present day English. In M. Hoey (Ed.), *Data Description Discourse* (pp. 39–49). London: Harper Collins.

Leech, Geoffrey, Rayson, Paul, & Wilson, Andrew (2001). *Word Frequencies in Written and Spoken English.* London: Longman.

Louw, B. (1993). The diagnostic potential of semantic prosodies. In M. Baker, G. Francis, & E. Tognini Bonelli (Eds.), *Text and Technology: In Honour of John Sinclair* (pp. 157–176). Amsterdam & New York: John Benjamins.

Lyons, John (1977). *Semantics.* Cambridge: Cambridge University Press.

Martin, James R. (2000). Beyond exchange. In Hunston & Thompson (Eds.), 142–175.

Mauranen, Anna (2000). *Reflexive Academic Talk: Observations from MICASE.* In Simpson & Swales (Eds.), 165–178.

McCloskey, Donald (1985). *The Rhetoric of Economics.* Madison: University of Wisconsin Press.

Nuyts, Jan (2000). *Epistemic Modality, Language and Conceptualization: A Cognitive-Pragmatic Perspective.* Amsterdam & New York: John Benjamins.

Nuyts, Jan (2001). Subjectivity as an evidential dimension in epistemic modal expressions. *Journal of Pragmatics, 33,* 383–400.

Quirk, Randolph, Greenbaum, Sidney, Leech, Geoffrey, & Svartvik, Jan (1985). *A Comprehensive Grammar of the English Language.* London: Longman.

Simpson, Rita (2001). *Statistical Analysis of Disciplinary Style in Transcripts of Spoken Academic English.* Conference paper at The Third North American Symposium on Corpus Linguistics and Language Teaching, Boston, MA.

Simpson, Rita C. & Swales, John M. (Eds.). (2000). *Corpus Linguistics in North America: Selections from the 1999 Symposium.* Ann Arbor: University of Michigan Press.

Simpson, Rita C., Briggs, Sarah L., Ovens, Janine, & Swales, John M. (1999). *The Michigan Corpus of Academic Spoken English.* Ann Arbor, MI: The Regents of the University of Michigan.

Sinclair, John M. (1996). The search for units of meaning. *Textus, IX* (1), 75–106.

Sinclair, John M. (1998). The lexical item. In E. Wiegand (Ed.), *Contrastive Lexical Semantics* (pp. 1–24). Amsterdam & New York: John Benjamins.

Swales, John & Malczewski, Bonnie (2001). Discourse management and new-episode flags in MICASE. In Simpson & Swales (Eds.), 145–164.

Tognini Bonelli, Elena (2001). *Corpus Linguistics at Work.* Amsterdam & New York: John Benjamins.

Aspects of identification and position in intertextual reference in PhD theses

Paul Thompson
The University of Reading, UK

This paper investigates some aspects of the complex interplay between averral and attribution in a corpus of PhD theses, through a study of citation practices, and through close analysis of a number of extracts from the theses. By skilful management of averral and attribution, a thesis writer makes clear who is responsible for a given proposition (identification) and develops a credible authoritative persona whose voice is dominant throughout the text (position).

Introduction

In a discussion of the problems faced by novice second language academic writers, Groom (2000) talks of the importance of what he refers to as *identification* and *position*. Identification is the indication of who is responsible for a given proposition within the text, while position is the dominant voice in a text. Groom argues that novice writers often fail to appreciate the need for clear identification of propositional responsibility, and also have difficulty in establishing a clear position. This can lead to ambiguity in the text, and, in more extreme cases, to charges of plagiarism.

Key terms in the discussion of identification are *averral* and *attribution*, terms introduced by Sinclair (1988), and also extensively applied in the work of Angele Tadros (1993), in relation to academic writing. Averral is the default condition of a text, where the reader assumes that the responsibility for each proposition rests with the speaker or writer. Attribution is the counterpart, the case where a proposition is indicated as deriving from a source. This source could be the writer, in which case it is self-attribution, or it could be writer-external. Attribution in academic texts can be marked by citation conventions, but it can also consist of a reference to an external source such as in the following:

> As with cocoa, concerns have been raised by the World Bank that expanding cotton exports as a consequence of project assistance or structural adjustment programs could eventually lead to a decline in world prices and a general decrease in export revenues.   [TAE-004][1]

The responsibility for the proposition that 'expanding cotton exports . . . could eventually lead to . . .' is here attributed to the 'World Bank'. The focus of this paper, however, is on uses of attribution as realised through citation of other texts, and within a particular genre of academic discourse, the PhD thesis, as instantiated in one university in the UK.

In academic writing, writers have to mix averral with attribution skilfully, showing that their averrals are justified, and invoking the voices and actions of others to indicate what is thought, and what has already been done (a form of intertextuality). Self-attribution (where the reference is *intra*textual) is important in the management of long texts as writers have to frequently remind their readers of what they have said in earlier (or later) sections of their texts, and this is particularly true of PhD theses.

Doctoral candidates are in a peculiar position of being both experts, as well as examinees. It is important therefore both to assume a tone of authority, and, at the same time, establish that the writer is entitled to adopt a tone of authority. Claims must be backed up with evidence, and a comprehensive understanding of thinking, approaches and knowledge in their chosen fields of specialisation must be demonstrated, in order to persuade the most immediate readers (the examiners) that the thesis is worthy of the award of a doctorate.

This paper presents both quantitative and qualitative analyses of theses contained in a corpus of academic texts. These analyses identify the citation practices most typically used in three disciplines represented in the corpus, and explore some of the strategies employed by thesis writers in managing intertextuality while maintaining a dominant voice (position) in the text. A key element of position is seen to be that of evaluation, in that the writer's voice guides the reader through the text, introducing what is known, what is not known, what the major issues are, reviewing methods, developing a framework, justifying decisions, reporting what has been done, and considering what remains to be done. In all this, the writer's clear and convincing evaluation of what is fact and what is not, what is an appropriate method, and what is not, how strong an argument is, what value an action has, and so on, are fundamental to the establishment of an authoritative persona.

Averral, intertextuality and intratextuality

An example of the complex interplay of averral, intertextuality and intratextuality can be seen in the following extract from the final chapter of a PhD thesis in Agricultural Economics:

> **Extract 1**
> The limitation of economic indicators in research assessment is of relevance to the interpretation of past studies of returns to research. For example, the fact that in many cases high IRRs are found may reflect either that technical service work is being assessed or that some other form of partial analysis is occurring, or that a model is being used where research has an effect on productivity within a year. This would argue that the apparent returns to research found in papers such as Nagy and Furtan (1978) and Akino and Hayami (1975), for example, might be re-examined, as the apparent time between the initiation of research and benefits appears very short for plant breeding work.
> Thirtle (1989) argues that the bulk of UK agricultural research is of a short term adaptive nature. However, apart from the fact that inspection of the AFRC index of research (AFRC, 1992) suggests that only a small proportion of this scientific effort has immediate effect on productivity, this argument implies that it is the returns to technical service which are being measured. Such work would be deemed 'near-market' and outside the remit of the AFRS. It is reiterated that the presence of 'high returns' in such circumstances is misleading.   [TAE-002]

The writer begins the first paragraph with an averral: "The limitation of economic indicators in research assessment is of relevance to the interpretation of past studies of returns to research", which makes a strong claim about the importance of an understanding of the limitation of economic indicators. The writer's position is clearly indicated in this paragraph-initial statement. The limitation, it is claimed, is of relevance when one assesses past studies of returns to research. The claim is then supported through exemplification, and reference to studies which the writer is criticising (in other words, negative evaluation).

The form of the reference to other studies is notable in this context: the citation reference, though apparently referring to other researchers, is actually referring to the research *work* of others, and takes on an ambiguous role where one could either take the reference to be to a textualisation of their work (the text in which the work is reported), or to the research work itself. The citation does not allow the cited authors a voice for themselves but introduces the names as references solely to the research as object. These objects in turn become entities that are capable of evaluation by the writer.

The second paragraph begins with a different form of intertextual reference. The citation in this instance affords an agency role to the cited name, and the citation form allows a different author a voice in the text. The proposition that 'the bulk of UK agricultural research is of a short term adaptive nature' is attributed to this other voice, but the writer maintains a position in relation to the proposition through the choice of reporting verb: *argue*. *Argue* in itself is not indicative of a writer's position but in context it can be seen to indicate a negative, neutral or positive appraisal of the author's proposition. In paragraph-initial position, it may be posited, the use of *argue* in present simple, and without any adverbial modification (consider the case of *convincingly argues*, where the adverb would mark the writer's stance) indicates that the ensuing proposition is held up for consideration and that judgment on the value will be given in one or more of the following sentences. In this case, the next sentence begins with a concessive *however* which reintroduces the writer's voice, and indicates that the proposition put forward in the preceding sentence is to be challenged. The voice of the other is now transformed into an 'argument', an entity to be observed and evaluated. Finally, in the concluding sentence of the paragraph, the writer sums up the assessment of the other's argument through a reference back to his own previous statement, *it is reiterated . . .*, in an instance of self-attribution.

In this extract, then, we have an example of a complex interplay between averral, attribution (intertextual reference) and self-attribution (intratextual reference), in which the writer's voice remains dominant.

It can also be seen that the form of a citation can be exploited in different ways. In Extract 1, the citations are what Swales (1986) terms *integral*. Such citations appear within the sentence and are integrated into the syntax of the sentence (as opposed to *non-integral* citations, which are typically separated from the sentence by parentheses, and do not perform an explicit syntactic role). In Extract 1, the first two citations are in the form of a noun phrase that does not control a lexical verb – in other words, no agency is directly ascribed to the noun phrase in this instance. Non-agentive citations can act in a number of ways within a sentence. They can function as (1) a modifier (for example, *the work of Fuller (1997)* or *Fuller's (1997) work*), (2) a noun phrase followed by a linking verb, as in *Fuller (1997) is the best example of this approach*, or (3) naming of texts, as in *papers such as Nagy and Furtan (1978) and Akino & Hayami (1975)*.

The second form of citation found in Extract 1 is the agentive integral citation. These citations either report the actions of others, or they introduce the voices of others into the text, as in *Miller (1990a) found no such correlation* ... or *Thirtle (1989) argues* .... These two examples feature the use of active voice, but passive is also commonly used: *It has been argued by Thirtle (1989)* .... While space does not permit an extended discussion of the reasons behind the choice of active or passive voice constructions in explicit intertextual reference, it should be noted that one reason is the decision to thematise either the object of the action, or the agent (Shaw 1992). More sophisticated models of these citation types can be found in Thompson and Ye (1991) and Thomas and Hawes (1994), for example, but for the purposes of this paper, a simplified account will be given. The two types of integral citation discussed here will be described as *Verb-controlling* (agentive) and *Naming* (non-agentive).

A second example of intertextual reference is given in Extract 2, which is taken from the Conclusions chapter of a thesis in Agricultural Botany:

> **Extract 2**
> Carbon dioxide is responsible for the activation of ACC oxidase (Chapter 4, Dong et al. 1992) but the mechanism involved remains unknown. The substrate ACC can form a carbamate directly with CO_2 as shown:
> -EQUATION-
> Carbamylation of the ACC molecule would alter its structure, and may in this way result in enzyme activation. However, the carbamylation of ACC has an alkaline pH optimum around 9 (Thompson et al. 1984) and does not occur to any significant extent at physiological pH.   [TAB-007]

The citations here are non-integral. In both cases, they refer the reader to other papers in which evidence to support the proposition made is given. In the first sentence, the evidence for the claim that carbon dioxide is responsible for a particular chemical reaction is attributed to a paper by Dong et al., but there is also intratextual reference in the mention of Chapter 4 of the writer's own text, in which he presented and discussed the evidence that he had obtained in his own research experiments. In fact, in Chapter 4, the writer had hedged the claim (*Carbon dioxide seems more likely than HCO_3^- to be the species responsible for the activation*), but in the concluding chapter he presents the proposition as a fact, reinforced by intertextual reference. The second citation in the extract similarly uses the reference as evidence for a statement, although in this case it may be more a case of identifying the source of an item of information.

In this extract, the dominant voice is that of the writer. Propositions from other sources are summarised in the words of the writer, and the non-integral citation forms allow the writer to justify his line of argument through reference to external evidence. The intertextual reference takes on interesting properties in that the evidence for the truth value of the statement is attributed to the other (the text referred to) but the voice of the text is that of the writer, in that the proposition (disregarding what appears within parentheses) is expressed in the words of the writer. This is an example of what Hunston (2000: 192) has termed a 'sourced averral'.[2]

Non-integral citations can take a number of forms, with a clear distinction existing between numerical references and references in which the author names and date of publication are given. The citation may refer to a proposition within the sentence, as expressed minimally through a non-finite clause:

> the carbamylation of ACC has an alkaline pH optimum around 9 (Thompson et al. 1984)

In some cases the citation identifies a verb-controlling agent within the clause. For example:

> the use of morphological markers has been criticised because ... (Smith & Smith 1989)   [TAB-002]

In this instance, Smith and Smith were the ones who made the criticism, but the writer has chosen to place the names in the background. A similar strategy is employed in the following sentence, in which the citations identify the studies referred to in the main proposition:

> RFLP studies (Jan et al. 1993; Gentzbittel et al. 1994) have both revealed high levels of DNA polymorphism in sunflower ...)   [TAB-002]

There are other types of non-integral citation (see Thompson 2000) but for the present study we shall restrict our attention to the first type shown here, which we will term a Source citation, and the latter two which we will refer to collectively as an Ident citation type. 'Ident' is an abbreviation for 'identifying'.

From the above, it can be seen that there is no simple equivalence between citation and attribution, when attribution is used as a specialised term to refer to the responsibility for a proposition. In many cases, a citation is attached to a summary of what other researchers found, or what they did, or what has happened in the 'real world'. The statement that *RFLP studies ... have both revealed high levels of DNA polymorphism in sunflower ...* is a report of one of the main findings in other studies, and does not directly suggest that the cited authors are responsible for the proposition (the writer is responsible, however, for the summary). The same holds true for many integral citations of the agentive type, such as:

> Experiment Four employed a lexical decision task with double and single string trials, as used by MacLeod and Mathews (1991).   [TPS-005]

where the agentive citation controls what can be termed a 'Research Verb' (following Thompson & Ye 1991); a verb that refers to mental or physical processes that are part of research work. On the other hand, where a Discourse Verb (in Thompson and Ye's terminology, a Textual Verb) is used, this typically introduces a proposition, as in:

> Fox (1993a) suggests that it is in fact the repressors ability to avoid processing threatening information which allows them to maintain low levels of anxiety.   [TPS-005]

This can be interpreted as an embedded attribution, in that the opening to the sentence is an averral, but the following proposition is attributed through the opening averral to 'Fox (1993a)'. The writer indicates an evaluation of the proposition through the choice of the verb *suggest*.

In Thompson and Ye's categorisation of what they term 'reporting verbs', it is sometimes difficult to distinguish between Research Verbs and Discourse Verbs. For example, it would seem logical to place *find* in the category of Research Verb, and *report* in the Discourse Verb category, but, as I have reported elsewhere (Thompson 2001), these two verbs are often used interchangeably, and the distinction between research processes and discourse processes may not be as clear as first thought. An alternative approach, which is adopted in the following analysis, is to tag the verbs that are controlled by agentive citations (both integral and non-integral) and then to search in the corpus for instances of these verbs (search by the tag) followed by a projecting *that* clause. In this case, *find* and *report* are treated equally as verbs introducing a projecting *that* clause.

A final point is that in non-agentive integral citation types, which we hereafter call 'Naming' citations, the citation is either used as a the modifier or is the subject of a linking verb, in which case it is at the level of an entity within the sentence that is open to evaluation in itself. An exception to this is the case of the *according to* + citation pattern, which is non-agentive, but which clearly attributes responsibility for the following proposition to the cited authors. However, this pattern only occurs 15 times in the corpus of 20 theses, and therefore is not discussed below.

Table 1. The relation between averral, attribution, and citation

	With citation (sourced)	Without citation
AVERRAL	Citation indicates source of information – Non-integral source citation – Agentive citation NOT using verb + *that* clause	Plain averral
ATTRIBUTION	Citation as source of proposition – Direct quotation – Agentive citation using verb + *that* clause – Self-attribution with citation	Report of others propositions without citation Self-attribution without citation

A tabular representation of the relations between averral and attribution, on one axis, and citation, on the other, is given in Table 1.

The corpus

The corpus used for this study is the Reading Academic Text (RAT) corpus. The major part of this corpus is made up of PhD theses written by students for whom English is their first language, and submitted to the University of Reading between 1989 and 1998.

In this study, the following were used:

– 8 Agricultural Botany theses (average 31,000 words)
– 8 Agricultural Economics theses (average 63,500 words)
– 4 Psychology theses (average 50,000 words)

The reason for choosing these three subject areas was to provide a perspective on variation across the disciplines. The choice of subject areas may seem odd in that it does not cover what may be considered core disciplines, but it was strongly influenced by the attitudes of departments at the University of Reading: these departments were more cooperative and their students were prepared to allow their texts to be included in the corpus, so there is a better representation of theses in these areas than in others.

In some countries, doctoral students are expected to publish chapters of their thesis prior to completion of the final thesis and it is possible for the writer then to insert the published papers exactly as they were originally published, into the final thesis. There is only one case within the 20 theses in this corpus of such a chapter: TAB-009 contains a chapter that is included verbatim as it appeared in an international journal. In all other cases, the thesis has been written as a unitary text, with chapters that contain research work that had been published before re-written for the thesis. In other words, all but one chapter had been written with a set of rhetorical purposes in mind that is different from those that are employed when addressing a journal audience.

The texts in the corpus were tagged for a number of features:

1. Citation type (Source, Ident, Verb-controlling, Naming)
2. Voice and tense
3. Verb controlled (in instances of Ident or Verb-controlling citations, the verb controlled was tagged)
4. Direct quotation

The reason for tagging citation type should be clear. It should be noted, however, that all mentions of names which invoked other texts were treated as citations, and that a further tag was created for uses of a name that had previously been introduced as a citation, but subsequently appeared without conventional citation information (not even the inclusion of *ibid.* or *op. cit.*). These references were tagged as 'Non-cit' and the reason for tagging them was that these still constitute intertextual reference (tagging of pronouns were not, however, included, although they should logically have been).

Results of analysis

It is important to remember that there is considerable variation in textual practices both between disciplines and also within disciplines. There is no space here to enter into discussion of the degrees of variation that exist between theses within one discipline (I have discussed this in more detail in Thompson 2001 and Thompson 2002). Table 2 summarises a quantification of the citation types described above in the sub-corpus of the RAT corpus.

As can be seen, the Agricultural Botany writers write substantially shorter texts, tend to use non-integral citations far more than writers in the other two disciplines, and use the Source type of citation most frequently (nearly 4 in 10 citations). Sourced averral appears thus to be a preferred form of citation in this discipline; it is also noteworthy that there is comparatively little use of direct quotation (approximately 2 direct quotations per thesis), which suggests, in combination with the other findings, that there is less introduction of other voices into the text than in the other two disciplines.

Table 2. Summary of quantification of citation types and density in PhD theses in three disciplines*

	Agricultural Botany	Agricultural Economics	Psychology
Av. length of thesis	31,000 words	63,500 words	50,000 words
Citation density (per 1,000 words)	9	5.25	8.5
Ratio of non-integral to integral	2:1	4:6	5:12
Direct quotation (per 100,000 words)	6	45	34
Most commonly used citation type (per 1,000 words and as percentage of all types)	Source – 3.4 (38%) Verb-controlling – 2.0 (22%) Ident – 1.7 (19%)	Verb-controlling – 1.9 (36%) Source – 1.25 (24%) Naming – 0.95 (18%)	Verb controlling – 2.7 (32%) Non-cit – 2.4 (28%) Ident – 1.0 (12%)
Number of agentive citations controlling verb + that clause	193	181	220

* The citation types listed in this table are discussed in this paper. In the analysis, a number of other categories were employed and they account for small percentages of the uses; for example, while non-integral citations account for 66% of the Agricultural Botany total, the two types of non-integral citation discussed in this paper make up only 57% – the remaining 9% are non-integral citation types that are excluded from the current discussion.

Both Agricultural Economics and Psychology writers show a preference for integral citations, and almost equal use of direct quotations per thesis. The cited authors are thus more frequently introduced as actors within sentences, and the number of verb-controlling citations is high, relative to that in the Agricultural Botany theses. In Psychology theses, there is also more extended discussion of particular papers/researchers in which the references to individuals lose their conventional citational forms, after a few mentions of the name. From this evidence, we can say that both Agricultural Economics and Psychology appear to foreground the researchers and the models that they have developed.

Voice and tense are not reported on here, although it is worth commenting that discourse verbs appear more in the Agricultural Economics and Psychology theses and tend to be in the present active, which allows for wider range of 'voices' to manifest themselves in those texts, compared to the Agricultural Botany texts which are more concerned with reports of experiments.

Table 3. List of 10 verbs most frequently used in agentive citation types (Verb-controlling and Ident) which are followed by a projecting *that* clause

Verb	Instances
Find	108
Suggest	75
Report	73
Show	70
Argue	33
Note	29
Conclude	28
Point out	23
Demonstrate	20
Propose	19
Total	478
Total all such verbs	594

Citation density varies between disciplines too, which could suggest that the longer the text, the lower the citation density (and consequently the higher proportion of averral). This is partially supported by the findings of Hyland (1999) who found levels of citation density ranging from 7.3 to 15.5 in journal articles, with figures of 10.1 to 12.5 in social science texts, which could be compared to the agricultural economics texts. However, in a small comparison study I conducted with a collection of agricultural economics journal papers (Thompson 2001), I found a citation density level of 6.7 per 1,000 words that suggests that the high level of averral is a feature of writing in this discipline, and that the length of text is not directly connected to levels of citation density.

Table 3 shows the 10 most frequently used reporting verbs followed by a *that* clause.

The most noticeable feature of Table 3 is that the majority of the verbs appear to be relatively neutral or positive. In the two disciplines in which experimental studies are common (Agricultural Botany, and Psychology), the most common verbs involve reports of findings (*report* and *find*). *Suggest* indicates that the following proposition was attributed provisional status by the cited researchers, and the writer's judgment on the proposition cannot be obtained from the choice of verb alone; the wider context will determine the status awarded to the proposition by the writer. *Show* and *demonstrate*, on the other hand, imply that the researchers cited were successful in their efforts to illustrate a point or theory, and *note* and *point out* also tend to indicate an acceptance by the writer of the following proposition. The only verb that could suggest a negative evaluation of the cited researchers is *argue*, but this, as we have noted above, also gains its evaluative load from the wider context.

These general quantitative data, as the previous point indicates, are useful in determining tendencies in the sample, but it is always important to refer back to the texts themselves, as the reality is usually far more complex. In the following section, we examine a number of extracts from the conclusions sections of the theses, and discuss the interplay of averrals and attributions.

Conclusions chapters

The overall organisation of a PhD thesis is subject to variation. Bunton (1998), for example, presents a three-stream model, Thompson (1999) extends to four, and Ridley (2000) describes five structural patterns for PhD theses, amongst which there is also considerable room for adaptation. The one regularity among PhD theses is that they are highly likely to feature an introductory chapter and a concluding chapter. Amongst the theses in the RAT corpus, there is greater similarity of organisation of the concluding chapter than of the introductory chapter, with the concluding chapter likely to contain:

 — A restatement of the research questions and hypotheses
 — A summary of the main findings, possibly chapter by chapter
 — A discussion of the implications of the research
 — A discussion of the limitations of the research
 — Suggestions for further research

For the simple reason that this is the only section that can be compared across theses, we turn now to an examination of a small sample of extracts from Conclusions chapters in the theses in the RAT corpus.

Figure 1 shows the citation density for the theses according to chapter, and demonstrates how theses in one group (Agricultural Economics) have a relatively low density of citations in the Conclusions chapter. An explanation for this is that work in applied economics is generally model-driven: the researcher develops a model, emanating out of discussion of previous models (which accounts for the high density of citation in earlier chapters of the thesis), then applies the model to a dataset, and finally, in the conclusions, evaluates the success of the model, in relation to its application.

Agricultural Botany and Psychology, by contrast, seem to fit into an hourglass model (as proposed by Hill et al. 1982), in which the Introduction and Conclusion sections contain references to other texts in order to place the

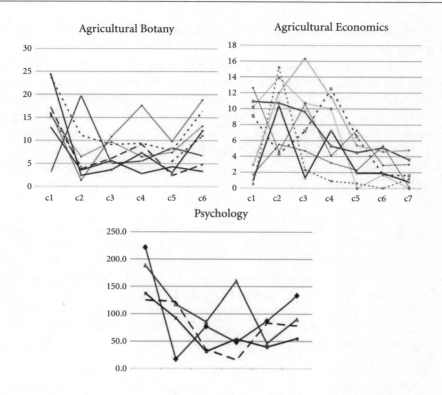

Figure 1. Graphs showing citation density per chapter in each of the theses in each discipline. The leftmost side of each graph shows the density in the first chapter and the rightmost that for the final chapter. Adjustments have been made to the intermediate figures as not each thesis has the same numbers of chapters. The main purpose of the graphs is to demonstrate the density of citations in the final chapter relative to the rest of the thesis.

text within the context of the current state of knowledge in that subject area; the image of the hourglass is used because the entry and departure points of the text are 'wider' while the middle sections take a narrow perspective, being more focused on the researchers' own text and work than on others. The hourglass model, it should be noted, describes the IMRD structure (Introduction-Methods-Results-Discussion) of the conventional scientific research paper, rather than the PhD thesis, and many of the Agricultural Botany and Psychology theses employ the IMRD structure for each of the middle chapters, each chapter describing a set of experiments. All the same, the tendency for theses in these two areas to have a relatively high density of citations in the final chapter can be seen.

The foregoing discussion has indicated that there is considerable variation between disciplines in the use of citation and that in the Conclusions chapters of Agricultural Economics theses, there is a comparatively low degree of citation density. The following pages return to discussion of extracts from Conclusions chapters to illustrate some of the uses of citation made in the closing pages of theses, and the strategies used by writers to assert their voice of authority. Extract 3 exemplifies a hedged negative evaluation of the proposition of a previous researcher:

Extract 3

Although these results do not explain the precise means of this introduction, they tend to refute the hypothesis put forward by Buddenhagen (1987) that *M. Fijiensis* arose in Honduras due to mutation and selection pressure from the population of *M. musicola* already present on that continent. **It is more likely that** *M. fijiensis* was introduced into Central America on contaminated banana foliage used as packing material as **suggested** by Stover (1978), or in the distribution of banana germplasm for the breeding programmes active at that time.   [TAB-005]

In this case, the writer is mitigating the force of the averred proposition ('they refute the hypothesis . . .') by the inclusion of *tend to*. The results obtained by the writer provide evidence that a previous hypothesis is incorrect, but the writer chooses to hedge the negative evaluation of the other researcher. Following Myers (1989), we can see this as motivated by a form of politeness strategy, in which a face-threatening act is diluted by the use of the hedge, and there is also an element of self-construction of the writer as a community member who is aware of the face needs of other members of the research community (cf. Hyland 2000).

Extract 4

In support of this theory Peiser et al. (1983) showed that [1-^{14}C] ACC was converted to ^{14}C-asparagine by mungbean tissue, inferring that the initial product was ^{14}C-cyanide processed by ß-cyanoaniline synthase. However this pathway does not conform with the observations of Adlington et al. (1983) who showed that during reaction, the hydrogen atoms of the carbons 2 and 3 of ACC underwent stereospecific scrambling. Pirrung (1983) has argued that such scrambling would require a ring open intermediate and therefore ethylene biosynthesis is most likely to occur, not in a con-

certed, but step-wise process. The availability of purified enzyme will now
allow the establishment of the true mechanism.   [TAB-007]

In Extract 4, the writer's voice is dominant and intertextual reference is made
primarily to indicate that there is an unresolved problem, which the writer can
then prescribe the solution to. The first citation introduces the finding of a
study which is presented as fact, but the conclusion drawn by those researchers
is problematised with the use of the verb *infer*, followed by the concessive *However* signalling the introduction of counter-evidence. An alternative argument
has been proposed by Pirrung, in terms of an hypothesis (*would require*) and
the final sentence of the paragraph states that the hypothesis can now be tested
with the use of purified enzyme. The sentence beginning *Pirrung (1983) has argued* ... temporarily introduces another voice into the text, one that the writer
endorses, and then the writer's voice is reasserted in the final sentence, in which
an explicit evaluation is made, through the use of *true*, implying that truth can
be established, and that previous efforts have failed to identify that mechanism.

In Conclusions chapters, it is rare for the writer to use direct quotation, in
the RAT corpus, at least. Working on the premise that thesis writers are aiming
to establish their own voices as authoritative, we can presume that they will
avoid ceding the floor to others, and that they will therefore restrict the introduction of other voices to minor roles in these final sections. Of the 20 theses,
only four have direct quotations in the final chapter, three of these being Psychology theses in which the quotations are either taken from the comments
of subjects about the experiments or are short extracts from general principles
stated by researchers in their field. The only thesis from the other two disciplines that contains a direct quotation is TAE-007, an exceptional thesis in that
the application of the theoretical model to a dataset showed that the model
developed in the thesis was flawed, and the tone of the Conclusions chapter is
consequently quite defensive. Much space is given to evaluation of the model
and to the identification of its flaws, and there is one extraordinarily long quotation of 60 words that identifies a problem in the way that growth has been
estimated in equivalent studies. The extensive discussion of the flaws can be
seen as a strategic ploy, answering the criticisms of the examiner in advance,
and the extensive quotation suggests that the writer does not want to assume
a wholly authoritative voice, as a consequence of the flawed nature of the research. It is possible once again to see this as a strategic ploy to forestall negative
reaction through the adoption of a suitably humble stance.

Openly evaluative adjectives are rare in the theses as a whole, but in Extract
5 we have an example of two unusually strong evaluative terms used (*spectacu-*

lar, exciting). A possible interpretation is that the writer felt able to make such assertions in the closing comments of the thesis, having established his author-ity in the foregoing chapter and sections. It should be reiterated, however, that such openly strong evaluative adjectives are rare in the exemplars of the PhD thesis genre in this corpus.

Extract 5

In the last three years, research on ACC oxidase has moved from being largely confined to studies *in vivo*, to concentrating on the enzyme *in vitro*. Over this period progress has been spectacular ... Important questions to be addressed include ... However, the exciting prospects of determining the structure, catalytic mechanism and the mechanism of CO_2 activation of ACC oxidase, means that research on the enzyme *in vitro* will continue to dominate this area in the near future.   [TAB-007]

A more common use of citation in the final chapter is to give a summary over view of the field, and indicate how the work reported on in the thesis fits into what has previously been done. An example of this can be seen in Extract 6.

Extract 6

Previous research shows some discrepancy in the reports of biases shown by individuals with low levels of trait anxiety. Some studies have reported that these individuals show no bias either towards or away from threat-ening stimuli (e.g. Mogg, Mathews, & Weinman 1989), whereas others report that low anxiety groups actually avoid attending to threatening stimuli (e.g. Eysenck et al. 1987; MacLeod & Mathews 1988). These results have been mirrored in the studies of this thesis ...   [TPS-005]

As suggested above, a technique by which writers could introduce a clearer evaluative role to the choice of reporting verb is by combining the verb with an adverb, as in *mistakenly recommends* (an invented example). Such adverb + verb combinations are however rare in the corpus. The few examples that exist are of temporal markers (*first, subsequently, later, previously, originally*) with a single instance of open evaluation in *was well reviewed*. The following extracts from a Psychology thesis show an interesting discoursal feature of the use of an apparent temporal marker:

Extract 7

Many studies (for example, Jonides & Naveh-Benjamin 1987; Maki & Ostby 1987; Sanders et al. 1987; Greene 1990 and others) have now shown that the storage of frequency information is not necessarily automatic, as originally suggested by Hasher & Zacks (1979, 1984).

Extract 8

The overall conclusion is that subjects do not abstract a semantic rule, at least not in this particular task, as originally suggested by McGeorge & Burton (1990). Rather, by processing individual exemplars, it seems that subjects come to acquire, in a non-conscious way, stochastic knowledge of string structure.   [TPS-001]

In both examples, the adverb *originally* is added to the reporting verb *suggested* to indicate that the writer's conclusions have disproved the interpretations propounded by earlier researchers. *Originally* typically activates the expectation that it will be contrasted with a later state of affairs that effectively supersedes the former.

The final extract comes from the final paragraph of the same psychology thesis. The writer begins the paragraph by averring that the usefulness of the term 'implicit learning' is open to debate. She then proposes a solution which she chooses to identify not only as her own (notice the use of *also*) but also as that of earlier researchers. The reasons for her choice can only be speculated on, but a possible explanation is that the writer wants to indicate clearly the origin of the idea (thus demonstrating her knowledge of thinking in this field, and also averting any accusation of adopting others' ideas as one's own) while maintaining the dominant position in the text, by taking the major responsibility for the statement *One solution is . . ..*

Extract 9

Finally, in view of the current debate over the nature of implicit learning, it can be asked whether the term is still valid and useful. One solution, also suggested by Shanks, Green, & Kolodny (1994), is to restrict the definition of implicit learning to non-conscious processes of knowledge acquisition, with non-conscious processes of retrieval being left to the province of implicit memory.   [TPS-001]

Conclusion

The analysis and discussion of the corpus data in this study has demonstrated the complexity of the interplay between averral, attribution and self-attribution in academic writing, as realised in PhD theses. As Groom (2000) suggests, the task of establishing a clear, authoritative position in one's writing is challenging and the skilful management of averral and attribution is integral to successful development of a position. Clearly, more is involved than can be discussed here, such as the complexities involved in deciding which propositions require support from evidence and also the motives that may underlie the decision to include a citation and in what light (especially when the cited author is one of the examiners for the thesis!). The quantitative analysis of the data has demonstrated the variation in citation practices between the disciplines, and has suggested that the tendency is to use citation as source of fact or information, with little use of clear attribution (the use of direct quotation and agentive verb + *that* clause), especially in Agricultural Botany. The qualitative analysis revealed a number of the rhetorical strategies used by thesis writers to interpolate intertextual references into their discourse in ways that demonstrate their authority and guide their readers.

Notes

1. The code at the end of each extract identifies the source of the extract, and the full list of theses appears at the end of the chapter. In this case, TAE stands for Thesis Agricultural Economics and '002' is the thesis identifier. Agricultural Botany theses are identified with codes beginning TAB and Psychology with TPS.

2. A problem with sourced averral can arise when the words in which the averral is stated are too close to the words of the source text. At this point, the line between averral and attribution becomes indistinct and the writer's position is not clear. At worst, the writer is open to charges of plagiarism.

The corpus

Reading Academic Texts (RAT) Corpus. http://www.rdg.ac.uk/app_ling/corpus.htm

The permission of the authors to use their texts for research purposes is gratefully acknowledged.

TAB-001: C. Darwen (1991). A study of fructan metabolism in the Jerusalem artichoke (*Helianthus tuberosus* L.).
TAB-002: S. Berry (1995). Molecular marker analysis of cultivated sunflower (*Helianthus annuus* L.).
TAB-003: A. C. Grundy (1993). The implications of extensification for crop weed interactions in cereals.

TAB-004: J. C. Peters (1994). Pattern and impact of disease in natural plant communities of different age.

TAB-005: A. Johanson (1993). Molecular methods for the identification and detection of the Mycosphaerella species that cause Sigatoka leaf spots of banana and plantain.

TAB-007: J. J. Smith (1993). Biochemistry of 1-aminocyclopropane-1-carboxylate (ACC) oxidase (the ethylene-forming enzyme) isolated from ripening fruits.

TAB-008: P. J. Harkett (1996). Studies on the use of cut seed tubers for the production of potatoes for French fry processing.

TAB-009: G. Champion (1998). The implications of integrated farming systems on arable weed floras.

TAE-001: R. J. Loader (1995). Investigating and assessing agricultural and food marketing systems.

TAE-002: H. S. Beck (1994). The economic value of long term agricultural research.

TAE-003: A. S. Bailey (1996). The estimation of input-output coefficients for agriculture from whole farm accounting data.

TAE-004: M. A. Gadbois (1997). The effects of exchange rate variability and export instability on selected exports from sub-Saharan African countries.

TAE-005: Y. J. G. Khatri (1994). Technical change and the returns to research in UK agriculture 1953–1990.

TAE-006: Steve L. Wiggins (1991). Managing the implementation of agricultural and rural development in the Third World.

TAE-007: D. Hadley (1997). Estimation of Shadow Prices of Undesirable Outputs: An Application to UK Dairy Farms.

TAE-008: R. M. Bennett (1992). The Economics of Livestock Disease Control.

TPS-001: J. Cock (1996). Implicit learning: Number rules and invariant features.

TPS-002: N. Martin (1997). Behavioural Effects of Long-Term Multi-Sensory Stimulation.

TPS-005: R. Magee (1994). Anxiety: An information processing perspective.

TPS-006: S. L. Catt (1997). Early perceptions and behavioural effects of fats in human infants.

References

Bunton, D. (1998). Linguistic and textual problems in PhD and MPhil theses: An analysis of genre moves and metatext. Unpublished PhD thesis, University of Hong Kong.

Groom, N. (2000). Attribution and averral revisited: Three perspectives on manifest intertextuality in academic writing. In Thompson (Ed.), 15–26.

Hill, S., Soppelsa, B., & West, G. (1982). Teaching ESL students to read and write experimental research papers. *TESOL Quarterly, 16*, 333–347.

Hunston, S. (2000). Evaluation and the planes of discourse: Status and value in persuasive texts. In S. Hunston & G. Thompson (Eds.), *Evaluation in Text: Authorial Stance and the Construction of Discourse* (pp. 176–207). Oxford: Oxford University Press.

Hyland, K. (1999). Academic attribution: Citation and the construction of disciplinary knowledge. *Applied Linguistics, 20* (3), 341–367.

Hyland, K. (2000). *Disciplinary Discourses: Social Interactions in Academic Writing.* Harlow: Longman.

Myers, G. (1989). The pragmatics of politeness in scientific articles. *Applied Linguistics, 10* (1), 1–35.

Ridley, D. (2000). The different guises of a PhD thesis and the role of a literature review. In Thompson (Ed.), 61–76.

Shaw, P. (1992). Reasons for the correlation of voice, tense, and sentence function in reporting verbs. *Applied Linguistics, 13* (3), 302–319.

Sinclair, J. (1988). Mirror for a text. *Journal of English and Foreign Languages (Hyderabad, India), 1.*

Swales, J. (1986). Citation analysis and discourse analysis. *Applied Linguistics, 7* (1), 39–56.

Tadros, A. (1993). The pragmatics of text averral and attribution in academic texts. In M. Hoey (Ed.), *Data, Description, Discourse.* London: HarperCollins.

Thomas, S. & Hawes, T. (1994). Reporting verbs in medical journal articles. *English for Specific Purposes, 13* (2), 129–148.

Thompson, G. & Ye, Y. (1991). Evaluation in the reporting verbs used in academic papers. *Applied Linguistics, 12* (4), 365–382.

Thompson, P. (1999). Exploring the contexts of writing: Interviews with PhD supervisors. In P. Thompson (Ed.), *Issues in EAP writing research and instruction* (pp. 37–54). Reading, UK: CALS, The University of Reading.

Thompson, P. (2000). Citation practices in PhD theses. In L. Burnard & T. McEnery (Eds.), *Rethinking Language Pedagogy from a Corpus Perspective: Papers from the Third International Conference on Teaching and Language Corpora* (pp. 91–102). (Lodz Studies in Language.) Hamburg: Peter Lang.

Thompson, P. (Ed.). (2000). *Patterns and Perspectives: Insights for EAP Writing Practice.* Reading, UK: CALS, The University of Reading.

Thompson, P. (2001). A pedagogically-motivated corpus-based examination of PhD theses: Macrostructure, citation practices and uses of modal verbs. Unpublished PhD thesis, The University of Reading.

Thompson, P. (2002). Modal verbs in academic writing. In B. Kettemann & G. Marko (Eds.), *Teaching and Learning by Doing Corpus Analysis* (pp. 305–324). Amsterdam: Rodopi.

Authorial presence in academic genres

Céline Poudat and Sylvain Loiseau
CORAL, Université d'Orléans / Modyco, Université Paris X Nanterre

This paper considers different styles of authorial presence in linguistic and philosophical writings and looks in particular at personal pronouns in French which are regularly used to indicate the first person. Academic texts are analysed in philosophy and linguistics, showing that philosophical papers prefer a universalist stance, while linguistic papers choose less formal styles of self-reference, giving a personal or neutral flavour to the writing. The study shows how a sensitive analysis of a few pronominal choices can reveal genre differences that would be difficult to explain without the evidence.

Introduction

Scientific discourse has traditionally been considered as "objective", "matter-of-fact" and "only marginally characterised by authorial presence, commitment and open argumentation" (KIAP project, www.hit.uib.no/kiap); as such it tends to be written in an impersonal style. However, various studies centred on the textual analysis of acknowledged papers have demonstrated the opposite. The "subjectivity" of academic discourse is now generally acknowledged (cf. Swales 1990; Hyland 1998; etc.).

As authors are increasingly subjected to the considerable pressure of social norms (acknowledgement and scientific positioning in the domain, quota of published articles, academic norms, editorial tradition, etc.), the different ways in which they manifest their presence are many. Various markers realise these authorial manifestations: personal pronouns and adjectives, modals, imperatives, etc.

As academic discourse is not a homogeneous entity, these manifestations are quite difficult to consider without taking into account the notion of *genre*. Indeed, very few linguistic markers are univocal or at least stable enough to be characterised "in language", independently of genres. The first singular personal pronoun may for instance be endowed with different values: in modern philosophical texts, it hardly ever refers to the author. Authorial presence and markers are particularly subjected to genre constraints as they are socially regulated: the same markers might involve different degrees of presence, according to the author presence, whether expected or otherwise.

As a consequence, genre classifications have to be taken into account. The genre is here considered as a correlation between a socialised discursive practice and a corresponding regularity of linguistic features (Rastier 2001). Texts belonging to the same genre share a set of conventions, expressed through a set of linguistic norms that concern all types of linguistic markers: a genre is thus a level of systematic organisation of linguistic features and carries out a significant function of disambiguation. Taking genres into account also enables the analyst to make the most of markers; this descriptive capacity increases the value of using large corpora in qualitative analysis: genre-based corpora enable quantitative data to be qualified in a far more precise way.

The stabilisation provided by a genre might enable the analyst to better evaluate authorial presence in academic genres since the latter are highly regulated genres. The most obvious regulations are social and "bureaucratic" constraints weighing on research papers, such as *peer reviewing*, anonymous selections, stylesheets or even stylistic demands, such as the more and more common requirement for a *reader-friendly* style, which highly regulates authorial manifestations. Studying authorial presence in these genres is thus easier than in less regulated ones.

In that prospect, we chose to consider for this study two very different French academic genres: scientific articles in the field of linguistics and philosophical essays. Scientific articles are much more regulated than philosophical essays, which, on the other hand, are more author-centred and closely related to academic discourse, in spite of being regulated by academic conventions and philosophical traditions. However, the two genres share a common tradition in spite of their different social evolution and they are quite interesting to compare.

A set of low-level variables and correlations was selected: French personal pronouns (PP), which are traditionally acknowledged as authorial markers – JE, ON and NOUS, as well as the impersonal pronoun IL.[1] As we were particularly interested in the correlations between different parameters, rather than on a specific marker or a predefined type of authorial presence, we chose to concentrate on Subject PP[2] and their correlations to verb tenses and types.

Data and methodology

The corpus

The corpus is composed of linguistic and philosophical academic texts. The linguistics corpus is made up of six issues of three linguistic journals (*Cahiers du CIEL 1994–1995, 1996–1997, Cahiers de Praxématique 33 et 36, Revue de Sémantique et Pragmatique 6 et 8*), totalling 42 articles. We should note that none of the articles were co-written by different authors, and this fact excludes the use of the *NOUS* pronoun as referring to several authors. The corpus of philosophical texts is composed of ten texts, all of them published works by G. Deleuze and P. Macherey, making it very homogeneous and representative of classical contemporary philosophy (the selected Deleuze texts were published before his avant-garde shift in 1968). This focus on two different authors enables us to observe the incidence of personal style. The commentary and essay genres are equally represented.

A quantitative analysis was first carried out on the corpus, and the results were clarified and extended thanks to a context analysis based on selected sub-corpora.

The texts of the corpus were carefully marked up in XML (eXtensible Markup Language) according to the TEI Guidelines (Sperberg-McQueen et al. 2001). The tagging was necessary to extract certain elements that might have limited the use of computational linguistics tools and the analysis of authorial presence (foreign words or expressions, examples, quotations, examples, etc.).

Table 1 illustrates how the distribution of the PP in scientific articles varies according to the different sub-corpora.

As we can see in Table 1, in the linguistics corpus, the percentage of *JE* falls by 9.63% in full texts to 7.99% in texts without examples, quotations, foreign elements, etc. This difference is considered significant because *JE* is in fact fre-

Table 1. PP distribution in linguistics corpus[3]

	First singular PP *JE* (%)	Third singular PP *ON* (%)	First plural PP *NOUS* (%)
Full text	9.63	23.63	15.72
Texts w/o extracted elements	7.99	24.30	17.32
Quotations	4.59	20.54	17.83
Footnotes	9.20	27.87	14.34
Examples	25.58	11.16	5.19

Table 2. PP distribution in philosophical corpus

	First singular PP *JE* (%)	Third singular PP *ON* (%)	First plural PP *NOUS* (%)
Commentaries	0.63	71.04	7.29
Essays	1.01	77.41	2.8
Footnotes	3.68	12.28	16.59
Commentaries footnotes	0.84	71.07	7.84
Essays footnotes	1.75	80.63	2.39
Corpus w/o footnotes	2.75	10.83	21.23

quently used in examples[4] (25.58%), whereas there the *ON* and *NOUS* PP are little employed.

Elements which would have hindered a parsing of the texts were extracted: proper nouns, foreign words, metadiscursive elements such as *JE* in utterances as in *elle rapporte la représentation au JE comme à une libre faculté*,[5] in which *JE* – marked in capitals – is mentioned and not used, etc.

It should be noted that the philosophical essay appears to be less structured than the scientific article, and the text attempts to give the impression of continuity and to avoid any irregularity or disparity that might disturb the reasoning. However, the difference between texts with and without footnotes is too minimal to justify a quantitative analysis in this context (see Table 2).

Quantitative and qualitative analysis

As we are working on relatively large corpora (3 million words), we decided to use a morphosyntactic parser and chose Cordial Analyseur ® 8.1, developed by *Synapse development*. Although Cordial has its limits and, for example, cannot identify impersonal and anaphoric *IL*, it is an established tool and its efficiency has been proven in various corpus linguistics studies (Malrieu & Rastier 2001). The extracted sub-corpora were then tagged and parsed.

The results obtained with Cordial are quite interesting, as they provided precious genre indications; we did not, for instance, have to search for certain tenses which are not genre representative). In order to quality and refine the results, we worked at the same time on the sub-corpora to analyse the contexts of the utterances for each correlation.

Results

Results obtained on whole corpora: General tendencies

Table 3 and 4 illustrate the distribution of person[6] and verb tenses[7] in both corpora. We should mention, first of all, that the results are not really relevant for the philosophical texts, for the reasons already mentioned above.

Generally speaking, personal pronoun choice is strongly correlated to the choice of the present tense (80% verbs) and this is not surprising, since the present is the tense favoured in academic genres. In scientific articles, the 3rd person singular pronoun is noticeably correlated to the present tense. Although 3rd person pronoun here does not have the role of impersonal PP, the correlation might nevertheless indicate a general propensity of the authors to adopt the impersonal and objective style as recommended by tradition.

The first person pronouns (*JE* and *NOUS*), which display the presence of the author most visibly,[8] is highly correlated with the future tense. The 1st singular pronoun *JE* is the most frequently used with the *conditionnel* tense. Thus,

Table 3. Distribution of persons and verb tenses in linguistics corpus[9]

	First singular PP JE (%)	Third singular PP ON (%)	First plural PP NOUS (%)
Indicatif présent	54.52	79.80	51.47
Indicatif futur	14.10	2.43	20.45
Indicatif passé composé	17.47	9.47	23.52
Indicatif imparfait	5.89	1.76	1.06
conditionnel présent	4	3.19	2.27
subjonctif présent	1.47	1.88	0.13

Table 4. Distribution of persons and verb tenses in philosophical corpus

	Deleuze essays			Deleuze commentaries			Macherey commentaries		
	% JE	% ON	% NOUS	% JE	% ON	% NOUS	% JE	% ON	% NOUS
Indicatif présent	85.88	83.75	69.94	71.43	83.41	79.68	NA	77.53	75.70
Indicatif futur	0.00	1.07	4.08	3.30	2.22	4.73	4.71	1.14	3.74
Indicatif imparfait	2.35	3.93	6.80	6.59	3.02	4.25	NA	0.97	4.92
Indicatif passé simple	1.18	0.53	0.15	3.30	0.35	0.00	NA	0.74	0.00
Conditionnel présent	0.00	2.54	1.81	1.10	2.00	1.42	0.52	3.08	2.12
Subjonctif présent	1.76	1.93	0.91	3.30	2.10	1.04	1.83	3.33	1.38

the author seems to become more visible in his discourse when this is forward-looking or hypothetical. In philosophical texts, the 1st person plural pronoun *NOUS* seems to be more correlated to modals than the singular: indeed, while *NOUS* is more frequently used with the *future*, the *imparfait* and the *conditionnel* tenses, *JE* is more frequent with the *passé simple* and *present* tenses, which are often used in examples and short narratives.

These first general tendencies of course have to be clarified and extended with a systematic analysis of the verb types which are correlated with this choice.

Context analysis of the correlations between PP, verbal tenses and verb types

Self-reference
Scientific articles first differ from philosophical essays in the use of the *JE* pronoun. In French research papers, authors often use *JE* to refer to themselves, although in our data the *NOUS* PP, which used to be exclusively employed in that purpose, turned out to be less employed (*JE* was used in all texts, whereas *NOUS* was used in half of them). However, the *JE* PP is not often employed in the texts and it generally refers to the author as a scientific authority (four texts out of six).

In articles in which *JE* has no self-reference purpose (see the concept of universalisation below), *NOUS* may fulfil this function. Since authors usually disambiguate between pronouns by supplying them with a specific and set value, self-reference is in most cases expressed with one single pronoun.

JE is usually found with the present tense in both corpora (Linguistics Corpus: 64.7%; Philosophical Corpus: 85%). Although many regularities concerning verb type became apparent, no relevant regularities were found for the *JE*/Present tense correlation. In the Linguistics corpus authors use the *JE* PP to promote their scientific choices and findings or to define the scope of their research whereas *NOUS* is the only pronoun used by philosophical authors to refer to themselves. Consider the following examples:

(1)   Nous ne suggérons aucune ressemblance entre le Dionysos de Nietzsche et le Dieu de Kierkegaard. (*We do not suggest* any resemblance between Nietzsche's Dionysos and Kierkegaard's God.)   (DR)

(2)   Finalement, cette quête d'indices de contextualisation conduit, au plan de la méthode, à rassembler en premier lieu ce que j'appelle des sous-corpus

d'énoncés. (This search for contextualization signs leads to gather first *what I (would) call . . .*)   (Moirand, PRAX 33)

The author of philosophical essays seems to take on a role of "argumentation director", and this can be seen if we consider the verb lemmas combined with *NOUS*: *constater, chercher, considérer, invoquer, supposer, distinguer, apprendre, rencontrer, invoquer, demander, suggérer, vouloir dire, etc.* In the present tense, *NOUS* has an inclusive function and includes the reader. It is interesting to note that, on the other hand, it exclusively refers to the author when used in the *imparfait* and *conditionnel* tenses. It is worth mentioning that inclusive or "universalisation" values are specific to the present tense (cf. 3.2.1.1). Consider for example:

(3)   "c'est ce que nous voulions montrer..." (this is *what we wanted* to show...)   (DR)

The relationship between author and reader
In scientific articles, the correlations between *ON* and the *future* (10.4%) and *ON* and the *passé composé* (5.62%) perform a function which we could call *"reader-friendly"*. In the case of the *future*, the author directs the reading of the subsequent text with definitions and clarification:

(4)   On entendra par "description" l'énumération d'un ensemble de propriétés ne constituant pas explicitement un sous-type. (Description *will be understood* as the enumeration of . . .)   (François, CIEL 94)

The author seems sometimes to want to 'put the reader's mind at rest' about the subsequent clarification of certain issues:

(5)   On reviendra sur cette assimilation. (*we will return* to this comparison)
                                                                         (Bouquet, PRAX 33)

The correlation between *ON* and the *passé composé* is frequently used for reminders with the purpose to ensure text cohesion:

(6)   comme on l'a vu dans la seconde section ("as said in Section 2"), etc.

The correlation *JE/future* also has a *"reader-friendly"* function although, of course, *JE* does not include the reader. Only one occurrence of the *NOUS/future* correlation was identified and the author was the only one who did not employ the *ON/future* one.

In the philosophical corpus, the *ON/future* correlation allows the author to address the reader and it is worth mentioning that, in most cases, this is in order to refer him to a book. Consider:

(7)   On consultera également l'article de Michel Butor sur Roussel. (The article of Michel Butor on Roussel will also be consulted.)   (DR)

In spite of this, no dialogical relationship is established, and the absence of such a relationship is in fact a characteristic of academic philosophical style.

So, rather than with the *ON* PP, some kind of *reader-friendly* relation might be observed with the *NOUS/future* correlation in philosophical texts:

(8)   Toute la philosophie de Tarde, nous le verrons plus précisément, est fondée sur les deux catégories de différence et de répétition (we shall see it more precisely).   (DR)

Here, rather than a reader-friendly relation, we can say that philosophical discourse seems to have a more rhetorical function and this is shown in structures such as *nous devons* ('we must/have to'), in which the author points out a philosophical duty common to both author and reader:

(9)   Nous devons alors reconnaître l'existence de différences non conceptuelles entre ces objets. (We have to acknowledge the existence of . . .)   (DR)

Let us finally underline the point that the *JE/conditionnel* correlation also seems to be *reader-friendly* in scientific articles. In the following utterance, the author apologises to the reader for clarifying an issue that had already been expressed before:

(10)   En conclusion, je voudrais repréciser brièvement la notion de signifié construit d'un lexème, en la différenciant de celles de signifié prototypique et de signifié de puissance avant d'en risquer une définition. (To conclude, *I would like to* clarify again. . .)   (Pérennec, CIEL 94).

Universalisation
Contrary to the evidence found in the Linguistics corpus, in philosophical texts the pronoun *JE* never refers to the author: it always performs a universalisation function, which relies on the referential indeterminacy of the first person (Benveniste 1966). As the function of *JE* is to refer to 'any subject', we should note that both author and reader are included in this universal reference. The author acts as both the narrator and the 'actor' of what they describe and using the *JE* pronoun enables them to represent a common universe to both them-

self and the reader. Thanks to this rhetorical device, the reader's support is called upon. The pronoun relates to verb types which are not discursive but rather concrete action verbs, such as *dissoudre, refouler, mourir, voir, etc.* ('dissolve, repress, die, see'). The few epistemic-valued verbs collected always refer to 'naïve' experiences and are thus negatively valued in a philosophical perspective; these include verbs such as *percevoir, imaginer, sentir, souvenir,* etc. ('perceive, imagine, feel, remember').

It is thus possible to propose that authors refer to themselves with the *JE* pronoun only indirectly. The proportion of *JE* in the essays (4%) and the commentaries (1.6%) might validate this, as the author shows himself more in the former as he outlines his stances, whereas he mainly cites philosophical traditions in the latter.

Following the example of philosophers, two authors included in the Linguistics Corpus employ *JE* in the same way:

(11)   derrière le mur, on "voit" la maison; une *tache*, c'est une discontinuité sur une continuité anticipée: j'aperçois le fond comme constitutif de la figure. (*I see* the back as constitutive of the figure.)   (Cadiot, RSP6)

Thus, the ambiguity is all the more obvious since one of them uses *JE* both to refer to herself as well as to generalise.

A universalisation-value of the *NOUS* pronoun, similar to the one we identified for the pronoun *JE*, also came to light. The pronoun *NOUS* is only used in the present tense and in contexts where the content of the experience described is not really obvious. The author enlists the support of the reader using *NOUS*:

(12)   Nous sommes toujours Actéon par ce que nous contemplons, bien que nous soyons Narcisse par le plaisir que nous en tirons. (We are always Actéon by what we contemplate although we are Narcissus by the pleasure we get from it.)   (DR)

Objectivity/neutrality

Although the two corpora are more limited in size, the quantitative results presented in earlier can be improved upon and qualified. We note, among other things, the use of impersonal pronouns *IL* and *ON*, which were not distinguished before. The pronoun *ON* appears to be employed much more frequently than impersonal *IL* in the Linguistics corpus (249 vs. 148 occ., all occurrences taken together). Both PP are usually employed with the present tense but their use varies a lot according to verb tenses. *ON* is more often employed with the *future* tense (26 occ.) than with the *passé compose* (14 occ.) and *conditionnel* (13 occ.) tenses, whereas the choice of impersonal *IL* appears not to be correlated with the *future* tense[10] but rather with the *conditionnel* tense (9 occ.). The philosophical corpus also exhibits a clear predominance of the *ON* over the *IL* PP: *ON* has a greater dialogical and modal function and is usually employed with the *present, conditionnel* and *future* tenses, whereas *IL* is almost only employed with the present tense and with a limited number of expressions.

Impersonal *IL* is clearly associated with an objectivation and depersonalisation/de-responsabilisation function in both corpora. The author's scientific choices are all the more visible as he makes himself less visible:

> (13)   (. . .) il n'est toutefois pas certain que les déterminants, les prépositions, les auxiliaires, voire les conjonctions constituent des listes réduites et fermées, du moins en français (however, *it is not certain that* determiners. . .).
>
> (Cadiot, RSP 8)

Furthermore, impersonal structures with the pronoun *IL* clearly have a less modal function in scientific articles: 17% of the verbs are employed with an either epistemic (*sembler, apparaître*) or deontic (*falloir*) modal, and 60% of the occurrences are used with objective verbs such as *s'agir de, y avoir* and *être* (+ adjectif). It is also worth noting that these verbs are exclusively employed in the present tense.

The *conditionnel* tense is mostly employed in conjunction with deontic modality: *falloir, devoir, y avoir lieu de*, in 6 occurrences out of 9. In the three other utterances, authors reaffirm or introduce a hypothesis. In so far as the conditional is taken to be the tense of doubt and hypothesis, the *conditionnel* tense in these data seems to be incompatible with an objective impersonal structure unless there is an intention to clarify.

With the personal pronoun *ON*, the author relies on a kind of ambiguous subjectivity that is found in research papers. Although *ON* usually refers to a certain community, this sense is scarcely used in the scientific articles in the Linguistics Corpus. *ON* has usually the status of 'non-person', as it does not refer to a specific author, neither to reader nor to any given community. Contrary to impersonal *IL, ON* can be taken to refer to a prototypical individual, any competent analyst in the field, someone who can *observe, compare, découvre, retrouve* or *trouve*. The individual is of course the author, but the latter seldom employs *JE* or even *NOUS* in that perspective, as the first person pronouns are generally only used to refer to – and underline – more important scientific discoveries.

This may explain why this pronoun is often employed with the *pouvoir* modal: 38.6% occurrences in the present tense, that is, 73 occurrences collected in six papers, and 46% occurrences in the *conditionnel* tense. The following utterance is quite representative of the ones observed: here *ON* can be replaced by *quiconque* 'anyone', and this enables the author to objectivise his conclusion:

(14)   On peut en conclure que *sanft* exprime une propriété intrinsèque du terme avec lequel il entre en connexion, alors que *mild* exprime une propriété relationnelle du dit terme de connexion (*we can conclude* that...).
                                                                 (Pérennec, CIEL 94)

It is quite interesting to notice that the same correlation *ON* + modal *pouvoir* is clearly pejorative in philosophical essays: the author clearly distinguishes himself from the *ON* PP:

(15)   On peut toujours "représenter" la répétition comme une ressemblance extrême ou une équivalence parfaite. Mais, (...) (*we can always represent...*)
                                                                 (DR)

In philosophical texts on the contrary, *ON* is not combined with philosophical conceptual operations but with concrete actions – like the universalising *JE*. The pronoun *ON* refers to 'anyone', unlike *JE* and *NOUS* which refer to any member of the philosophical community or to any 'competent philosopher'. The described experience is more neutral and is not based on philosophical experience.

(16)   Mais, qu'on passe par degrés d'une chose à une autre n'empêche pas une différence de nature entre les deux choses. (*going* through different degrees ...)
                                                                 (DR)

In both corpora, *ON* is employed with epistemic verbs such as *on sait*, and this refers to common linguistic knowledge in scientific articles in the Linguistics Corpus and to factual book knowledge – in contrast to philosophical competence – in the texts in the Philosophical Corpus:

(17)   On sait qu'Aristote ne parle pas lui-même d'analogie à propos de l'être. (*It is well-known* that Aristotle does not himself mention...)   (DR)

The correlation of the pronoun *ON* with the *conditionnel* tense is in both corpora related to a position the author considers as conflicting and 'wrong':

(18)   Certes, on pourrait concevoir que les deux répétitions entrent dans un cycle où elles formeraient [...] (of course *it would be possible to* imagine...)
                                                                 (DR)

(19)   c'est dans la narrativité que se forge, comme le montre Jérôme Bruner, l'identité – l'idéal du moi pourrait-on dire dans un autre lexique (*one would say...*)

(Bouquet, PRAX 33)

Evaluation grids

Considering the evidence discussed, we can claim that certain values are common to both the linguistic scientific article genre and the philosophical one. In terms of functions related to verb tenses, for example, we notice that the *future* tense is most often employed to direct reader interpretation and to warrant text cohesion, while the *conditionnel* is used instead to express doubt or mistake. If we consider the functions related to verb types we observe that epistemic verbs are employed with impersonal *ON*/Present tense or with *NOUS*/Present tense.

However, many differences are also observed between the two genres. Let us consider the *author-reader relationship*. We notice here that in scientific articles, the style employed is quite close to the Anglo-Saxon *reader-friendly* one. In philosophical essays, on the contrary, the author only mentions his reader through an imprecise *NOUS*. This underlines the fact that the author-reader relationship seems to be on a rather egalitarian basis in scientific articles (peer relationship), whereas it appears to be asymmetrical in philosophical texts (the author possesses knowledge and the reader receives it). This can be analysed along three parameters:

a.   *Self-reference.* Linguistics authors tend to manifest themselves as *researcher-individuals* and they use the *JE* or *NOUS* pronouns a lot in a promoting purpose, whereas philosophical authors tend to limit their presence to methodological indications, although they also refer to themselves as "ideal philosophers" using the *NOUS* pronoun;

b.   *Neutrality.* As a matter of fact, the *ON* PP in linguistics articles is endowed with an "any competent researcher" value to ensure objectivity and neutrality, whereas this value was not encountered in philosophical texts. This is particularly clear with regard to the *on peut* value, which refers to "any competent researcher" in linguistics texts and to ideas the author deems to be "wrong" in philosophical essays;

c.   *Universalisation.* Philosophical genres use more universalisation techniques than linguistics articles. Although they might display a personal stance, the experience soon becomes "universalisable". Similarly, the mention of common values and duties enables the researcher to present himself

Table 5. Authorial presence in linguistics scientific articles

Correlation PP/Verb tense[11]	Verb type	Description	Frequency	Main function
JE/Présent NOUS/Présent	Variable	Either JE or NOUS I DON'T THIN THIS NOTE ADDS ANYTHING	Variable according to authors	Promoting oneself
JE/Conditionnel	S'excuser, etc.		Rare	Deference
ON/Passé composé	Appeler, trouver, voir, envisager, etc.	Reminders by author to ensure text cohesion	Moderately frequent	Reader-friendly
ON/Futur JE/Futur NOUS/Futur	Interpretation verbs: entendre, comprendre Metadiscursive verbs: développer, voir, trouver, etc.	Guidance from author of reader's interpretation of the subsequent text (explanation, clarification); attention to text cohesion.	Frequent	Reader-friendly
ON/Présent	Epistemic verbs: savoir	Invocation of a knowledge common to both author and reader	Frequent	Invocation of a common universe
JE/Présent NOUS/Présent ON/Présent	Open list of activity, perception verbs, etc.	Universalisation technique including both author and reader	Variable	Universalisation
ON/Présent	Open list of scientific activity verbs: observer, comparer, découvrir, retrouver, trouver, etc.	Reference to "any competent researcher" including both author and reader	Very frequent	Neutralisation/ Objectivity
ON/Présent	Pouvoir	Reference to "any competent researcher" including both author and reader	Extremely frequent	Neutralisation/ Objectivity
IL/Conditionnel	Modals: falloir, devoir, y avoir lieu, etc.	Scientific hypothesis/clarification proposition	Rare	Neutralisation/ Objectivity
IL/Présent	S'agir de, y avoir, être+ADJ	Foregrounding of scientific choices and backgrounding of author	Very frequent	Withdrawal
ON/Conditionnel	Pouvoir		Rare	Opposition

Table 6. Authorial presence in philosophical essays

Correlation PP/Verb tense	Verb type	Description	Frequency	Main function
NOUS/Imparfait	Closed set of discursive verbs	Comment by author on his approach	Rare	Self-reference
NOUS/Présent *NOUS/ Conditionnel*	Closed set of verbs referring to philosophical discursive activity: *constater, chercher, considérer, invoquer, supposer, distinguer*, etc.	Reference to author, but may also include reader	Frequent	Self-reference
NOUS/Futur	Metadiscursive verbs	Reader-oriented, but distance is maintained	Rare	Reader oriented
ON/Futur	Closed set: *lire, dire*	Recommendation to reader	Frequent	Reader oriented
NOUS/Présent *IL/Présent*	*Devoir* + discursive verbs; *falloir*	Reference to a common duty	Frequent	Appeal to common knowledge
ON/Présent	Epistemic verbs: *savoir*	Book knowledge	Rare	Appeal to common knowledge
NOUS/Présent	Open set of non-discursive verbs	Universalisation of an experience all philosophers can have	Rare	Universalisation
JE/Présent	(Non-philosophical) activity verbs	Universalisation; no direct reference to author	Frequent	Universalisation
ON/Présent	Activity verbs	Universalisation; reference to "anyone" and not to any philosophical community in particular	Frequent	Universalisation
IL/Présent	*Y avoir, s'agir de, être*+ADJ		Frequent	Withdrawal
ON/Conditionnel, présent, futur	Open set of verbs such as *dire, pouvoir* often expressing a hypothesis	Expression of a conflicting or "wrong" position	Frequent	Opposition

as expressing the opinion of all philosopher rather than his own. Universalisation is marginal in linguistics papers and tends to depend on the scientific sub-domains the texts belong to.

The differences highlight different strategies: in order to win the reader's support, philosophical essays invoke intimate experience and a common philosophical community, whereas linguistics articles implement a procedural exposition pattern – which accounts for why articles are so structured – and require the reader to belong to a (sub)scientific community.

These differences are synthesised in Tables 5 and 6: in linguistics papers, the *reader-friendly* and *neutralisation* poles are quite important whereas the *self-reference* as "personalisation" and *universalisation* ones are salient in philosophical essays.

Finally, evaluating authorial manifestations in linguistics articles may be done in a *functional* framework with "communicative functions" categories whereas philosophical essays are better described with rhetorical figures supporting argumentation. This situation is due to the intermediate position of philosophical genres, between academic and literary discourses.

Conclusion

Genre impact on texts is obvious if we consider the stable correlations we identified between low-level variables. This enables us to evaluate and characterise authorial manifestations in both genres. No PP indicates by its sole usage a precise type of authorial manifestation and this was based on correlations rather than on single variables.

In this study we highlighted several common configurations in the two genres. For example, concerning the use of impersonal structures with the pronoun *IL*, the correlation seemed to indicate authorial withdrawal in certain cases, while in others it was common a universalising function. We generally observed in both genres a regular correlation between potential modality, negative evaluation and personalisation.

The influence of Anglo-Saxon academic standards is quite visible in French linguistics papers, as most authors use *JE* to refer to – and to promote – themselves, as well as to express a preference for a rather *reader-friendly* style. On the contrary, philosophical essays are characterised by the absence of an established relationship between author and reader. As linguistics articles are written for *peers*, the author-reader relationship favours the egalitarian tone and neutrality is foregrounded with the use of the impersonal *ON* pronoun that refers to any competent scientist, either author or reader. In philosophical essays, the common philosophical universe in which author and reader are included also implies a common philosophical duty which is defined by the author; the relationship between author and reader, here, is far less egalitarian than in linguistics articles. Moreover, philosophers scarcely use *JE* to promote themselves as "competent philosophers" but only to refer to themselves as authors.

It is finally worth mentioning that linguistics articles and philosophical essays do not use the same strategies to win the reader's support: we have identified *neutrality* as the main strategy in linguistics scientific articles and *universalisation* in philosophical essays.

The descriptive categories were derived in an empirical way using an inter-genre comparative method. It is worth mentioning that the categories derived from linguistics articles tend to be more of the functional type and this may be due to the specificities of the genre. The corresponding categories are much less operational in philosophical texts. The establishing of common operative categories across different genres has to be seriously thought out.

Finally, the possibility of identification based on low-level criteria is very interesting with regard to different areas of computational linguistics, and automatic summarisation and information retrieval in particular. Indeed, modeling discursive configuration is still in question; this would nonetheless greatly improve identification and retrieval of relevant information.

Notes

1. Indeed, structures such as *Il va de soi qu'il ne s'agit pas d'étudier ces prépositions systématiquement/It goes without saying that there is no question of studying these prepositions in a systematic way* (Cadiot, RSP8) cannot be considered as *objective* and *impersonal*, as the *aller de soi* construction is a modal one.

2. Taking into account other markers (object personal pronouns, possessives, etc.) would have required a consideration of an almost unlimited set of correlations (themes, syntactic structures, etc.) and would have prevented us from implementing computational linguistics methods which are useful when working with large corpora because of the fine granularity of the variables.

3. Linguistics Scientific Articles.

4. More precisely when they are constructed by the author (Poudat 2003a).

5. 'It relates the representation to the I as to a free faculty'. All philosophical examples are extracted from *Différence et répétition*, PUF, 1968, henceforth *DR*.

6. After extraction of quotations, foreign elements, examples and bibliographical references.

7. The "person" here is the person of the verb, not the personal pronoun.

8. "Persons" refer to verb persons (and not to PP).

9. One of the most obvious and important ways writers can represent themselves to readers is to explicitly affirm their role in the discourse through first person pronouns (Hyland 2001, 2002; Kuo 1999; Tang & John 1999).

10. *IL* is hardly or ever unemployed with the future tense as it might suggest that the study is incomplete. Only one occurrence was collected.

11. Correlations in the same box are sorted according to their frequency.

References

Bazerman, C. (1988). *Shaping written knowledge: The genre and activity of the experimental article in science.* Madison: University of Wisconsin Press.

Benveniste, E. (1966). *Problèmes de linguistique générale 1.* Paris: Gallimard.

Biber, D. (1988). *Variation across speech and writing.* Cambridge: Cambridge University Press.

Breivega, K. R., T. Dahl, & K. Fløttum (2002). Traces of self and others in research articles. A comparative pilot study of English, French and Norwegian research articles in medicine, economics and linguistics. *Journal of Linguistics, 12* (2).

Cossutta, F. (1995). Pour une analyse du discours philosophique. *Langage, 119,* 12–38.

Fløttum, K. (2001). Le résumé scientifique – texte monophonique ou polyphonique? *Technostyle* (Sherbrooke), CATTW/ACPRTS *17,* (1), 67–86.

Fløttum, K. & F. Rastier (Eds.). (2003). *Academic discourse, multidisciplinary approaches.* Oslo: Novus forlag.

Hyland, K. (1998). *Hedging in scientific research articles.* Hong Kong: City University of Hong Kong.

Hyland, K. (2001). Teaching and researching writing. Pearson ESL.

Hyland, K. (2002). Authority and invisibility: Authorial identity in academic writing. *Journal of Pragmatics, 34* (8), 1091–1112.

Kuo, C. H. (1999). The use of personal pronouns: Role relationships in scientific journal articles. *English for Specific Purposes, 18* (2), 121–138.

Loiseau, S. (2003a). Philosophical discourse from autonomy to engagement: Deleuze commentator of Spinoza. In Flottum & Rastier (Eds.), 36–54.

Loiseau, S. (2003b). Thématique et sémantique contextuelle d'un concept philosophique. In G. Williams (Ed.), *Actes des 2nd journées de linguistique de corpus de Lorient.* Rennes: PUR.

Malrieu, D. & F. Rastier (2001). Genres et variations morphosyntaxiques. *TAL, 16,* 548–558.

Poudat, C. (2003a). Characterization of French linguistic research papers using morphosyntactic variables. In Flottum & Rastier (Eds.), 77–96.

Poudat, C. & G. Cleuziou (2003b). Genre and domain processing in an information retrieval perspective. In *Proceedings ICWE.* Oviedo, Spain: July 14–18, 2003. *Forthcoming.*

Rastier, F. (2001). *Arts et sciences du texte*. Paris: PUF.
Sperberg-McQueen, C. M. & L. Burnard (Eds.). (2001, 2002, 2004). *TEI P4: Guidelines for Electronic Text Encoding and Interchange*. The TEI (Text Encoding Initiative) Consortium. http://www.tei-c.org/P4X/
Swales, J. (1990). *Genre Analysis: English in Academic and research settings*. Cambridge: Cambridge University Press.
Tang, R. & S. John (1999). The 'I' in identity: Exploring writer identity in student academic writing through the first person pronoun. *English for Specific Purposes, 18*, S23–S39.

The Corpus

Works by Deleuze

Différence et répétition, PUF, 1968.
Qu'est-ce que la philosophie?, Minuit, 1991.
Critique et clinique, Minuit, 1993.
Spinoza et le problème de l'expression, Minuit, 1968.
Spinoza, philosophie pratique, Minuit, 1981.

Works by Macherey

The five volumes of *Commentaire de l'éthique*, Minuit, 1994, 1995, 1997, 1997, 1998.

Pragmatic force in biology papers written by British and Japanese scientists

Akiko Okamura

Takasaki City University of Economics, Japan

This study has been conducted to analyse type and tense of verbs with *we* in British and Japanese scientists' research articles in English. This is to examine non-English speaking scientists' difficulties in emphasising their role and their findings in their published work. I examined 23 biology papers (9 British and 14 Japanese) section by section.

The analysis indicates some general tendencies among the scientists. However it also showed subtle differences between the British and Japanese papers, which indicate possible disadvantages for Japanese scientists. For example, the Japanese mostly use past tense verbs with *we* throughout their papers, while the British change the main tense of verbs from present perfect in the introduction, to past in the results and present in the discussion. The findings suggest that the Japanese may not pay as much attention to the type of verbs and their tense to go with *we* as the British, to maximise the effect of *we* in their research articles.

Introduction

Non-English speakers' language and cultural backgrounds may affect their language use and text construction in writing academic texts in English (for example, Martin 2003; Mauranen 1993; Moreno 1997), which may create difficulties for their papers to be accepted in international journals in English. However, once published, we may assume little difference between English and non-English speakers' writing, as they have to conform to the expected norms of the journals in the field. In international disciplines such as science where English writing skills play a crucial role in professional survival and success, a question arises whether non-English speaking writers have difficulty in staking a claim and emphasising the importance of their contribution to the discourse community. It is worth paying attention to differences between English and non-English speakers in this respect.

In this study, I examine scientific research articles in biology written by English speaking and non-English speaking writers to compare the way in which they present their research findings. For this purpose, we first need to understand what these scientists share as members of the same discourse community.

In science their shared knowledge of linguistic features may be associated with the impersonal construction of sentences, which represents a positivist ideology of scientific discourse (Bazerman 1988; Halliday & Martin 1993; Swales 1990). In English, although impersonality is often associated with passive voice in scientific texts (for example, Riley 1991; Tarone et al. 1981, 1998; Wingard 1981), the choice of passive is not so simple; it depends on the combination of subjects and verbs (Master 1991), and information structure such as end focus (Rodman 1994; Tarone et al. 1981, 1998) and the maintenance of the flow of argument (Shaw 1992). In fact, it is important to note that impersonality can be realised by active voice with various linguistic features such as the use of inanimate subjects (Master 1991) and nominalisation (Halliday 1994).

To analyse the role of subjects in active voice, Rodman categorised subjects into 5 types (1994:315) and examined their frequency in scientific articles. She found that the most frequently used subject was the real world subject (32%) such as *alkaline granites*, which corresponds to the impersonal and objective nature of scientific discourse. However, human subjects such as *Smith, we*, were the second most frequently used type. Among them, 37% were the pronoun *we* although she agreed that "there was considerable variation in the use of the personal pronoun *we* from article to article" (1994:317). Why do writers use human subjects, in particular with the use of *we*, in supposedly impersonal scientific texts? Referring to Gosden's (1993) work on the analysis of subjects in scientific texts, Rodman (1994) describes the role of *we* as a device to provide maximum visibility and implied authority of the writers.

It seems that whereas the impersonal sentence construction itself is often described as a rhetorical means to shift responsibility from a human agent to factual data (Bazerman 1988; Martin & Halliday 1993; Swales 1990), *we* is also used as a rhetorical device to foreground the writers' contribution in the discourse community. It can be hypothesised that non-English speakers have difficulties in using *we* for this purpose.

To analyse the rhetorical use of *we* any further, it is necessary to clarify the meaning of *we* as it can refer either to readers and writers (inclusive *we*) or writers only (exclusive *we*) (Quirk et al. 1985). Through the analysis of computer science papers, Kuo (1999) found that 65.5% of the use of *we* in the analysed papers was exclusive use. In scientific texts, exclusive *we* may be a dominant pattern of use (Hyland 2001; Kuo 1999; Harwood 2005).

While *we* can be used to put forward the writers' role in research activities, it may also have a hedging effect to make the claim more tentative (Martinez 2001). The difference in the effect of *we* seems to depend on the choice of verbs that accompany *we*. We need to examine *we* in relation to its accompanying verbs in research articles to understand how writers maximise the effect of *we* on readers.

Reporting verbs have been studied to examine how writers evaluate previous studies and present their own findings through the use of tense (Gunawardena 1989; Salager-Meyer 1992) or that of type (Hyland 1999, 2001; Thomas & Hawes 1994; Thompson & Ye 1991).

Hyland (1999) compared the disciplinary differences across various disciplines such as arts, social sciences, natural sciences in the use of citation forms and that of reporting verbs. According to the type of activity, he categorised reporting verbs into three types, based on the findings of Thompson and Ye (1991) and Thomas and Hawes (1994):

(1) Research (real-world) Acts, which occur in statements of findings (*observe, discover, notice, show*) or procedures (for example *analyse, calculate, assay, explore*).

(2) Cognitive Acts, concerned with mental processes (*believe, conceptualize, suspect, view*).

(3) Discourse Acts, which involve verbal expression (*ascribe, discuss, hypothesize, state*).   (Hyland 1999:149)

Hyland's study (1999) showed that disciplinary principles seem to affect the choice of reporting verbs employed with *we*. For example, engineering and scientific papers favoured research act verbs while social science papers displayed a liking for discourse act verbs.

Obviously writers follow the norms of the field in their general use of linguistic forms. However, a detailed analysis would reveal some differences between English and non-English speaking writers.

It seems useful to examine type and tenses of verbs accompanying *we* section by section.

Research questions

This study aims to examine how English speaking and non-English speaking scientists use the pronoun *we* with certain types of verb and certain tenses in order to promote their research findings in impersonal scientific research articles. The pedagogical objective is to help non-English speaking writers construct a persuasive argument in a highly competitive field.

I will ask the following two questions in this study:

1. What do English and non-English speaking scientists share as members of the same discourse community?
2. How do they differ in their use of type and tense of verbs with *we* in emphasising their work?

Data collection and data analysis

23 biology papers (9 British and 14 Japanese papers) were collected from two American journals (*Journal of Plant Biology* and *Journal of Plant Physiology*) to avoid any differences due to the country of publishing institutions of the journals. English speakers were British researchers and non-English speakers were Japanese researchers. The criteria for identifying British and Japanese papers were writers' affiliation and/or names of the writers. As there are many collaborative works between two institutions, I avoided papers written as a result of collaboration between English-speaking countries and Japan. The reason for the choice of biology papers was because they all had the same sections: introduction, method, results and discussion (IMRD). In fact, it was not easy to locate the same sections in other fields. The difference in the number of British and Japanese papers analysed is due to the difficulty in identifying British papers according to the criteria set for British and Japanese papers. Because of this difference, it seems necessary to count not only the token number but also the type number of verbs employed with *we*.

I examined verbs with *we* separately in the three sections (introduction, results and discussion) excluding the method section because *we* is not a common feature in the method section and recently it has not been given the same importance as other parts in the research papers (Tarone et al. 1998). In fact, in all the biology papers analysed, the method section was placed at the end of the paper in reduced font.

The difficulty in categorising some of the reporting verbs, as acknowledged by Thomas and Hawes (1994), should be mentioned. Some verbs, such as *show* and *demonstrate*, may belong to the category of research act verbs as they show research process, but may also be considered discourse act verbs when presenting a result. Thus it seems necessary to examine examples rather than simply count numbers. In this study I categorised *show* and *demonstrate* as discourse act verbs because the combination of *we* and these verbs carry a verbal aspect of reporting. As I intend to examine the tense of verbs, I treated the same verb in present tense and past tense as a different item.

Findings

Common features between British and Japanese papers

The first common feature was the number of different verbs with *we* as subject ('Types' in Table 1), which may indicate the standardised nature of the use of verbs employed with *we* in biology papers.

The second was the rank order of the occurrence of tenses of verbs with *we*. Table 2 shows that British and Japanese writers used past tense most, which supports other findings on the nature of experimental research papers (Salager-Meyer 1992), followed by present and present perfect tense.

The third was that both papers mainly used *we* with research act verbs such as *examine* and *provide* as shown in Table 3, as was also found in Hyland's (1999) study.

Table 1. Type and token number of verbs with *we*

Researchers	Type	Token	Total number of papers analysed
British	63	132	9
Japanese	68	191	14

Table 2. Number of reporting verbs employed with *we* (token number)

Tense	British papers (9 papers)	Japanese papers (14 papers)
Past	66 (50%)	144 (76%)
Present	37 (28%)	33 (17%)
Present perfect	23 (17%)	12 (6.5%)
Auxiliary + verb	6 (5%)	1 (0.5%)
Total	132	190

Table 3. Number of research, discourse and cognitive act verbs used with *we*

	Number of research act verbs with *we*	Number of discourse and cognitive act verbs with *we*	Total number
British papers	109	23	132
Japanese papers	154	37	191

Table 4. Number of uses of verbs with *we* in the active voice, with inanimate subjects in the active voice, and in the passive voice

Verbs	Number of uses with *we* in active voice		Number of uses with inanimate subject in active voice		Number of uses in passive voice	
	British	Japanese	British	Japanese	British	Japanese
Discourse act verbs						
show	5	10	69	69	12	22
suggest	2	2	58	47	1	5
indicate	0	0	55	23	1	0
demonstrate	3	6	9	7	3	3
report	1	6	5	6	13	3
explain	0	0	1	5	0	4
propose	7	3	0	0	5	3
Cognitive act verbs						
know	2	1	0	0	17	5
think	0	2	0	0	8	4
consider	1	0	0	0	5	3
believe	0	4	0	0	4	1

Because both papers used a relatively small number of discourse and cognitive verbs with *we*, to understand the whole picture of the use of these verbs, I widened the study to include the same verbs that occurred with *we* in all their occurrences, and I examined all the type of subjects and voice these verbs took. Instead of examining all the verbs of these types, I focused only those employed more than five times in total in both British and Japanese papers (see Table 4). For the analysis of the combination of subjects and discourse act verbs, types of subject were divided into two: *we* and inanimate subjects which present the same information (*we show* as opposed to *this study shows*). Thus there were three sentence patterns for discourse act verbs presenting the same information such as "we suggest", "this study suggests..." or "it is suggested that...". For cognitive verbs, two sentence patterns appeared: *we* + active voice verbs and passive voice verbs such as "it is thought...". This data did not include any occurrence of *we* + passive voice of research and discourse act verbs.

Table 4 shows that the majority of discourse verbs such as *show, suggest, indicate* tended to be employed in active voice with inanimate subjects, while cognitive verbs were likely to be in passive voice. A relatively few discourse verbs such as *propose* took only *we* instead of inanimate subjects.

Differences between British and Japanese papers

Although both papers shared the general pattern of the use of verb and subject, a close examination revealed differences in relation to type and tense of verbs.

Type and tense of verbs

Table 4 also shows differences in the use of discourse and cognitive act verbs. First British papers used *propose* with *we* twice as many times as Japanese ones to stake a claim tentatively, while only Japanese papers used an objective verb, *report* with *we* to present their findings. The difference may be small but it nonetheless shows how the writers present themselves to readers.

Second, British papers seem to be more selective of the combination of *we* and verbs. For example, British papers used *we* with cognitive verbs much less than Japanese. British papers mainly used cognitive verbs in the passive voice. A similar tendency to avoid the use of *we* also appeared with research act verbs in British papers. Table 5 shows that British papers never used *we* with the following five research act verbs (*reveal, confirm, provide, imply* and *support*). It is interesting that *confirm* with *we* appeared in 4 Japanese papers but not in a single British paper.

Further analysis of verbs with *we* showed that British writers often combined two verbs such as *we attempt to examine* and *we decided to examine* to emphasise the active role of *we* as thinkers and decision makers (Table 6). British writers employed 6 types with 16 tokens of this construction, while

Table 5. Research act verbs with *we* in the active voice, with inanimate subjects in the active voice, and in the passive voice

Reporting verbs	Number of uses with *we* in active voice		Number of uses with inanimate subject in active voice		Number of uses in passive voice	
	British	Japanese	British	Japanese	British	Japanese
reveal	0	2	14	10	2	0
confirm	0	4	5	5	2	3
provide	0	0	5	3	0	0
imply	0	0	5	1	0	0
support	0	0	5	4	2	4

Table 6. Use of two-verb constructions

Section	Type of verb (token)
(a) British writers	
Introduction	1. We wish to *discover* (1)
	2. We need to *know* (1)
	3. We have attempted to *determine* (1)
Results	1. We decided to *use* (2)
	2. We attempt to *rescue* (1)
	3. We are/were unable to *provide/grow* (2)
	4. We may be unable to *detect* (1)
	5. We attempted to *express* (1)
	6. We tried to *establish* (1)
Discussion	1. We wanted to *establish* (1)
	2. We were not able to *demonstrate* (1)
	3. We did not attempt to *insert* (1)
	4. We do not wish to *endorse* (2)
	5. We will attempt to *answer* (1)
(b) Japanese writers	
Results	We decided to *use* (2)
	We succeeded in *detecting* (3)
Discussion	We need to *elucidate* (1)

Japanese writers used only 3 types with 6 tokens, never using this construction in the introduction.Considering the number of papers analysed, British papers seem to have used more than four times as many two-verb construction than Japanese papers.

Tense of verbs with we in each section

A section by section analysis reveals another difference between British and Japanese papers. Table 7 shows that in British papers the most frequently used tense changes from present perfect in the introduction, to past in the results and present in the discussion, while Japanese papers simply stick with past tense throughout the paper. Differences in the use of tense occurred in the two most rhetorically charged sections: introduction and discussion (Hyland 2001), also referred to in other studies as argumentative sections (Riley 1991; Rodman 1994).

The use of tense observed here in the British papers has also been documented in previous studies: Salager-Meyer (1992) showed that in abstracts in medical papers the main tense is present perfect in the introduction and present tense in discussion, while Gunawardena (1989) found the domi-

Table 7. Use of tense in each section

Tense/Section	Introduction	Results	Discussion	Total
(a) British				
Past	3	55	8	66
Present	4	9	24	37
Present perfect	9	5	9	23
Aux	0	2	4	6
Total	16	71	45	132
(b) Japanese				
Past	21	99	24	144
Present	13	5	15	33
Present perfect	0	3	9	12
Aux	0	1	0	1
Total	34	108	48	190

Table 8. Proportion of discourse and cognitive act verbs out of total number of verbs used in a particular tense

Tense	Past	Present	Present perfect
Japanese	22/69 (31%)	39/69 (57%)	8/69 (12%)
British	4/38 (11%)	26/38 (68%)	8/38 (21%)

nant tense in the introduction of biology and biochemistry papers to be the present perfect.

This large number of examples of past tense in Japanese papers may be attributed to their use of discourse and cognitive verbs with *we* in past tense as shown in Table 8. The British papers used only 4 of 38 discourse and cognitive act verbs in past tense (11%), while the Japanese papers used 22 of 69 of these verbs in past tense (31%).

Discussion

Shared use and differences between British and Japanese papers

This study has examined what British and Japanese writers share and differ in the use of type and tense of verbs with *we* to identify Japanese writers' difficulties in promoting their role.

Table 9.

Type of subject	Voice	Type of verb
Inanimate subject (*this study*)	Active	Discourse act verbs (*demonstrate, indicate, suggest*, etc.)
Inanimate subject (*it*)	Passive	Cognitive act verbs (*believe, conclude*, etc.)

Type of subjects and verbs

Overall British and Japanese writers seem to share the similar combination of subject, verb and voice. They used the majority of *we* with research act verbs suggesting that this is the most acceptable combination in impersonal scientific discourse. Discourse act verbs tend to have inanimate subjects such as *this study*, possibly because this combination lets the results speak for themselves. Cognitive act verbs tend to be in the passive voice with inanimate subjects, which may not be surprising if we consider the positivist-empirical principles of scientific norms. Cognitive act verbs such as *think* and *consider* were most likely to be realised, if at all, in passive voice. The general pattern of the combination can be summarised in Table 9.

However, differences also emerged between British and Japanese writers. British combined *we* with fewer cognitive act verbs such as *think* and *believe* than Japanese. British writers seem to be able to maximise the effect of *we*, which was shown in the following examples.

First, British writers used the two-verb construction much more than the Japanese writers; this construction highlights the writers' intention such as "We wish to …" and "We decided to …" and sometimes carries hedging tone to make the claim more tentative such as "We are unable to …". It seems that this two-verb construction helps to emphasise the role of writers as decision makers in conducting research and to represent them as humble members of the discourse community who acknowledge their limitations.

Second, British writers used *we* with *propose* as opposed to *report*, unlike Japanese papers which mainly used *report* with *we*. Although *propose* and *report* can be interchangeable in some contexts, *propose* seems to be used to strengthen the role of *we* as an investigator of research. It is interesting that in both types of writers in this study, *propose* only had *we* as subject while *report* had both inanimate subjects and *we* (see Table 4).

Third, British writers never used *we* with certain research act verbs. Although this difference may perhaps be due to language proficiency, other factors may also be involved. For example, the British never used *confirm* with *we*, while 4 Japanese papers did. *Confirm* is certainly an important verb to be used in research articles as it draws attention to the fact that writers found the same results as others. However, if *we* is used to emphasise writers' unique contribution to the discourse community, *confirm* may not be the most suitable verb to use with *we*. The tendency to use *confirm* with *we* by Japanese writers may be related to their cultural background in which people are educated to conform to expected social norms (Nakane 1970).

Thus the combination of *we* and verbs seems to create a different effect on readers. Another difference is shown in the use of verb tenses with *we*.

Tense of verbs

In all the papers, the most frequently used tense of verbs with *we* was the past, and this was likely to be employed in the results, as is also shown in the analysis of abstracts of medical texts (Salager-Meyer 1992) and results sections of medical research articles (Williams 1999).

However a close examination again has revealed subtle differences. Compared to Japanese papers, British papers seem to choose the type and tense of verbs depending on the purpose of a sentence; descriptions of the research procedure can be shown in research act verbs in the past tense, while the presentation of findings and their interpretation may be in discourse and cognitive act verbs in present tense (see Table 8). Consequently there seems to be a strong link with a particular tense in each section in the British papers, while Japanese papers stick with the past. In the introduction, where the present perfect seems to help to create a gap between previous studies and the writers' current work (Salager-Meyer 1992), only British writers used this tense to introduce the topic of research. It can be said that Japanese writers are disadvantaged in creating a research gap possibly due to their language difficulties (Gunawardena 1989). In the results and discussion, as past tense is normally used to report the writers' own research (Salager-Meyer 1992), Japanese seem to follow what may be expected as norms of the community. In fact, readers of three discussion sections written by Dutch biologists suggested changes most often from present to past (Burrough-Boenisch 2003). However, when writers are trying to stake a claim and seek the generalisation of findings in the discourse community, they may prefer to use present tense (Burrough-Boenisch 2003; Salager-Meyer 1992). Thus the Japanese papers' lower use of the present tense may weaken the strength of a claim. In contrast, British writers may deviate from the norms to attract the attention of readers and to produce some rhetorical effect on them.

Conclusion and implications

This study has been conducted to examine how British and Japanese research article writers emphasise their roles through the analysis of tense and type of verbs to go with *we*. Results suggest that tense and voice of sentences need to be examined in relation to the type of verbs employed with subjects. Being in the same discourse community, British and Japanese writers obviously share the norms for the use of linguistic forms in their specific field. However British writers seem to be more selective in their use of tense and type of verbs with *we*. In British papers, *we* plays a limited but active role of an investigator, interpreter, thinker, presenter or promoter, depending on the combination of *we* and tense and type of verbs. In sharp contrast, in Japanese papers, *we* may be used more widely but the role seems to be limited to that of an agent of the sentence or an actor in the sentence; this illustrates Japanese scientists' disadvantage when emphasising their claims and appealing to readers.

As the number of the analysed papers is limited, more studies are necessary to further clarify the difficulties Japanese scientists may face. Nonetheless, the findings in this study of differences can help Japanese writers to better construct persuasive scientific arguments, as they may now be alerted to paying more attention to the type and tense of verbs that combine with *we* in both the writing and reading of papers in their field.

References

Bazerman, C. (1988). *Shaping Written Knowledge*. Madison: University of Wisconsin Press.

Burrough-Boenisch, J. (2003). Examining present tense conventions in scientific writing in the light of reader reactions to three Dutch-authored discussions. *English for Specific Purposes, 22* (1), 5–24.

Gosden, H. (1993). Discourse functions of subject in scientific research articles. *Applied Linguistics, 14* (1), 55–75.

Gunawardena, C. N. (1989). The present perfect in the rhetorical divisions of biology and biochemistry journal articles. *English for Specific Purposes, 8* (2), 265–273.

Halliday, M. A. K. (1994). *An Introduction to Functional Grammar* (2nd ed.). London & Baltimore: Edward Arnold.

Halliday, M. A. K. & Martin, J. R. (1993). *Writing Science. Literacy and Discursive Power*. London: The Falmer Press.

Hanania, E. A. S. & Akhtar, K. (1985). Verb form and rhetorical function in science writing: A study of MS theses in biology, chemistry, and physics. *English for Specific Purposes, 4* (1), 49–58.

Harwood, N. (2005). We do not seem to have a theory – the theory I present here attempts to fill this gap: Inclusive and Exclusive Pronouns in Academic Writing. *Applied Linguistics, 26* (3), 343–375.

Hyland, K. (1999). Academic attribution: Citation and the construction of disciplinary knowledge. *Applied Linguistics, 20* (3), 341–367.

Hyland, K. (2001). Humble servants of the discipline? Self-mention in research articles. *English for Specific Purposes, 20* (3), 207–226.

Kuo, C.-H. (1999). The use of personal pronouns: Role relationships in scientific journal articles. *English for Specific Purposes, 18* (2), 121–138.

Lackstrom, J. E., Selinker, L., & Trimble, L. (1972). Grammar and technical English. *English Teaching Forum* 105. (Part reprinted in J. Swales (Ed. 1985), *Episodes in ESP*. Oxford: Pergamon.

Martin, M. P. (2003). A genre analysis of English and Spanish research papers abstracts in experimental social sciences. *English for Specific Purposes, 22* (1), 25–43.

Martinez, I. A. (2001). Impersonality in the research article as revealed by analysis of the transitivity structure. *English for Specific Purposes, 20* (3), 227–247.

Master, P. (1991). Active verbs with inanimate subjects in scientific prose. *English for Specific Purposes, 10* (1), 15–33.

Mauranen, A. (1993). Contrastive ESP rhetoric: Metatext in Finnish-English economics texts. *English for Specific Purposes, 12* (1), 3–22.

Moreno, A. I. (1997). General constraints across languages: Causal metatext in Spanish and English research articles. *English for Specific Purposes, 16* (3), 161–179.

Nakane, C. (1970). *Japanese Society*. Berkley, CA: University of California Press.

Quirk, R., Greenbaum, S., Leech, G., & Svarvik, J. (1985). *A Comprehensive Grammar of the English Language*. London: Longman.

Riley, K. (1991). Passive voice and rhetorical role in scientific writing. *Journal of Technical Writing and Communication, 21* (3), 239–257.

Rodman, L. (1994). The active voice in scientific articles: Frequency and discourse functions. *Journal of Technical Writing and Communication, 24* (3), 309–331.

Salager-Meyer, F. (1992). A text-type and move analysis study of verb tense and modality distribution in medical English abstracts. *English for Specific Purposes, 11* (2), 93–113.

Shaw, P. (1992). Reasons for the correlation of voice, tense, and sentence function in reporting verbs. *Applied Linguistics, 13* (3), 302–319.

Swales, J. (1990). *Genre Analysis: English in Academic and Research Settings*. Cambridge: Cambridge University Press.

Tarone, E., Dwyer, S., Gillette, S., & Icke, V. (1981). On the use of the passive in two astrophysics journal papers. *English for Specific Purposes, 1*, 123–139.

Tarone, E., Dwyer, S., Gillette, S., & Icke, V. (1998). On the use of the passive and active voice in astrophysics journal papers: With extensions to other languages and other fields. *English for Specific Purposes, 17* (1), 113–132.

Thomas, S. & Hawes, T. P. (1994). Reporting verbs in medical journal articles. *English for Specific Purposes, 13* (2), 129–148.

Thompson, G. & Ye, Y. (1991). Evaluation in the reporting verbs used in academic papers. *Applied Linguistics, 12* (4), 365–382.

Williams, I. A. (1999). Results sections of medical research articles: Analysis of rhetorical categories for pedagogical purposes. *English for Specific Purposes, 18* (4), 347–366.

Wingard, P. (1981). Some verbs forms and functions in six medical texts. In L. Selinker, E. Tarone, & V. Hanzeli (Eds.), *English for Academic and Technical Purposes: Studies in Honor of Louis Trimble* (pp. 53–64). Rowley, MA: Newbury House.

Evaluation and pragmatic markers

Karin Aijmer
Göteborg University

This study argues that pragmatic markers expressing stance are generally multifunctional and can become involved with confrontation and persuasion. In order to explain this multifunctionality the paper focuses on the properties indexicality and heteroglossia. The paper also aims to show how corpora can be used to analyse pragmatic markers. In particular it demonstrates that translation corpora can be a tool to test hypotheses about meaning and functions. Thus, the various uses of *really* in modern English are presented, based on its translations derived from a bidirectional parallel Swedish/English corpus. Although the meanings are not always tidily distinct, the intuitions of the translators make a satisfying tripartite classification into a 'reality' use, a hedging use and a conclusion from a number of alternatives.

Introduction

When we engage in interaction, our purpose is not only to convey information. At the same time we frequently express an evaluation towards the contents or the addressee. Evaluation and its realisations in language have tended to be neglected by linguists. This tendency reflects what Lyons (1995) calls "the intellectualist – and objectivist – prejudice that language is essentially an instrument for the expression of propositional thought" (Lewis 2001:4). However, in recent years linguists have become increasingly interested in how evaluation is expressed and how it should be integrated in linguistic theory.

Evaluation can be described negatively as that part of linguistic meaning which is not concerned with truth conditions or with propositions. It is a cover term for the expression of the speaker's or writer's attitude or stance towards, viewpoint on, or feelings about the entities or propositions that he or she is talking about (Thompson & Hunston 2000:5).

In order to study evaluation we need to separate out what is written about or talked about (the basic message) from the writer's or speaker's opinion or evaluation of that. In a programmatic article Michael Stubbs (1986) speaks about the need to 'strip off' all the surface markers of speaker's point of view and the need to classify these according to the degree and manner of commitment. However he warns that building up a grammar of evaluation (a modal grammar) to complement a grammar for the proposition calls for "prolonged fieldwork", "keeping armies of doctoral students" busy for years.

A start has been made on studying evaluation under different names such as Biber & Finegan's category of stance (1988, 1989), Ochs' (1996) 'epistemic and affective stance', Quirk et al.'s (1985) 'disjunct', Chafe & Nichols' (1986) 'evidentiality' and Fraser's (1996) 'commentary markers'. However more work needs to be done both from an empirical point of view and theoretically. Some of the problems or questions we need to face are the following:

–   The lack of generally accepted terminologies and classifications in this area. For example: How can these elements be classified in functional terms? How can they be defined formally?
–   What are the elements (lexical and grammaticalised structures) which fulfil pragmatic or evaluative functions in the languages of the world?

Terminological matters are less crucial than the other problems but they need to be tackled. The term which will be used here for elements expressing evaluation is *pragmatic marker*. This term is useful as a superordinate or umbrella term for elements which do not have propositional meanings but have the procedural or indexical meaning of signalling the writer's or speaker's evaluation or opinion.

It goes without saying that there is a large number of lexical and grammaticalised elements whose main function is to adopt interpersonal positions. We can try to describe the expressions formally and functionally. Formally pragmatic markers are usually placed outside the proposition, in the pre-front field, in the end-field or parenthetically. *Well* is a typical example of a pragmatic marker normally placed initially. However many pragmatic markers seem to be on the boundary between adverbs/adjuncts and pragmatic markers and are therefore more flexible with regard to position. Adverbs like *really, actually, of course*, etc. can be fused with the rest of the sentence although they are not part of the propositional meaning but their function is to comment on the proposition.

Functionally, pragmatic markers can be analysed along different parameters such as good/bad or certain/uncertain. Fraser (1996) suggests that 'commentary markers' (i.e. pragmatic markers) include value-laden markers (judgements whether something is good or bad) and epistemic/evidential markers having to do with the likelihood of an event or a proposition being true. The adverb *clearly* illustrates another parameter along which markers can be evaluated. In 'Clearly, the results from the two hospitals are unlikely to be the same' (an example from Thompson & Hunston 2000: 23), the adverb indicates not only how certain the writer/speaker is of what is to follow, but whether the information is expected or not. In this case the discourse is being evaluated in relation to its expectedness. Evaluation markers such as *certainly, of course, clearly* may also acquire textual functions in addition to the interpersonal ones. They can for instance function on the local level to link together steps in an argument or to signal how a proposition fits in with the preceding discourse or the speaker's assumptions. Some interesting studies in this area are Angela Downing's analysis of *surely* (2001), Diana Lewis' work on *of course* (2003) and the work by Scott Schwenter and Elisabeth Traugott on *in fact* (2002).

Research on evaluation faces some major challenges. On the theoretical side, there is a clear need for a model of communication which is rich enough to integrate different types of evaluation and explain them. It is obvious that such a theory is lacking and that research findings regarding various aspects of the functions of pragmatic markers have as yet not been accommodated within an overarching framework. The second challenge for research in this area is to deepen our insight into the multifunctionality of these elements in order to arrive at a satisfactory account of their semantic values and meaning relations.

In this paper I am going to discuss some aspects of evidential markers (pragmatic markers concerned with epistemic modality/evidentiality). As illustrated by *clearly*, such markers are interesting because their function can go beyond the epistemic or evidential marking of commitment or source of knowledge to signal, for example, that something is unexpected. There is a wide range of evidential markers which express a position to something which is expected. As an application of my analysis I will focus on *really* and its multifunctionality. Most of my paper will however be taken up by describing a model used for studying the functions of pragmatic markers and its theoretical underpinnings.

In line with the suggestions in previous work on pragmatic markers by Anne-Marie Simon-Vandenbergen and myself (Aijmer & Simon-Vandenbergen 2003, 2004; Simon-Vandenbergen & Aijmer 2002/2003; cf. also Aijmer et al. forthcoming), pragmatic markers can be placed under the heading of deixis or indexicality together with elements like tense and certain adverbs. By this I mean that they can indexically establish ties with the components of the speech event such as the speaker, hearer and affective or epistemic stance.

Pragmatic markers will also be discussed as a dialogic and textual phenomenon.

A further aim of my paper is to discuss methods for analysing the multifunctionality of pragmatic markers. It goes without saying that the basic
methodology for analysing the different functions of pragmatic markers involves natural discourse. An additional methodology is the use of translation
corpora. It has been amply demonstrated in the past that translation corpora
can be a valuable tool for exploring semantic and pragmatic phenomena in a
source language and that they can provide answers to questions that cannot
easily be answered on the basis of the analysis of a single language (see e.g.
Altenberg & Granger 2002; Hasselgård & Oksefjell 1999; Johansson & Oksefjell
1998). To begin with, I will discuss the indexicality of the pragmatic markers.

Pragmatic markers and indexicality

Deixis or indexicality is not restricted to language systems such as (certain)
pronouns, adverbs and tense which refer to participants, time and space in the
communication situation. Indexicality can also explain in what manner pragmatic markers refer to what is said or written. Regarding pragmatic markers as
indexical is not a new idea. Levinson (1983) considers markers such as *actually*
as deictic since they point backwards or forwards in the text. However indexicality is a broad notion which explains that pragmatic markers can be linked
not only to preceding and following discourse but that they can adopt stances
to hearers and to the content itself.

Indexicality is omnipresent in language; it explains that pragmatic stance
markers can convey information about social dimensions such as the social
identity of the participants and social acts in addition to other contextual dimensions. Because of its indexicality, stance could be regarded as a universal
linguistic phenomenon although the linguistic encodings of it differ cross-
linguistically.

According to Ochs (1996:419),

> ... linguistic structures that index epistemic and affective stances are the basic
> linguistic resources for constructing/realizing social acts and social identities.
> Epistemic and affective stance has, then, an especially privileged role in the
> construction of social life. This role may account in part for why stance is
> elaborately encoded in the grammars of many languages.

Heteroglossia

Speakers use pragmatic markers to report beliefs, certainties, feelings, etc. There is another, more rhetorical and interactive, aspect of pragmatic markers which is reflected in the way they are used to intensify what is said, to persuade or confront the reader or hearer, in addition to the epistemic function, to express a degree of uncertainty. To explain this open-endedness of pragmatic markers we have found it useful to refer to texts as heteroglossic (White 1999, 2000, 2003) and to use this insight to explain the function of pragmatic markers. The heteroglossic perspective on texts, which has been proposed by Peter White (1999, 2000, 2003), draws its inspiration from Bakhtin's dialogic view of language (cf. Bakhtin 1981) and is used by White to explain that a large number of resources can be used with a semantic or rhetorical orientation. In this approach, all texts respond to or incorporate other texts. As a result, an utterance does not only express a propositional content but also expresses an attitude to other texts.

Pragmatic markers get their meanings from being used in the communication situation. In particular, speakers indicate by means of pragmatic markers their awareness that different viewpoints exist and their willingness to align or disalign themselves with a claim or with a proposal in the preceding discourse.

It follows that the functions or attitudes ascribed to adverbial markers such as *clearly* or *really* should not in the first place be seen as expressing states of knowledge but as reflecting the process of interpersonal positioning and repositioning taking place within a text. In this view we can explain that pragmatic markers can express both agreement and disagreement with the preceding discourse or claim and that they can have both strong and weak force.

The multifunctionality of *really* – an illustration

So far I have tried to show that pragmatic markers are indexical and that they function to take up interpersonal stances towards previous discourses or expectations. I will now use this framework to demonstrate how we can account for the multifunctionality of pragmatic markers using *really* as an illustration. *Really* is one of the most frequent adverbials in spoken language and it has received a great deal of attention in the literature because of its different meanings (Paradis 2003; Simon-Vandenbergen 1988; Stenström 1986, 1999). The adverb illustrates a type of evaluation we can call 'expectedness' (Thompson & Hunston 2000); it is a pragmatic marker signalling "expectations of some kind against which knowledge may be matched" (Chafe 1986:271). Thus it is similar to *clearly* although its coded meaning is related to reality and truth rather than to perception (what is clearly seen).

Previous research on *really* has shown that it is functionally highly flexible. In what follows I will illustrate how a translation corpus can be used to get more information about the functions of *really* or to test hypotheses about its functions arrived at by other means. I am calling a *translation corpus* a bidirectional parallel corpus, that is a collection of translations in both directions (e.g. between English-Swedish and Swedish-English). Such a corpus could be regarded as a repository of translators' judgements about the meanings of words and constructions. If words are multifunctional, translators are forced to consider a number of factors such as the context, text type and situation in order to come up with an appropriate translation. The translations can therefore be regarded as tangible empirical data about the meanings and functions of pragmatic markers. For example, *really* does not have a single translation but corresponds to a paradigm of partially overlapping or discrete meanings or functions mirroring the complexity of functions of the word in the original text. Such a paradigm is illustrated in Tables 1 and 2 (Appendix). The material is taken from the English-Swedish Parallel Corpus (see Altenberg & Aijmer 2000). The corpus consists of nearly three million words of fiction and nonfiction texts which can be used for studying translations in both directions (English-Swedish and Swedish-English).

Really translated by '*verkligen*'

The epistemic/evidential meaning of *really* is associated with reality, actuality and truth.[1] This meaning is illustrated in (1) with its translation into Swedish. As seen from Table 1, *verkligen* (a semantic cognate of *really*) was the most frequent translation into Swedish.

The truth expressed by *really* can be asserted or questioned. In questions the translator uses the epistemic *verkligen* when the speaker asks whether something is really the case (whether it is true that something is the case).

(1)   Could you *really* drive a car without reversing?   (AT1)
        Går det *verkligen* att köra bil utan att backa?

(1) could be paraphrased as 'is it really true that' you could drive a car without reversing.

In (2), the truth is questioned since it is clear from the context that the speaker does not believe it:

(2)   "He *really* is dead, then," as if she hadn't thoroughly believed it before.

(DF1)

"Han är *verkligen* död, alltså", som om hon inte riktigt trott det tidigare.

(2) is paraphrasable as 'It is really true that he is dead then'.

Really has a disclaiming function (cf. White 2003:272). The claim 'that he is dead' is seen as surprising or unexpected since it is something the speaker had not believed before. The example illustrates that new functions can be derived from the meaning of 'reality' or truth because of the interactional possibilities open to speakers in the dialogic framework.

When *really* is translated by *verkligen*, it can also have a more general kind of modal meaning situated within a rhetorical, evaluative perspective on the text. Fraser (1996:184) analyses *really* as an emphasis marker since it has the function of emphasising the force of the basic message (what is written or said). In a heteroglossic or interactive perspective on *really* it could be seen as a resource used by a speaker taking stock of or confronting a contrary option as shown by the translation above. The meaning of *really* is similar to emphatic markers such as *I insist* or emphatic *do*. Some proof for the emphatic interpretation is that when the translator has used *verkligen*, it co-occurs with other emphatic markers such as *must*:

(3)   Oh, I *really* must go.   (RDA1)
       Åh, nu måste jag verkligen gå.

Really is emphatic as is apparent from the pseudo-cleft construction in which it is found:

(4)   "Well," he said.
       "All right.
       If that 's what you *really* want."   (AT1)
       "Jaså", sade han.
       "All right.
       Om du verkligen vill ha det på det viset."

Similarly in (5), the presence of the emphatic *does* signals that *verkligen* is used emphatically in the presence of some considered alternative action:

(5)   Then when I'm sure that he does understand, that he *really* does realize,
       that he feels just terrible, I'm going to open my purse and pull out a gun
       and shoot him between the eyes.   (AT1)

Sedan när jag är säker på att han fattar, att han *verkligen* begriper, att han känner sig avskyvärd, då ska jag öppna handväskan och ta fram en revolver och skjuta honom mellan ögonen.

Really translated by '*i själva verket*', '*egentligen*'

In the examples I have discussed, *really* was translated by *verkligen* and has emphatic or disclaiming meaning depending on whether the claim is interpreted as concurring with the speaker's view or as countering a speaker belief. Translations help us to discover other meanings which may be less closely related to the literal meaning. For example, *really* may be a hedge with a weaker, deemphasising (apologising, corrective) meaning.

The Swedish translations of the hedging *really* are *i själva verket* or *egentligen* but not *verkligen*. 'I själva verket' suggests that the speaker has considered an alternative view (interpretation, expectation) before making a replacement or correction:

(6)   We arrived at the island and the woman with glasses lifted me out of the canoe, and led me to a hut.
       It was *really* a bathroom.   (BO1)
       Vi kom fram till ön, och kvinnan med glasögan lyfte upp mig ur kanoten och ledde mig till en hydda. Det var *i själva verket* ett badrum.

By allowing for negotiation, *really* extends the semantic potential of the text. What is actually said is not the only alternative but the text opens up the possibility of many other options. *Egentligen* (the translation chosen in (7)) means almost the opposite of *verkligen* since it de-emphasises an option (it may not be the best alternative) and opens up the dialogic space for alternatives:

(7)   "All right, you want more toast or coffee?" she offered, as way of apology.
       He *really* didn't, but he let her fix him another cup to show that he was no longer annoyed.   (GN1)
       "Vill du ha lite mer kaffe eller rostat bröd?" frågade hon, som ett slags ursäkt. Egentligen ville han inte det, men han lät henne göra i ordning en kopp till för att visa henne att han inte var irriterad längre.

In (7) *egentligen* signals that the speaker has considered both having more toast and coffee and not doing so. The adverb does not generally express certainty or uncertainty but the speaker implies that there are other alternatives which may be equally good as in (8):

(8)   "I 'm not *really* complaining," said Kate.   (MD1)
      "Jag klagar *egentligen* inte", sade Kate.

Egentligen is used in the situation where the speaker contemplates both 'I am complaining' and 'I am not complaining'. Since both viewpoints are possible *egentligen* may signal some degree of non-commitment or de-emphasis. This is clearly the case in (9):

(9)   "I 'm not *really*.   (SG1)
      "Det gör jag *egentligen* inte.

Really translated as *'faktiskt'*

The translation as *faktiskt* represents a different meaning of *really*. *Faktiskt* ('in fact') is used when the speaker has taken stock of a variety of alternative situations or scenarios and assesses a situation which is contradictory to expectations as the alternative. *Faktiskt* could therefore implicate that an alternative is surprising or remarkable.

A sentence like (10) is typically used when the speaker has considered the alternative position ('it is like that'). As a pragmatic marker *faktiskt* underlines the fact that something is not the case although it may be expected as a reasonable alternative to the real one. In (10) it appears from the context that you could have believed there would be a different outcome:

(10)   It 's not *really* like that.   (JB1)
       Men det är *faktiskt* inte så.

Men ('but') *faktiskt* expresses that something is unexpected or remarkable in some way. In (11) the assumption is that you would have thought that I would take serious advantage of her. This assumption or expectation is rejected by *faktiskt*:

(11)   In a way it was inevitable, I suppose, in that restricted space.
       And I 'm no sexless angel.
       But I think I *really* felt more, well, fatherly towards her.   (BR1)
       På sätt och vis var sådant oundvikligt, antar jag, med det begränsade utrymmet. Men jag tror *faktiskt* att jag kände mig mera, skall vi säga, som en far för henne.

Again in (12), *faktiskt* marks an utterance as unexpected or remarkable ('you wouldn't believe it') presumably contradicting an assumption which is shared by the speaker and hearer:

(12)   "They must have been there when I bought it – overpriced anyway", was
        all Arthur said. So *really* she gave up.   (FW1)
        "De måste ha legat där när jag köpte den – den var förresten alldeles för
        dyr", var det enda Arthur sa. Så hon gav *faktiskt* upp.

Faktiskt does not serve an epistemic function but it is used to strengthen the expected option that she would not give up.

Conclusion

All utterances express an attitude or evaluation to a text or towards the hearer (reader). When the speaker uses a pragmatic marker, this is unlikely to express only a degree of commitment to the truth of what is said, but the pragmatic marker is used interactively, enabling the speaker to consider a number of alternatives opened up by the preceding discourse and assumptions about the hearer. An alternative meaning is subsequently suppressed, replaced, rejected, challenged or strengthened depending on the speaker's or writer's goals in the conversation and the particular marker which is used. *Really* has for instance illustrated that the pragmatic marker can strengthen what is said or replace assumptions by more correct ones.

Bakhtin's notion of heteroglossia can explain why pragmatic markers are multifunctional, for example, why *really* can be used to both to emphasise and to hedge what is said. For example, when *really* is emphatic, the speaker/writer must have considered different alternatives which are 'less true' before emphasising an option within this diversity. The term 'hedge' reflects the fact that the speaker or writer has failed to achieve a straightforward commitment to the truth of the utterance and that what is said is replaced or adjusted by a more correct alternative. *Really* as a hedge has the function of softening or de-emphasising rather than persuading, as shown by the translations. When *really* is translated by *faktiskt* or *men faktiskt*, its rhetorical force is persuasive. It pragmatically reinforces the opposition to a point of view which is assumed in the context.

Evaluation has been studied from different approaches. The aim of this paper has been to outline a method of dealing with the multifunctionality of pragmatic markers and to propose a theory relating pragmatic markers to other deictic elements in language. The theory of indexicality explains that texts are embedded in social life. What studies like the one described here do is to show that there are lexical or grammaticalised resources with indexical meaning which can be used interactively to respond to previous discourse or assumptions which can be inferred from the context.

Appendix

Table 1. Range of Swedish translations of *really* in English originals in the ESPC (fiction)

Swedish translation	No. of occurrences
verkligen ('really')	47
riktigt ('really')	16
verkligt	4
egentligen ('actually')	45
faktiskt ('in fact')	19
i själva verket ('as a matter of fact')	2
särskilt mycket ('very much')	2
ändå ('anyhow')	1
mycket ('much')	1
i grund och botten ('basically')	1
är det säkert ('is it certain')	1
är det sant ('is it true')	1
alldeles ('quite')	1
banne mig ('in truth')	1
allt ('indeed')	1
i praktiken ('in practice')	1
på allvar ('seriously')	1
direkt ('directly')	1
alls ('at all')	1
en riktig ('a veritable')	1
förstås ('of course')	1
i sanning ('in truth')	1
men ('but')	1
bara (inte) ('only not')	1
på hedersord ('on my word of honour')	1
omission	41
Total	194

Table 2. Range of Swedish originals translated as *really* in English in the ESPC (fiction)

Swedish original	No. of occurences
verkligen ('really')	58
riktigt ('really')	48
egentligen ('actually')	28
faktiskt ('in fact')	10
verkligt ('really')	5
väl ('surely')	5
nog ('probably')	4
i själva verket ('as a matter of fact')	4
alldeles ('quite')	4
så ('so')	3
synnerligen ('particularly')	2
ordentligt ('properly')	2
direkt ('directly')	2
alltså ('thus')	2
alls ('at all')	2
uppriktigt ('sincerely')	1
särskilt mycket ('very much')	1
så noga ('so important')	1
så mycket ('so much')	1
på allvar ('in seriousness')	1
nu ('now')	1
mycket ('much')	1
mest ('most')	1
med bestämdhet ('with certainty')	1
liksom ('like')	1
knappast ('scarcely')	1
ju ('as you know')	1
helt ('quite')	1
gärna ('willingly')	1
ens ('even')	1
enormt ('enormously')	1
other	12
omission	81
Total	288

Note

1. *Really* also serves as an intensifier before an adjective in a use where it is not a pragmatic marker. This use, which will not be commented on further, is reflected in many of the translations into Swedish.

References

Aijmer, K. & Simon-Vandenbergen, A.-M. (2003). The discourse particle *well* and its equivalents in Swedish and Dutch. *Linguistics, 41* (6), 1123–1161.

Aijmer, K. & Simon-Vandenbergen, A.-M. (2004). A model and a methodology for the study of pragmatic markers: The semantic field of expectation. *Journal of Pragmatics, 36*, 1781–1805.

Aijmer, K., Foolen, A., & Simon-Vandenbergen, A.-M. (forthcoming). Discourse particles in the perspective of heteroglossia. In K. Fischer (Ed.), *Approaches to Discourse Particles*. (Studies in Pragmatics.) Amsterdam: Elsevier.

Altenberg, B. & Aijmer, K. (2000). The English-Swedish Parallel Corpus: A resource for contrastive research and translation studies. In C. Mair & M. Hundt (Eds.), *Corpus Linguistics and Linguistic Theory. Papers from the 20th International Conference on English Language Research on Computerized Corpora (ICAME 20), Freiburg im Breisgau 1999* (pp. 15–33). Amsterdam & Philadelphia: Rodopi.

Altenberg, B. & Granger, S. (2002). *Lexis in contrast*. Amsterdam & Philadelphia: John Benjamins.

Bakhtin, M. M. (1981). *The Dialogic Imagination. Four Essays by M. M. Bakhtin*. Edited by M. Holquist. Translated by C. Emerson & M. Holquist. Austin: University of Texas Press.

Biber, D. & Finegan, E. T. (1988). Adverbial stance types in English. *Discourse Processes, 11*, 1–34.

Biber, D. & Finegan, E. T. (1989). Styles of stance in English: Lexical and grammatical marking of evidentiality and affect. *Text, 9*, 93–124.

Chafe, W. (1986). Evidentiality in English conversation and academic writing. In Chafe & Nichols (Eds.), 261–272.

Chafe, W. & Nichols, J. (Eds.). (1986). *Evidentiality: The Linguistic Coding of Epistemology* (pp. 261–272). Norwood, NJ: Ablex.

Downing, A. (2001). "Surely you know!" *Surely* as a marker of evidentiality and stance. *Functions of Language, 8* (2), 251–282.

Fraser, B. (1996). Pragmatic markers. *Pragmatics, 6* (2), 167–191.

Hasselgård, H. & Oksefjell, S. (Eds.). (1999). *Out of Corpora. Studies in Honour of Stig Johansson*. Amsterdam & Atlanta, GA: Rodopi.

Johanssson, S. & Oksefjell, S. (Eds.). (1998). *Corpora and Cross-Linguistic Research: Theory, Method and Case Studies*. Amsterdam & Atlanta, GA: Rodopi.

Levinson, S. C. (1983). *Pragmatics*. Cambridge: Cambridge University Press.

Lewis, D. (2001). Review of Hunston, S. & Thompson, G. (Eds.), *Evaluation in Text. Authorial Stance and the Construction of Discourse*. Oxford: Oxford University Press in Linguist List 12.1637.

Lewis, D. (2003). Rhetorical motivations for the emergence of discourse particles, with special reference to English *of course*. In T. van der Wouden, A. Foolen, & P. van de Craen (Eds.), *Particles. Belgian Journal of Linguistics, 16* (pp. 79–91).

Lyons, J. (1995). *Linguistic Semantics*. Cambridge: Cambridge University Press.

Ochs, E. (1996). Linguistic resources for socializing humanity. In J. Gumperz & S. C. Levinson (Eds.), *Rethinking Linguistic Relativity* (pp. 407–437). Cambridge: Cambridge University Press.

Paradis, C. (2003). Between epistemic modality and degree: The case of *really*. In R. Facchinetti, F. Palmer, & M. Krug (Eds.), *Modality in Contemporary English* (pp. 197–220). Berlin & New York: Mouton de Gruyter.

Quirk, R., Greenbaum, S., Leech, G., & Svartvik, J. (1985). *A Comprehensive Grammar of the English Language*. London: Longman.

Schwenter, S. & Traugott, E. C. (2000). Invoking scalarity: The development of *in fact*. *Journal of Historical Pragmatics, 1* (1), 7–25.

Simon-Vandenbergen, A.-M. (1988). What *really* really means in casual conversation and in political interviews. *Linguistica Antverpiensia, XXII*, 206–225.

Simon-Vandenbergen, A.-M. & Aijmer, K. (2002/2003). The expectation marker *of course* in a cross-linguistic perspective. *Languages in Contrast, 4* (1), 13–43.

Stenström, A.-B. (1986). What does *really* really do? Strategies in speech and writing. In G. Tottie & I. Bäcklund (Eds.), *English in Speech and Writing* (pp. 149–163). Uppsala: Acta Universitatis Upsaliensis.

Stenström, A.-B. (1999). *He was really gormless – She's bloody crap*. Girls, boys and intensifiers. In Hasselgård & Oksefjell (Eds.), 69–78.

Stubbs, M. (1986). A matter of prolonged fieldwork: Towards a modal grammar of English. *Applied Linguistics, 7* (1), 1–25.

Thompson, G. & Hunston, S. (2000). Evaluation: An introduction. In S. Hunston & G. Thompson (Eds.), *Evaluation in Text. Authorial Stance and the Construction of Discourse* (pp. 1–27). Oxford: Oxford University Press.

White, P. (1999). A quick tour through appraisal theory. Background paper for Appraisal workshop, University of Ghent, March 1999.

White, P. (2000). Dialogue and inter-subjectivity: Reinterpreting the semantics of modality and hedging. In M. Coulthard, J. Cotterill, & F. Rock (Eds.), *Working with Dialogue* (pp. 68–80). Max Niemeyer Verlag: Tübingen.

White, P. (2003). Beyond modality and hedging: A dialogic view of the language of intersubjective stance. *Text, 23* (2), 259–284.

"This seems somewhat counterintuitive, though…"

Negative evaluation in linguistic book reviews by male and female authors

Ute Römer
University of Hanover

This study, using a corpus of book reviews in linguistics, considers the ways in which academic book reviewers make negative evaluations, and in particular it examines whether there are systematic differences between male and female reviewers. The paper focuses on their use of adjectives such as *surprising* and *disappointing*, and concludes that our stereotypes of language and gender relations are not entirely reliable.

Introduction: Book reviews, evaluation, and gender

In an introductory article on evaluation in text, Thompson and Hunston describe "the expression of the writer's or speaker's opinion" as "an important feature of language" (2000:2). What they say about language in general is true in particular for a special type of language: the language of book reviews. In book reviews, a genre that so far has been rather neglected in the study of academic writing (cf. for instance Motta-Roth 1996:99; Hyland 2000:43), the expression of opinions is a central feature. Authors of reviews provide the research community with valuable information about new publications in their area of study and thus help us choose from the wide range of books available those books which we might most profit from. Reviewers do this by commenting on the book and by telling potential readers what they think about it.

In the guidelines for submitting reviews for Linguist List issues, prospective reviewers are explicitly asked to "point out merits and defects, identify problems, ask questions, and present positive or negative implications of the analysis", in addition to summarising the book's contents (Linguist List 2003: 2). In an article entitled 'Reviewing books for scholarly journals', Erwin states something very similar to this when he claims that "[t]he two components that epitomize a traditional book review are a summary of the book's content and an evaluative commentary" (1992: 113). Hyland even puts the expression of opinions at the heart of any text of this academic genre by saying that "reviews are centrally evaluative" (2000: 41). The present paper focuses on evaluation, or, more precisely, on negative evaluation in book reviews, and looks at ways in which review authors refer to defects, problems, or weaknesses of the work under scrutiny.

My main interest lies in the expression of *negative* evaluation (e.g. *this position is somewhat confusing*, attested example) as it seems to be more problematic to find an appropriate way to comment negatively on a book than to praise its positive features. Reviewers, including myself, may often find it difficult to express criticism of other researchers' works in a polite way, face-saving in the sense of Brown and Levinson (1987), both for the reviewer and for the author of the book. One part of the analysis will therefore discuss the use of downtoning devices or so-called hedges (e.g. the adverbial *somewhat* in the above example) as a means of reducing the impoliteness or face-threat of a critical comment.

In addition to this pragmatic part of the analysis, I will also include a sociolinguistic dimension and look at reviews produced by female authors separately from those produced by male authors to see whether women and men evaluate differently, without assuming beforehand that they do. While a number of sociolinguistic studies deal with the distribution of features in the spoken discourse of women and/or men (e.g. Coates 1996; Tannen 1990), we know little about the language and gender relation in written texts (but see Meinhof 1997). Besides, a large number of the analyses of spoken language and gender are either based on intuitive subjective data or on small samples of authentic material collected from conversations in specific contexts (e.g. Cameron 1997; Lakoff 1975). There is, hence, certainly a need for larger-scale empirical investigations on the relationship between language and gender in spoken and, in particular, in written English. The present study can be regarded as a first step in this direction, in that it uses authentic non-intuitive corpus data to investigate an important part of the written academic discourse of men and women.

The empirical study: Exploring BRILC

The starting point for the empirical analysis of negative evaluative expressions in male and female writing is an explorative approach to a corpus of linguistic book reviews. Before I report on the actual corpus-analytic procedure and present the central findings of the investigation, I will give a brief outline of the corpus and describe its most important features.

The Book Reviews In Linguistics Corpus (BRILC): Design and compilation

The Book Reviews In Linguistics Corpus (BRILC) was specifically compiled for the present study. It is an electronic collection of English language reviews published on the internet in issues of the Linguist List, an online mailing list and forum for exchanging information on the study of language and languages. BRILC is designed as an open-ended monitor corpus which does not have a fixed size but to which new texts are added periodically. The research reported on in this article is based on a 500,000-word corpus (size in February 2003), consisting of 222 book reviews, 111 written by female and 111 by male authors.

All texts in the corpus are kept in plain text file format, and so far no meta-linguistic annotational material (like word class labels or paragraph markers) has been added. In the compilation of BRILC I decided to include full texts instead of text samples because it seemed likely that evaluative expressions were not evenly distributed across each review (cf. also Motta-Roth's 1996 findings). Hence, text sampling may have meant skewing the data and probably also the results of the analysis.[1] However, some minor textual editing was carried out: review headers (including date of publication, email address and affiliation of the author), footnotes, and references were cut and any kind of information about the reviewer (name, affiliation, research interest) was deleted. In connection with this editing process the text files were sorted into two subfolders: "BRILC texts written by female authors" (BRILC female) and "BRILC texts written by male authors" (BRILC male). The resulting internal structure of BRILC thus allows corpus searches by reviewer gender.

Tracing negative evaluative expressions in BRILC

Following Thompson and Hunston's general definition of evaluation (2000: 5), I regard negative evaluation in book reviews as a cover term for the reviewer's expression of a negative attitude towards, a negative viewpoint on, or negative

feelings about the book under review. What I did to trace negative evaluative expressions in BRILC was take a corpus-driven approach to the topic of
negative evaluation, i.e. a let-the-data-guide-you approach without any pre-
formulated ideas or fixed categories in mind (for a detailed account of the
corpus-driven approach see Tognini-Bonelli 2001). In this context the cen-
trality of any kind of corpus work in the examination of evaluative devices in
language ought to be stressed. I would like to join Joanna Channell in her argument and show that "analysis of evaluation can be removed from the chancy
and unreliable business of linguistic intuitions and based in systematic observation of naturally occurring data" as it "allows observations which go beyond
what intuitions can achieve" (2000: 39).

I started my investigations from the corpus data. First of all I ran a BRILC
query on the search term *book* to see how the noun is pre- or postmodified and
what kinds of comments are usually made about "the book". Of course, not all
instances of *book* referred to the work under review. Thus, a careful manual
sorting of the concordance lines was necessary. In a second step I read through
ten of the 222 files included in the corpus, five written by male and five by female reviewers. By carrying out these two initial analytic steps, I found different
types of lexically based negative criticism which can be grouped according to
word classes:

1. nominal criticism, e.g. *problems, shortcomings, weaknesses, the absence of X*
2. verbal criticism, e.g. the book + *does not X, would have benefited from X,
   suffers from X, seems to lack X, might hinder readers from X, could have been
   made more readable*
3. adverbial criticism, e.g. *abruptly, unnecessarily*; a positive comment + a
   concessive adverb (*however, though*)
4. adjectival criticism, e.g. *clear* + negation, *confusing, unclear, vague*.

This last type of criticism seemed on the one hand to provide a greater lexical variety than types 1 and 3 (nominal and adverbial criticism), while on the
other hand being easier to trace and handle than the rather complex verbal
constructions I found (type 2). This was especially so when studying an unan-
notated plain text corpus. I therefore decided to look at adjectival criticism in
some more detail and centre all further analytic steps on negative evaluative
adjectives.

The next task was then to find a larger number of critical adjectives in
BRILC. While determining a local grammar of evaluation in text, Hunston and
Sinclair found that language "patterns may be used to identify evaluative ad-
jectives" (2000: 91). A pattern that was noticeable in the reviews I read involved

N	Concordance
18	ther sections, for instance 5.5, remain somewhat opaque because formal con
19	cated and theoretically informed, albeit somewhat out of date, analysis.
20	d yet, the essay devoted to his work is somewhat outdated: It deals extensivel
21	oundary between lexicon and syntax is somewhat porous, since some linguisti
22	personality Thoughts of Edward Sapir, somewhat puzzling in nature, are pres
23	ur through eight. This makes the book somewhat repetitive in the presentatio
24	e, and a single interview and therefore somewhat skewed. Although the excer
25	thors' treatment of these two topics is somewhat superficial because they did
26	ker." This is a rather vague statement, somewhat surprising for a work which i
27	r analyses of specific speech acts. It is somewhat surprising to see more tha
28	he phenomenon of "speech acts". It is somewhat surprising that only 21 page
29	approaches to demonstratives. This is somewhat surprising, given the importa
30	nd the answer given is both vague and somewhat unclear (pp. 5-6). The disc
31	formance be characterized. It remains somewhat unclear, if the speakers of
32	int" in "ne ... pas" construction) is also somewhat unexpected. The authors
33	strands of research, however, is Bell's somewhat vague proposal (p. 168) of
34	from all three sites the presenter was somewhat wooden and failed to achie

Figure 1. Part of a BRILC concordance of *somewhat*, sorted to the right (1R, 2R)

the co-occurrence of negative evaluative adjectives with either a form of the verb SEEM or a premodifying adverb, like *somewhat*, *rather*, or *quite*, which has a softening or downtoning effect. This pattern (downtoning adverb or form of SEEM + negative evaluative adjective) was hence used as a means of adjective identification. I compiled and examined BRILC concordances of *quite*, *rather*, *somewhat*, and *seem**, including the forms *seem*, *seemed*, *seemingly*, *seems* (see Figure 1 for a concordance of the downtoner *somewhat*), the result of which was a list of 70 critical adjectives that occurred as collocates of one or several of these search items.[2] The automatic compilation and sorting, and the manual filtering of concordances of each of these 70 adjectives led to the results reported on in the following sections.

Focussing on negative evaluative adjectives: Adjectival criticism and the value system of linguists

As Knowles (1989) states in his study on the "suasive nature" of the language in tourist brochures, there is a close connection between evaluation in a text and the ideology of the group of people the text is aimed at. Evaluative expressions usually mirror ideological features of a social group or discourse community and need "to be discussed in terms of the value system of the community" (Hunston 1993:71). A similar statement is made by Bolívar, who observes that "evaluation is more than expressing feelings and opinions, it concerns attitudes and value systems" (2001:135). Thus, when we look at features of evaluation in book reviews written by linguists, we automatically get an insight into the value system of the linguistic community, which can be regarded as a community of practice, "an aggregate of people who come together around mutual engagement in an endeavour" (Eckert & McConnell-Ginet 1992b:434; also in Eckert & McConnell-Ginet 1992a).

According to Hyland, the construction of knowledge takes place inside particular communities of practice which "exist in virtue of a shared set of assumptions and routines about how collectively to deal with and represent their experiences" (1999:121). I will be trying to show that corpus research on the use of negative evaluative adjectives in texts written by and for linguists can provide us with information about the shared assumptions and the central norms of the linguistic community. For this purpose, BRILC concordances of the 70 adjectives traced by the preceding analytic steps were compiled and filtered manually. This manual filtering process was necessary to make sure that only such occurrences of the adjectives were included in which a critical comment was made on the book under review, and not on other sources like texts or theories the book referred to. Figure 2 shows an example of such a filtered concordance.

The result of the concordancing, filtering, and counting process was a frequency list of critical adjectives. The following are the top 20 items in this list

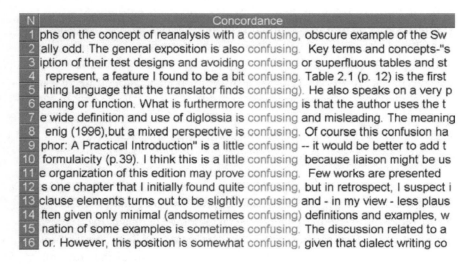

N	Concordance
1	phs on the concept of reanalysis with a confusing, obscure example of the Sw
2	ally odd. The general exposition is also confusing. Key terms and concepts-"s
3	iption of their test designs and avoiding confusing or superfluous tables and st
4	represent, a feature I found to be a bit confusing. Table 2.1 (p. 12) is the first
5	ining language that the translator finds confusing). He also speaks on a very p
6	eaning or function. What is furthermore confusing is that the author uses the t
7	e wide definition and use of diglossia is confusing and misleading. The meaning
8	enig (1996),but a mixed perspective is confusing. Of course this confusion ha
9	phor: A Practical Introduction" is a little confusing -- it would be better to add t
10	formulaicity (p.39). I think this is a little confusing because liaison might be us
11	e organization of this edition may prove confusing. Few works are presented
12	s one chapter that I initially found quite confusing, but in retrospect, I suspect i
13	clause elements turns out to be slightly confusing and - in my view - less plaus
14	ften given only minimal (andsometimes confusing) definitions and examples, w
15	nation of some examples is sometimes confusing. The discussion related to a
16	or. However, this position is somewhat confusing, given that dialect writing co

Figure 2. BRILC concordance of *confusing*, filtered and sorted to the left (1L, 2L)

(with absolute frequencies of occurrence in BRILC behind each adjective in brackets):

1. *clear* + negation (40)	11. *convincing* + negation (7)
2. *confusing* (16)	12. *narrow* (7)
3. *unclear* (16)	13. *mysterious* (6)
4. *difficult* (15)	14. *odd* (6)
5. *vague* (15)	15. *awkward* (5)
6. *unfortunate* (14)	16. *disappointing* (5)
7. *lengthy* (12)[3]	17. *obscure* (5)
8. *surprising* (10)	18. *puzzling* (5)
9. *hard to* + verb (9)	19. *superficial* (5)
10. *misleading* (8)	20. *circular* (4)

This frequency ranking can certainly provide us with some interesting information about the value system of the linguistic community. The list can teach us something about the requirements for good academic writing and about the ideology behind it in that it shows which characteristics of a book are usually criticised by reviewers. It is probably a clever move to first find out what is considered a bad feature of linguistic writing and is hence to be avoided, if the aim is to write a book that meets the norms for a good piece of linguistic writing. Judging from the negative evaluative adjectives frequently used in BRILC texts, linguists[4] value highly clarity in writing, as the token numbers of *clear* + negation, *confusing*, *unclear*, and *misleading* show. Other features that determine the quality of a good book are brevity or the avoidance of redundant information ($\neq$ *lengthy*), information which is to the point ($\neq$ *vague*), coherence and logical connections ($\neq$ *surprising*), convincing argumentation ($\neq$ *convincing* + negation), development of thoughts ($\neq$ *circular*), thoroughness ($\neq$ *superficial*), and what I would term 'easy informational access' ($\neq$ *difficult, obscure*).

A data-guided approach to evaluation in book reviews thus tells us something about ideology in linguistics and reveals, to use Motta-Roth's words, "what is considered to be desirable or undesirable, important or unimportant in the intellectual apparatus of the field" (1996:115).

In the next part of the paper, I will investigate whether, within the community of linguists, male and female members of the group emphasise different values or favour different critical adjectives in assessing the quality of a book.

Adjectival criticism and reviewer gender

In this section I shall address the question "Do women and men, in the context of linguistic review writing, criticise differently?" It has to be stressed again that this question clearly differs from traditional questions on language and gender in that it does not presuppose that there *are* in fact differences between the use of criticism by male and female reviewers. We have to be aware of the dangers which lie in approaching language data with preconceived ideas and certain expectations about the findings in mind, because the outcome of the research is likely to be influenced by these initial expectations and by the type of questions asked. We should thus take Bing and Bergvall seriously when they state that

> Linguists must realize that when they publish answers to the question, 'How do women and men speak differently?', their discoveries of difference may be co-opted for the purpose of strengthening gender polarization.   (1996: 18)

To facilitate the comparison of the ways in which female and male linguists use negative evaluation, each of the 70 manually filtered concordances of critical adjectives was automatically sorted according to reviewer gender. Figure 3 shows such a gender-sorted concordance of the search word *lengthy*.

As can be seen in Figure 3, equal shares of concordance lines (6/6) come from texts written by women and men respectively. Although this is not the case for all adjectives under investigation, this result mirrors the general findings of the gender-related part of the present analysis. Of 297 instances (tokens) of critical adjectives in BRILC, going back to the list of the 70 different search items (types), 147 entries (49.5%) are from the male reviewers subcorpus and

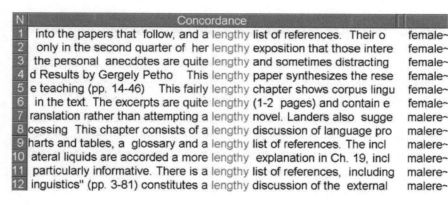

Figure 3. BRILC concordance of *lengthy*, sorted according to reviewer gender

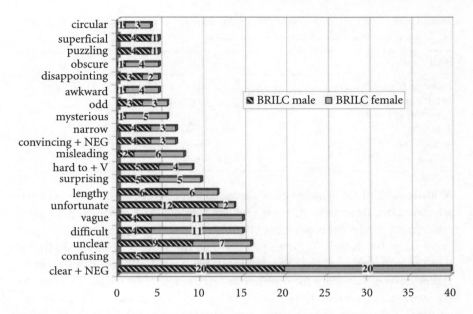

Figure 4. Gender-differentiated distribution of the 20 most frequent critical adjectives in BRILC

150 (50.5%) from the female reviewers section. There are thus no significant gender-related differences with respect to overall token frequencies. In the case of the distribution of types, the difference between the female and male sub-corpora is slightly bigger but still not statistically significant (according to the chi-square statistical test). Of the 70 adjectives under analysis, 54 occur in male-authored reviews whereas a smaller set of 46 adjectives is used by female authors. More significant differences can be found when we look more closely at the distribution of individual adjectives across texts in the two components of BRILC. Figure 4 graphically displays the frequencies of occurrence of the 20 most often used critical adjectives in BRILC male and BRILC female.

As we can see, some of the adjectives (e.g. *unfortunate, puzzling*) occur more frequently in male-authored reviews, while others (e.g. *difficult, misleading*) are preferred by female review writers. However, a comparison of the top six frequency lists of negative evaluative adjectives in BRILC female and BRILC male reveals similarities rather than discrepancies (cf. Table 1). Four of these higher frequency adjectives (*clear* + negation, *confusing, lengthy, unclear*) appear in both lists, whereas only two of the items in the male list (*unfortunate, hard to* + verb) and in the female list (*difficult, vague*) are found in positions

Table 1. Most frequently used negative evaluative adjectives in the BRILC subcorpora (absolute frequencies of occurrence in brackets)

BRILC male	BRILC female
1. *clear* + negation (20)	1. *clear* + negation (20)
2. *unfortunate* (12)	2. *confusing* (11)
3. *unclear* (9)	3. *difficult* (11)
4. *lengthy* (6)	4. *vague* (11)
5. *confusing* (5)	5. *unclear* (7)
6. *hard to* + verb (5)	6. *lengthy* (6)

of lower rank in the female and male charts respectively. Also, a look at a few selected adjectives shows that what we are tempted to deduce from Figure 4 concerning gender differences may be misleading. Four of the 11 instances of *vague* in BRILC female, for example, occur in the same review. This indicates that the preferences of individual authors for certain adjectives must not be neglected and that there may well be at least as much *intra*-gender variation (i.e. variation within the male or female sex group) as there is *inter*-gender variation.[5] Certainly, a larger collection of texts is needed for the retrieval of higher absolute token numbers if more reliable statements on qualitative adjective specific differences between negative evaluation strategies of male and female reviewers are to be made. However, even then we cannot be entirely sure whether differences really arise from the preferences of women and men (as members of two gender groups) or rather from the preferences of individual reviewers.

Hedged adjectival criticism and reviewer gender

One of the definitions under the entry "hedge (verb)" in the Cobuild English Dictionary says that "[i]f you **hedge**, you avoid [...] committing yourself to a particular action or decision" (Sinclair et al. 1995:784). The idea of 'avoiding commitment' is also central to the concept of hedging in linguistics (cf. e.g. Hyland 1999:103).[6] By refusing to fully commit themselves to what they write, e.g. by using *seems* instead of *is* in the sentence *This seems quite anachronistic for a book published in 2000* (BRILC), writers make their statements appear less forceful, convey indeterminacy or vagueness, and put themselves in a detached position. In this context, Hyland (1998:1) lists "the kind of caveats like *I think, perhaps, might* and *maybe*" as hedging devices and stresses their expression of tentativeness or softening which goes hand in hand with a reduction of the speaker/writer commitment. As "the review is a potentially threatening genre"

N	Concordance
1	constructions" and "contexts", and it is surprising that this question has not be
2	y attempt to make it an 'Irish joke'. It is surprising to me that it was related in
3	f our participants" (p.7). This is a little surprising, as one would expect that e-
4	ir insistence on this point is particularly surprising given that the preceding pap
5	E, SUCCEED, TOGETHER may seem surprising at a first glance, but the auth
6	is a rather vague statement, somewhat surprising for a work which is otherwis
7	s to demonstratives. This is somewhat surprising, given the important role play
8	enon of "speech acts". It is somewhat surprising that only 21 pages are devot
9	of specific speech acts. It is somewhat surprising to see more than 340 pages
10	f grammaticalization, and it is therefore surprising that the term grammaticalizat
11	on different multilingual corpora, it was surprising that practically all the article

Figure 5. BRILC concordance of *surprising*, including hedged and un-hedged examples

(Hyland 2000: 56) and as criticism inevitably creates a certain amount of tension, hedges are needed as a means of softening this tension and weakening the threat of the criticism, hence minimising the risk of loss of face, and at the same time making the utterance more polite.[7] Politeness can thus be regarded as the main motivating factor for the use of hedging. Figure 5 illustrates how *somewhat*, *may seem*, *to me*, and *a little* are used as hedges in some of the reviews to soften the force of the critical adjective *surprising*.

It is a common belief that in general women are more polite than men and that female language contains more hedges than male language (see for instance Holmes 1995). For the present analysis this would mean that the percentages of hedged negative evaluative statements should be significantly higher in BRILC female than in BRILC male. However, if we determine the shares of hedging in the subcorpora of BRILC, we do not find any significant differences between the numbers of [hedge + negative adjective] combinations in reviews written by women and men but almost equal percentages. In BRILC female, hedging devices (like *rather, somewhat, it seems, I think*) were found in 83 of 150 examined concordance lines (55.3%). With 53.7% (79 out of 147 instances) the relative number of hedged critical statements in texts written by male reviewers is only slightly lower. Thus, concerning the shares of hedging of all analysed adjectives as a group, no significant gender-related differences could be found.

A look at the adjectives whose shares of hedging lie far above average (i.e. above 53.7% or 55.3%) reveals similarities as well as differences between BRILC female and BRILC male (cf. Table 2). Apparently, reviewers in both gender groups feel a need to hedge their statements when they use [*convincing* + negation] or [*clear* + negation]. While male reviewers show particularly high shares

Table 2. Adjectives showing particularly high shares of hedging in reviews by male and female authors

BRILC male	BRILC female
convincing + negation: 100% (4 in 4)	*convincing* + negation: 100% (3 in 3)
misleading: 100% (2 in 2)	*disappointing*: 100% (2 in 2)
confusing: 80% (4 in 5)	*unfortunate*: 100% (2 in 2)
surprising: 80% (4 in 5)	*awkward*: 75% (3 in 4)
clear + negation: 75% (15 in 20)	*clear* + negation: 75% (15 in 20)

of hedging with *misleading, confusing,* and *surprising,* female authors score above average for the percentages of softened utterances e.g. with *disappointing, unfortunate,* and *awkward.* However, it has to be noted that, because of the very small absolute numbers of [adjective + hedge] occurrences in BRILC male and BRILC female (cf. Table 2), the results have to be treated with extreme caution and must not be overrated. Generalisations about the hedging preferences of women and men on the basis of these findings are hence rather problematic. Besides, as was the case with adjectival criticism in general, it is likely that results on hedged adjectival criticism which hint at inter-gender differences in fact refer back to possibly gender-independent preferences of individual review authors. These findings support Poos and Simpson's observation, based on a subsection of the Michigan Corpus of Academic Spoken English (MICASE), that "there is no significant gender-related effect on speakers' hedging frequencies" (2002: 20).[8]

Theoretical implications: Rethinking language and gender relations

According to the results of the present analysis, there are no significant differences between female and male writers concerning their use of adjectival criticism in linguistic book reviews.[9] Traditional assumptions that in general women are less critical than men and that there is more mitigation and less aggravation in female than in male language can not be supported. While our empirical analysis showed remarkable similarities between the groups of male and female reviewers, it pointed to some dissimilarities among the members of these apparently homogeneous groups. In other words, the reader's attention was directed to "intragroup differences and intergroup similarities [which] often go unreported" in the literature (Bing & Bergvall 1996: 13). Our findings thus imply the necessity of rethinking traditional beliefs about the relations between language and gender.

Previous sociolinguistic findings related to gender contrasts and politeness phenomena in conversational interaction do not seem to be valid in the context of academic (or at least review) writing. Often language divergences which are ascribed to gender may depend on other factors like aims of the discourse, power relations, or the context of the actual speech or writing situation. As has been hinted at in recent sociolinguistic studies, we probably have to include "the perceived norms of the CofP [community of practice]" in our analyses of language and gender (Mills 2002: 84). Depending on which community of practice we belong to in a certain situation and depending on who we want to be in that situation, we perform differently in different contexts. When I sit down to write a book review, I do not perform as the university teacher, the sister, friend, or running companion (all of which identities I have in other life situations), but as the critical academic who participates in the linguistic community and tries to evaluate another community member's writings. In such a specific situation gender may be a less influential factor on the language I use and on the lexical choices I make than writing task and community membership are.

Freed, whose empirical study on discourse features also revealed striking gender similarities concerning language behaviour, found that often "speech patterns are products of the activities that people are engaged in" (1996: 67). What she states about spoken language probably holds true also for written discourse. The present analysis has demonstrated that certain language patterns, e.g. the pattern [downtoning adverb + critical adjective] as in *somewhat surprising*, are repeatedly used in negative evaluative statements by men and women alike. Hence, gender appears to be a less relevant variable than task or activity (in this case the activity of review writing and the task of commenting on somebody else's book). I therefore agree with Freed when she says that we

> should hesitate before attributing to sex or gender linguistic differences which can more accurately be accounted for by economic privilege, subcultural phenomena, setting, activity, audience, personality, or by *the context-specific communicative goals of the particular speakers* who are being studied.
>
> (1996: 56; my emphasis)

These observations support a recent trend in gender studies which stresses gender dynamicity and challenges the clear-cut male-female dichotomy (cf. the contributions in Bergvall et al. 1996 and in Litosseliti & Sunderland 2002; also cf. Butler 1999). If it is true that we perform differently in different situations and constantly switch between different context-dependent identities, it may well be that these identities, rather than falling into two gender classes, are situated somewhere on a scale going from "stereotypically male" to "stereo-typically female". As is often the case with dichotomies, these two classes are abstractions and not ideal to capture reality. A continuum, perhaps with pro-totypes, may serve better to explain empirical real-life findings than a binary system does.

This trend towards continuity and dynamicity goes hand in hand with a welcome shift from focussing on dissimilarities to looking at (and for) simi-larities between the language of women and men. We need to be aware of the fact that as long as we approach the data with preconceived ideas about dif-ferences between male and female language in mind, it will be difficult to find out more about the real origins of linguistic variation and about the ways in which language is really used in spoken and written discourse. For the present analysis this means that new observations about negative evaluation strategies in academic writing by women and men probably would not have been made if our research question had been *"How* do male and female review authors criticise differently?" Instead, the data were approached with the question *"Do* male and female review authors criticise differently?"

Conclusion: The need for corpus-driven sociolinguistics

The present empirical analysis was intended to shed light on the expression of negative evaluation in linguistic book reviews and to see whether male and female reviewers differ considerably in their use of critical adjectives and politeness-conveying hedging devices. I hope to have shown (a) that corpus-driven investigations of the language of a certain academic discourse genre (here linguistic book reviews) can reveal interesting facts about the value sys-tem of the discourse community (here the community of linguists), (b) that they can lead to unexpected findings concerning the use of criticism and hedged criticism in reviews written by men and women, and (c) that these findings might challenge existing conceptions about language and gender rela-tions. We obviously need to be more cautious with over-generalisations about and stereotyped interpretations of these relations.

Some of the results presented above, especially those related to similari-ties in the language of female and male authors, may indeed seem "somewhat counterintuitive" to the reader. They demonstrate rather nicely, though, one of the major strengths of corpus research: to enable us to discover things about the language that remain hidden to our intuition.[10] However, it cannot be taken for granted at this stage that the results obtained are fully representative of review language and of male and female review writing in general, as the data sets which my investigations are based on may not be large enough. Two future tasks will therefore be (1) an expansion of BRILC (from 500,000 to several million words) and (2) a comparison of the data collected from this corpus with data from other (linguistic) review corpora.

It has to be stressed that the present study could not do much more than scratch the surface of a wide newly emerging research field, a field which I would like to call 'corpus-driven sociolinguistics'. In the future, a lot of research in this area will be necessary in order to provide a larger empirical basis for the study of language and society. I suspect that if researchers take large amounts of data seriously and approach them in an unprejudiced way, i.e. without certain preconceived ideas, concrete expectations or biased questions in mind, exciting new discoveries about the factors that influence our linguistic behaviour will be made. As long as we go on asking traditional questions and start with theories instead of data, we will find what we want to find and not what is actually there to be found.[11] My suggestion would hence be that we ask different questions, base our research on more data, and let the data guide us to discover facts hidden so far and maybe even to make some revolutionary findings about the language. More corpus-driven comparative analyses of the writing of men and women in different settings and in different written registers will probably further challenge the oversimplified male-female dichotomy and lead to a more contextualised, more complex, and less binary approach to gender studies (or variation studies in general) in linguistics.

Acknowledgements

I would like to thank Jennifer Coates and Marion Gymnich for helpful comments on an earlier version of this paper. I am also grateful to a number of colleagues in my audience at the *Evaluation in Academic Discourse* conference in Siena, 14–16 June 2003, especially to John Sinclair, for some very interesting questions and remarks after my presentation.

Notes

1. For a discussion on sampling and the advantages and drawbacks of sample corpora see Sinclair (1991: 19 and 23f.).

2. For more information on *somewhat,* its unfavourable contexts and negative connotations, the reader is referred to Bublitz (1996).

3. In the case of *lengthy* I was not absolutely sure whether the adjective really expressed negative evaluation (most dictionaries give rather neutral definitions). Hence, before *lengthy* was put on the critical adjective list, two large reference corpora of written British English, the written part of the British National Corpus (BNC, 90 million words) and the online searchable British English part of the Bank of English (BoE, 26 million words; accessible via http://www.collins.co.uk/Corpus/CorpusSearch.aspx consulted: 05.05.05), were consulted to see how the adjective is used in context. The BNC and BoE concordances demonstrated that *lengthy* often appears in negative contexts and repeatedly co-occurs with nouns like *ban, battle, debate, jail sentence, torture, war* and *warning*. The same procedure (with comparable results) was carried out for *surprising.*

4. The use of the collective term "linguists" is not supposed to give the impression that each member of this group treasures exactly the same values to the same degree. However, despite some intra-group variation, agreement can probably be found concerning most of the values.

5. Another possible variation factor in this context might be a regional or ethnic one. Unfortunately, though, the originally intended subdivision (in the compilation of BRILC) of text files according to the cultural and linguistic backgrounds of the review authors could not be carried out, as in most cases it was impossible to determine whether the writers were native speakers of English and which regional variety of English they were using. Besides, it is likely that Linguist List editors make minor alterations on the reviews and do not fully preserve the original style.

6. The use of the term goes back to Lakoff (1972) for whom "hedges" were devices like *rather, very,* or *sort of* that can make an utterance fuzzier or less fuzzy. Since then the concept has been widened and defined differently by discourse analysts and pragmaticists. For more information on the development of the notion see Markkanen and Schröder (1997) or Hyland (1998).

7. Mauranen also discusses hedging in academic writing and describes academic discourse as "a world [...] where it is natural to cultivate hedges" (1997:115).

8. More support on absent gender differences with respect to politeness can be found in Deutschmann (2003). In his detailed study on apologising in British English the author states that "[n]o significant gender differences in the apology rates were observed" (2003:112).

9. Another piece of evidence for missing gender differences is the result of a BRILC male and BRILC female frequency word list comparison. On top of both female and male keyword lists we find lexical items which are closely related to the topics of the individual books under review (e.g. *bilingual, formulaic, grammaticalisation, literacy*) and names of the book authors or editors (e.g. Davidson, Wray, Aijmer). No typically male or typically female key vocabulary emerged from the word lists.

10. This is a generally acknowledged central pro-corpus argument which is discussed in any good introductory corpus linguistic textbook. See e.g. Hunston (2002:20) and Sinclair (1991:4).

11. The idea that "analysts find what they expect to find" is also one of Stubbs's major criticisms of a number of studies carried out in the field of CRITICAL DISCOURSE ANALYSIS (1997:102).

References

Bergvall, V. L., Bing, J. M., & Freed, A. F. (Eds.). (1996). *Rethinking Language and Gender Research. Theory and Practice*. London: Longman.

Bing, J. M. & Bergvall, V. L. (1996). The question of questions: Beyond binary thinking. In Bergvall et al. (Eds.), 1–30.

Bolívar, A. (2001). The negotiation of evaluation in written text. In M. Scott & G. Thompson (Eds.), *Patterns of Text. In Honour of Michael Hoey* (pp. 129–158). Amsterdam & Philadelphia: John Benjamins.

Brown, P. & Levinson, S. C. (1987). *Politeness. Some Universals in Language Usage*. Cambridge: Cambridge University Press.

Bublitz, W. (1996). Semantic prosody and cohesive company: 'Somewhat predictable'. *Leuvense Bijdragen (Leuven Contributions in Linguistics and Philology)*, 85 (1–2), 1–32.

Butler, J. (1999). *Gender Trouble: Feminism and the Subversion of Identity*. New York: Routledge.

Cameron, D. (1997). Performing gender identity: Young men's talk and the construction of heterosexual masculinity. In S. Johnson & U. H. Meinhof (Eds.), *Language and Masculinity* (pp. 47–64). Oxford: Blackwell.

Channell, J. (2000). Corpus-based analysis of evaluative lexis. In Hunston & Thompson (Eds.), 38–55.

Coates, J. (1996). *Women Talk*. Oxford: Blackwell.

Deutschmann, M. (2003). *Apologising in British English*. Umeå: Umeå University Press.

Eckert, P. & McConnell-Ginet, S. (1992a). Communities of practice: Where language, gender and power all live. In K. Hall, M. Bucholtz, & B. Moonwomon (Eds.), *Locating Power: Proceedings of the Second Berkeley Women and Language Conference* (pp. 89–99). Berkeley, CA: Women and Language Group.

Eckert, P. & McConnell-Ginet, S. (1992b). Think practically and look locally. Language and gender as community-based practice. In C. Roman, S. Juhasz, & C. C. Miller (Eds., 1994), *The Women and Language Debate. A Sourcebook* (pp. 432–460). New Brunswick, NJ: Rutgers University Press.

Erwin, R. W. (1992). Reviewing books for scholarly journals. In J. M. Moxley (Ed.), *Writing and Publishing for Academic Authors* (pp. 111–118). Lanham, Maryland: University Press of America.

Freed, A. F. (1996). Language and gender research in an experimental setting. In Bergvall et al. (Eds.), 54–76.

Holmes, J. (1995). *Women, Men and Politeness*. London: Longman.

Hunston, S. (1993). Evaluation and ideology in scientific writing. In M. Ghadessy (Ed.), *Register Analysis. Theory and Practice* (pp. 57–73). London: Pinter.

Hunston, S. (2002). *Corpora in Applied Linguistics*. Cambridge: Cambridge University Press.

Hunston, S. & Sinclair, J. (2000). A local grammar of evaluation. In Hunston & Thompson (Eds.), 74–101.

Hunston, S. & Thompson, G. (Eds.). (2000). *Evaluation in Text. Authorial Stance and the Construction of Discourse.* Oxford: Oxford University Press.

Hyland, K. (1998). *Hedging in Scientific Research Articles.* Amsterdam & Philadelphia: John Benjamins.

Hyland, K. (1999). Disciplinary discourses: Writer stance in research articles. In C. Candlin & K. Hyland (Eds.), *Writing: Texts, Processes and Practices* (pp. 99–121). London: Longman.

Hyland, K. (2000). *Disciplinary Discourses. Social Interactions in Academic Writing.* London: Longman.

Knowles, M. (1989). Some characteristics of a specific language. The language of tourism. In C. Laurén & M. Nordmann (Eds.), *From Office to School. Special Language and Internationalisation* (pp. 59–66). Clevedon, Philadelphia: Multilingual Matters Ltd.

Lakoff, G. (1972). Hedges: A study of meaning criteria and the logic of fuzzy concepts. In P. M. Peranteau, J. N. Levi, & G. C. Phares (Eds.), *Papers from the Eighth Regional Meeting of the Chicago Linguistic Society* (pp. 183–228). Chicago: Chicago Linguistic Society.

Lakoff, R. (1975). *Language and Women's Place.* New York: Harper Colophon Books.

Linguist List (2003). *Review Guidelines.* Available online at: http://saussure.linguistlist.org/ cfdocs/new-website/LL-WorkingDirs/pubs/reviews/guidelines.cfm (consulted: 05.05.05)

Litosseliti, L. & Sunderland, J. (Eds.). (2002). *Gender Identity and Discourse Analysis.* Amsterdam & Philadelphia: John Benjamins.

Markkanen, R. & Schröder, H. (Eds.). (1997). *Hedging and Discourse. Approaches to the Analysis of a Pragmatic Phenomenon in Academic Texts.* Berlin & New York: Mouton de Gruyter.

Markkanen, R. & Schröder, H. (1997). Hedging: A challenge for pragmatics and discourse analysis. In Markkanen & Schröder (Eds.), 3–18.

Mauranen, A. (1997). Hedging in language revisers' hands. In Markkanen & Schröder (Eds.), 115–133.

Meinhof, U. H. (1997). 'The most important event of my life!' A comparison of male and female written narratives. In S. Johnson & U. H. Meinhof (Eds.), *Language and Masculinity* (pp. 208–228). Oxford: Blackwell.

Meldrum, G. (2000). I know I have to be critical, but how? In G. M. Blue, J. Milton, & J. Saville (Eds.), *Assessing English for Academic Purposes* (pp. 169–187). Bern: Lang.

Mills, S. (2002). Rethinking Politeness, Impoliteness and Gender Identity. In Litosseliti & Sunderland (Eds.), 69–90.

Motta-Roth, D. (1996). Same genre, different discipline: A genre-based study of book reviews in academe. *The ESPecialist, 17* (2), 99–131. Available online at: http://lael. pucsp.br/especialist/172motta-roth.ps.pdf (consulted: 05.05.05)

Poos, D. & Simpson, R. (2002). Cross-disciplinary comparisons of hedging. Some findings from the Michigan Corpus of Academic Spoken English. In R. Reppen, S. M. Fitzmaurice, & D. Biber (Eds.), *Using Corpora to Explore Linguistic Variation* (pp. 3–23). Amsterdam & Philadelphia: John Benjamins.

Sinclair, J. M. (1991). *Corpus, Concordance, Collocation.* Oxford: Oxford University Press.

Sinclair, J. M. (Ed.). (1995). *Collins COBUILD English Dictionary.* London: Harper Collins.

Stubbs, M. (1997). Whorf's children: Critical comments on Critical Discourse Analysis (CDA). In A. Ryan & A. Wray (Eds.), *Evolving Models of Language* (pp. 100–116). Clevedon: Multilingual Matters. Available online at: http://www.uni-trier.de/uni/fb2/anglistik/Projekte/stubbs/whorf.htm (consulted: 05.05.05)

Tannen, D. (1990). *You Just Don't Understand. Women and Men in Conversation.* London: Virago.

Thompson, G. & Hunston, S. (2000). Evaluation: An introduction. In Hunston & Thompson (Eds.), 1–27.

Tognini-Bonelli, E. (2001). *Corpus Linguistics at Work.* Amsterdam & Philadelphia: John Benjamins.

Is evaluation structure-bound?

An English-Spanish contrastive study of book reviews

Lorena Suárez-Tejerina
University of Léon, Spain

This study uses a personally-assembled corpus of academic book reviews. It considers the reviews *in toto* and approaches the question of how evaluation is related to the structure of the review. Working with a Move Analysis set up by Motta-Roth, the paper analyses a collection of academic papers on literature, half of which are in Spanish and half in English. The findings show considerable consistency in the two languages with respect to the occurrence and the expression of evaluations, but with some rather different attitudes from the underlying cultures.

Introduction

Thompson & Hunston (2000) give very convincing reasons why evaluation is "a topic worthy of study" (Thompson & Hunston 2000:6). Expressing one's opinion is not an easy matter. Studying evaluation is not easy either. Not only can evaluation be studied at several levels (mainly macro- and micro-linguistic levels); the focus of analysis can also vary. The number of units that can be taken as the object of study is very variable, including both long, elaborate clauses or sentences, and minimal categories such as adjectives, adverbs, lexical verbs and so on.

Given the subjectivity of the topic of evaluation, there is a range of ways of looking at it. This diversity is reflected in the number of divergent studies on evaluation that exist in the literature. Hunston & Thompson (2000) compile some of the most recent ones. They define evaluation as "the expression of the speaker or writer's attitude or stance towards, viewpoint on, or feelings about entities or propositions that he or she is talking about. That attitude may relate to certainty or obligation or desirability or any of a number of other sets of values" (Thompson & Hunston 2000: 5). Further, they state that "the expression of the writer's or speaker's opinion is an important feature of language. . .it needs to be accounted for in a full description of the meanings of texts" (Thompson & Hunston 2000: 2). That is, not only is evaluation the *expression of attitude or stance*, it may also play a part in the reader's/hearer's understanding of texts.

If evaluation plays as important a role in all texts in general, its function in genres such as the book review is necessarily much more crucial. The evaluative character of book reviews is emphasised by scholars such as Motta-Roth (1995) and Hyland (2000). This genre and others, such as reviews of research articles or "comment reviews" – in Belcher's (1995) words – are evaluative by nature.

The term evaluation overlaps, as Thompson & Hunston (2000) point out, with other concepts, namely *connotation* (Lyons 1977), *affect* (Besnier 1993), *appraisal* (Martin 2000) and *stance* (Conrad & Biber 2000). Barton (1993) establishes a link between 'evidentials',[1] argumentation and epistemological stance. The present study resembles Thompson & Hunston's (2000) in the choice of the concept *evaluation* to refer to "language expressing opinion". The reason for this is that *evaluation* is one of the most neutral terms. Apart from that, by picking the term *evaluation*, Thompson & Hunston adopt a 'combining' approach to the study of evaluation which includes a variety of parameters.[2] The combining approach to evaluation is opposed to the 'separating' approach (cf. Halliday 1994 and Martin 2000).

According to Thompson and Hunston (2000), evaluation has three functions: expressing opinion, maintaining relations between the writer/speaker and the reader/hearer, and organising the discourse, the first being the main function. The second function distinguishes between manipulation, hedging and politeness. The final function of organising the discourse can be linked to the idea[3] that "evaluation, in writing as in speech, tends to occur at the boundary points in a discourse, thereby providing a clue to ('monitoring') its organization" (Thompson & Hunston 2000: 11). Bolívar (2001) sees evaluation as a main text-structuring tool. In her corpus of newspaper editorials, a *triad* is to be taken as a recurrent "discourse unit that consists of three elements[4] of structure [or *turns*], in which the third element is an evaluation, obligatory in evaluative texts" (Bolívar 2001: 136).

Book reviews, for example, are more likely to present instances of evaluation in moves 3 (*Highlighting parts of the book*) and 4 (*Providing closing evaluation of the book*) than anywhere else in the text – though it may appear in other sections as well.[5] Thus, in the case of book reviews evaluation points up the structure of texts very often. As Thompson & Hunston (2000) say:

> ...evaluation tends to be found throughout a text rather than being confined to one particular part of it. [...] It is also true, however, that evaluation is identified in some cases because of its position in a text and the role that it plays because of that position. (Thompson & Hunston 2000: 19)

This and other issues related to the organising role of evaluation will be explored later on in the present paper.

The genre chosen in this paper for the study of evaluation is the book review. There are various reasons leading to the choice of such a genre. As Belcher (1995) states, book reviews are a useful guide for students to approach the complex task of being critical towards somebody else's texts. For Motta-Roth (1995) and Hyland (2000), the book review genre is also an evaluation-loaded genre in itself, especially when compared with the remaining genres of the academy. By concentrating on book reviews, the present study aimed at shedding some light on a "somewhat neglected genre" (Hyland 2000) or one of Swales' (1990) 'occluded genres'.

Besides providing further insight into the book review genre in general, it is hoped that this contrastive study will contribute to the field of contrastive rhetoric by offering interesting results, rhetorically speaking, as to the way English and Spanish book reviewers organise their texts. Another main aim of the present study is to contrast the rhetorical strategies used by English and Spanish writers to evaluate somebody else's works. Praise and criticism will be looked at both separately and in combination. When a speaker/writer resorts to praise-criticism or criticism-praise binomials, they go beyond the mere expression of an opinion: they are either constraining the positive opinion they have just posed or they are trying to mitigate the impact of a negative remark. This contrastive approach has also focused on the resources employed and preferred by English and Spanish book review writers in both their positive and negative remarks.

The pedagogical applications derived from this study will benefit professional book review writers as well as students in general. In relation to the latter, Stubbs (2003: 1) points out that book reviews are texts "which young scholars sometimes have the opportunity to do quite early in their careers". A study of the characteristics presented here will favour students' ability to compose book reviews both from the functional and from the formal viewpoints.

The study

Data

The corpus of the study consists of 40 book reviews – 20 in English and 20 in Spanish – of books belonging to the academic discipline of literature. In both languages, the book reviews were drawn from four different journals:

> English journals:
> *The Review of English Studies* (published in Great Britain; texts from 2002)
> *English Literature in Transition. 1880–1920* (published in North-America; texts from 2002)
> *Ariel: A Review of International English Literature* (published in Canada; texts from 2000)
> *Studies in Romanticism* (published in North-America; texts from 2001)
>
> Spanish journals:
> *España Contemporánea* (published in North-America; texts from 2001)
> *Anales de la Literatura Española Contemporánea* (published in North-America; texts from 2002)
> *Revista de Literatura* (published in Spain; texts from 2000)
> *Revista de Poética Medieval* (published in Spain; texts from 2001)

With the English journals, no distinctions were made between the British, American and Canadian varieties. However, since size and type of targeted audience may be a factor affecting the shape of language (as Fredrickson & Swales 1994 and Burgess 2002 suggest), it was decided that this complicating factor be controlled by balancing the Spanish corpus in terms of audience, with two of the journals chosen being published in a national setting, and two published internationally; the variable of the audience will not however be addressed in the present study.

Method of analysis

The study can be defined as an English-Spanish contrastive analysis of the resources and rhetorical ways in which evaluation, both positive and negative, is expressed by book review writers. Evaluation was analysed in its role in textual organisation. Instead of concentrating on a pre-established compendium of categories and resources, the analysis, clearly based on the functional role of language, aimed at identifying all those devices in the corpus that express

Table 1. Schematic description of rhetorical organisation of BRs (Motta-Roth 1995)

Move 1 Introducing the book

Sub-function 1 Defining the general topic of the book	and/or
Sub-function 2 Informing about potential readership	and/or
Sub-function 3 Informing about the author	and/or
Sub-function 4 Making topic generalizations	and/or
Sub-function 5 Inserting book in the field	

Move 2 Outlining the book

Sub-function 6 Providing general view of the organization of the book	and/or
Sub-function 7 Stating the topic of each chapter	and/or
Sub-function 8 Citing extra-textual material	

Move 3 Highlighting parts of the book
Sub-function 9 Providing focused evaluation

Move 4 Providing closing evaluation of the book
Sub-function 10A Definitely recommending/disqualifying the book or
Sub-function 10B Recommending the book despite indicated shortcomings

some kind of evaluation on the part of the reviewer. Two levels of analysis – the macro and the micro levels – were applied.

The choice of the book review as the object of analysis of the study presented here in the search for evaluative resources and strategies responds to the evaluative nature of the genre. As indicated above, a main concern of the study is the examination of evaluation and its role as discourse-organiser or structure-marker. In this respect, a representative structure of book reviews needs to be established before instances of evaluation are identified and accounted for in the corpus. There have not been many previous studies on book reviews in the literature. The most revealing approach to this genre from a structural point of view has been Motta-Roth's (1998). She identified four recurrent moves in her corpus of 180 book reviews (evenly distributed between the disciplines of linguistics, chemistry and economics), resulting in the scheme shown in Table 1.

It should also be noted that interesting rhetorical differences between the English and the Portuguese cultures were found by De Carvalho (2001) in the application of Motta-Roth's (1998) four-move model to her corpus of academic book reviews.

Motta-Roth's (1998) scheme has been taken to be the original model for the book reviews in the present study, not only because there are no similar studies in the literature to date (apart from De Carvalho 2001), but also, and more importantly, because it presents itself as a very adequate model.

Results

Move Analysis

The application of Motta-Roth's (1998) model to the corpus of the present study resulted in a slightly adapted scheme shown in Table 2 below.

Table 3 shows the frequency of the four moves as well as their respective sub-functions – non-exclusive – or options – exclusive – in the corpus.

Table 2. Moves, sub-functions and options in the English and Spanish corpora of BRs

M1 Introducing the book	
1.1 Defining the general topic of the book	and/or
1.1.1 Developing an aspect of the general topic	and/or
1.2 Informing about potential readership	and/or
1.3 Informing about the author	and/or
1.4 Making topic generalizations	and/or
1.5 Inserting book in the field	
1.6 Informing about the writing technique/methodology used by the writer	and/or
M2 Outlining the book	
2.1 Providing general view of the organization of the book	and/or
2.2 Stating the topic of each chapter	and/or
2.3 Citing extra-text material	
M3 Highlighting parts of the book	
3.1 Providing focused evaluation	
M4 Providing closing evaluation of the book	
A Definitely recommending the book	or
B Recommending the book despite indicated shortcomings	or
C Disqualifying the book despite indicated strengths	or
D Providing neutral summary-conclusion of the book	

Table 3. Frequency of the different moves, sub-functions and options in the corpora

	M1 and sub-functions							M2 and sub-functions			M3 and sub-function	M4 and options			
	1.1	1.1.1	1.2	1.3	1.4	1.5	1.6	2.1	2.2	2.3	3.1	A	B	C	D
	M1 total no.: 19							M2 total no.: 8			M3 total no.: 12	M4 total no.: 18			
English BRs (20)	19	0	0	1	4	5	0	4	5	2	12	3	11	3	1
	M1 total no.: 20							M2 total no.: 20			M3 total no.: 8	M4 total no.: 17			
Spanish BRs (20)	17	5	2	7	3	10	3	8	12	4	8	11	4	1	1

Table 4. Occurrences of moves 2 and 3 separately and in combination in English and Spanish BRs

	M2 alone	M3 alone	M2 & M3
English BRs	8	12	4
Spanish BRs	20	8	7

Move Analysis is quite relevant to the study because, apart from clarifying the structure of the book reviews (most of the time), the frequency counts – especially those representing moves 3 (*Highlighting parts of the book*) and 4 (*Providing closing evaluation of the book*) – are very indicative of the writers' evaluative behaviour in general.

Regarding the structure of the texts, it should first of all be noted that De Carvalho (2001) proposes a slightly different schema, reducing Motta-Roth's (1998) four moves to three. In her corpus, Motta-Roth's (1998) moves 2 (*Outlining the book*) and 3 (*Highlighting parts of the book*) are fused together in the same move (move 2). In the present study, although four moves have been identified (following Motta-Roth's 1998 model), moves 2 and 3 sometimes converge in a single move, as illustrated in Table 4; this is something that Mota-Roth also noted in her corpus and that it supports De Carvalho's (2001) model.

Concerning move 3, its absence in 9 Spanish book reviews is striking, especially considering that move 3 is characterised by its evaluative nature; moreover, in the English corpus it is missing only twice. The lack of such a move can be explained, as Motta-Roth (1998) suggests, by the fact that move 4, which is also a predominantly evaluative move in book reviews, is present in the corpus in almost a hundred per cent of the cases.

As the results in Table 4 show, move 4 is especially relevant to this work, because it can be realised through one rhetorical function out of four (instead of 2, as in the original model). That is, the analysis of the English and Spanish corpora of the present study led to the identification of two new possible options in move 4:

> **Option C:** Disqualifying the book despite indicated strengths
> **Option D:** Providing neutral summary-conclusion of the book

Option C[6] is the reverse of *option B* (*Recommending the book despite indicated shortcomings*). This option is extremely relevant because it is the only one by means of which the writers of the book reviews in the corpus do disqualify a book.

In the English corpus, *option A* (*Definitely recommending the book*) appears twice, while this same option appears on 12 occasions in the Spanish corpus. None of these occurrences in the two corpora implies a disqualification of the book under review. That is why Motta-Roth's (1998) *sub-function 10A* (*Definitely recommending/disqualifying the book*) has been formulated in the present study as *Definitely recommending the book*. Options A and B in this study reflect both the English and the Spanish reviewers' reluctance to disqualify books in a straightforward, severe way. As regards the general absence of *option A* in the English corpus, it could be argued that English reviewers tend not to make definite statements when judging the value of a book. They are more likely to hedge their verdicts by closing their reviews with *option B* (*Recommending the book despite indicated shortcomings*) or *option C* (*Disqualifying the book despite indicated strengths*).

The following are examples of option C from the corpora:

Option 10C in the English corpus
Given Jasper's method of treating his subject, I would suggest that it is his engagement with the minute particulars – the appropriate analogy, the engaging comparison, the startling reading of a particular text or painting – that will reward a patient reader. His claims for reconsidering the positions of Coleridge and Arnold as biblical critics, his fascinating analysis of Turner's paintings as biblical criticism, and his claims for a renewed understanding of the relevance of romanticism to modern theological issues are certainly parts that we all should be grateful for. For my part, however, I would prefer a more systematically developed and more historically informed argument; and thus I find that this volume in "Perspectives in Romanticism" – despite some strong individual parts – does not fully deliver what the series promises.

Option 10C in the Spanish corpus
Si bien se trata de un proyecto de amplias expectativas, tal y como se acaba de señalar, sus tres autores han logrado realizar un estudio científico y literario acerca de una tradición oral en la provincia de Burgos, una tradición que, por más que se intente rescatar – a través de investigaciones como la presente –, perecerá inevitablemente con la desaparición de los moradores de estos pueblos.

Option D is found only once in each corpus. In this case, the rhetorical strategy chosen by the writers to close the review is that of refusing to give a final judgement of the book. Instead, they decide to end the review with a brief summary or conclusion of the book; this is illustrated in the following examples:

Option 10D in the English corpus
In short, this is one man's testimony to a lifetime's appreciation of Thomas Hardy. It is not an intervention in any kind of contemporary critical discourse about Hardy. Reading Hardy's Landscapes places readers in Irwin's classroom – a pleasant space that is best suited to beginning readers of Hardy.

Option 10D In the Spanish corpus
En síntesis, queda demostrado que el género caballeresco no puede entenderse desligado del mundo editorial español, de donde el nombre de "género editorial" que permitirá comprender el desarrollo y los cambios de rumbo de esa tradición literaria.

Evaluation in the corpus

Due to the complexity of the topic of evaluation, some basic criteria were established before carrying out the textual analysis. An *instance of evaluation* was taken to be any grammatical category expressing the reviewers' stance. The level of evaluation was classified as follows:

a. Moves containing **fewer than three instances of evaluation** were considered **non-evaluative**
b. Moves containing **between three and six instances of evaluation** were considered **evaluative**
c. Moves containing **more than six instances of evaluation** were considered **highly evaluative.**

Table 5 shows the evaluative nature of the four moves identified in the study leaving aside the cases in which moves 2 (*Outlining the book*) and 3 (*Highlighting parts of the book*) appear fused in a single move.

From Table 5, one can infer that book review writers do not cluster their evaluative comments in only one move. Instances of evaluation are prone to appear in all the four moves identified in the corpus, though moves 3 (*Highlighting parts of the book*) and 4 (*Providing closing evaluation of the book*) are the most highly evaluative.

Regarding the question of which language is more evaluative than the other, the English corpus clearly stands out as much more evaluation-loaded. Table 6 shows the number of instances of evaluation in each corpus as well as the correspondent percentages of positive and negative evaluation.

Table 5. Evaluative nature of moves 1, 2, 3 and 4 in the corpora

	M1	M2 (detached from M3)	M3	M4
English BRs	19	8	12	18
Non-eval.:	13	1	0	1
Evaluative	4	3	2	9
Highly eval.:	2	1	16	8
Spanish BRs	20	20	8	17
Non-eval.:	11	10	0	1
Evaluative:	6	3	4	13
Highly eval.:	2	1	7	5

Table 6. Total, positive and negative evaluation in the corpora

	Total instances of evaluation	Instances of positive evaluation	Instances of negative evaluation
English BRs	454	283 (62,3%)	171 (37,6%)
Spanish BRs	317	270 (85,1%)	47 (14,8%)

Table reveals three important facts in relation to the present study:

i.   The English book reviewers tend to show their stance much more often than the Spanish book reviewers.
ii. Both the English and the Spanish book reviewers tend to praise rather than criticise other authors' works.
iii. However, the distribution of praise and criticism is much more balanced in the English corpus than in the Spanish one, i.e. the Spanish writers are more reluctant to condemn other authors' works.

As far as the rhetorical distribution of evaluation throughout the book reviews is concerned, both the English and the Spanish texts share the following characteristic: when they present instances of evaluation at the very beginning of the review (i.e. in the introduction) or in the first half of the review (in the introduction and the outline of the book chapters), those instances of evaluation are always positive or mostly positive, presenting a very small percentage of criticism. The second half of the texts is more revealing when comparing the English and the Spanish corpora: while the texts in both corpora present a tendency to end with a positive closing instead of disqualifying the book under review, the difference between the two languages is to be found in move 3 (*Highlighting parts of the book*). Whereas in the English corpus move 3 tends to present a mixture of positive and negative evaluation, in the Spanish corpus move 3 is almost always praise-loaded. In all the cases where praise and criticism appear together in move 3 in the two corpora, there are two possibilities of combination:

a. in chunks consisting of two or more sentences, with first praise and then criticism, or vice versa:

Chunks of criticism and praise in the English corpus

Though he says the "feud" between the two little magazines isn't important, he spends much of the book talking about it [criticism]. (...) Hand in hand with his dismissal of the feud comes Trehearne's overly harsh depiction of John Sutherland as a mere tactician and opportunist. By downplaying the feud, he is able to depreciate the importance of Sutherland 's critical writings, many of which were created in the context of opposition to Preview poetics. As an example of this supposed insincerity, he cites Sutherland's denigration of A. J. M. [criticism]. (...) The logic is superficial [criticism]. (...) Elsewhere Trehearne takes cheap shots and attributes venal motives to Sutherland, such as a shakily supported claim that Sutherland was critical of P. K. Page's verse because she had rejected him as a suitor (53) [criticism]. At best, he doles out backhanded compliments, such as presenting Sutherland as the decade's "chief nay-sayer" (318) [praise].

The most stimulating aspect of Trehearne's book is his pursuit of the development of integritas in Page, Klein, Layton, and Dudek. He brilliantly delineates the search for this integritas as the defining quality of these four poets' evolution from the forties to the fifties. . .[praise]

Chunks of praise and criticism in the Spanish corpus

El libro, escrito con un tono ameno [praise] (...) en el que no faltan explicaciones sobre los espacios más representativos – pórticos, plazas, corrales... –, las propuestas más innovadoras de cada momento o los nombres de los principales escenógrafos responsables de las mismas [praise]. (...) No obstante, uno de los aspectos más destacados de estas páginas, a nuestro juicio, sería el estrecho vínculo que Nieva establece entre los diferentes elementos escenográficos y la propia representación, sin necesidad de acudir de manera recurrente a la historia de la literatura dramática [praise]. (...) Aún más valioso resulta, en nuestra opinión, un apartado dedicado a ofrecer análisis prácticos que completa muchos de los capitulillos de esta primera parte del libro [praise]. En ellos vierte el autor sugestivas orientaciones sobre posibilidades de aprovechamiento de la escenografía, recupera algunos hitos de la historia del teatro y no escatima advertencias, consejos y reflexiones en voz alta destinados a los jóvenes escenógrafos que deben enfrentarse a géneros o piezas concretos [praise]. No faltan en ellas consideraciones personales [*praise*] una visión integradora del hecho teatral que trata de establecer lúcidas conexiones entre diversas formas del espectáculo de todos los tiempos [*praise*] (...) muestra, de modo igualmente esquemático, pero riguroso [*praise*] (...) quizás fuera susceptible de una actualización que incluyera, al menos de forma sucinta, algunas de las propuestas más innovadoras que han jalonado la segunda mitad de este siglo [*criticism*] (...) en esta primera parte parecería necesaria la inclusión de un cuerpo de notas y, asimismo, también sería deseable una mayor atención a la calidad del material gráfico [*criticism*] (...) unos criterios de ordenación algo discutibles [*criticism*] (...), seguimos echando en falta un necesario apartado de notas y una mayor atención al material gráfico, prácticamente inexistente en todo este apartado del libro [*criticism*]. (...) En este sentido, también parecería conveniente que... [*criticism*]. (...) Esta actualización podría ser completada... [*criticism*]

b. in binomials of praise and criticism (or vice versa), on most occasions connected by means of adversative and concessive metatext,[7] both intersentential and intrasentential, to explicitly mark the opposition:

Binomials of praise and criticism in the English corpus
Though it aims to be accessible to a wide readership [*criticism*], this is ultimately a careful and skilful scholarly edition that makes a number of contributions to the specialist's understanding [*praise*]. It is difficult to explain, therefore, why Gates opts to omit Hunt's cancellations – saying simply that "crossed-out words or phrases are left out and treated as nonexistent" (x) – while retaining misspellings and quirks of punctuation [*criticism*]. (...) It may be that not very much of importance is lost in what Gates has left out [*praise*], **but** the importance of scholarly evidence is always relative and by definition difficult to determine before the fact. Gates's own text provides one counterexample... [*criticism*]. (...) Gates wisely breaks her own rule here and prints the canceled word in square brackets [*praise*], **but** this very exception would seem to test the adequacy of the rule [*criticism*].

Binomials of praise and criticism in the Spanish corpus
...intenta justificar con ardor y erudición...[*praise*]. (...) No es ésta, desde luego, una teoría que pueda sonar a nueva ni a extraña a ningún crítico literario [*criticism*]. **Pero** las argumentaciones en su favor de Borges resultan tan fascinantes, tan eruditas y tan poéticas al mismo tiempo, que se puede afirmar sin temor a dudas que en estas páginas se encier-

> ran algunos de los avales más brillantes y más intuitivos que tal teoría ha encontrado nunca [*praise*]....

These two strategies mirror the writers' propensity to hedge or mitigate their negative remarks by surrounding them by, or intercalating them with, positive comments.

Taking move 3 (*Highlighting parts of the book*) separately, the order of the chunks and the sequences formed by praise and criticism could be significant in the cases in which the one coming last seems to be the strongest one. However, looking at the overall organisation of the texts, the order of such a sequence within move 3 in this study does not really matter because, as stated before, move 4 (*Providing closing evaluation of the book*) is predominantly positive. So, the main point is that, in general, in this corpus of English and Spanish book reviews on literature, reviewers tend to open and close their reviews with positive remarks; in the case of closings, this would imply the recommendation of the book. When there is criticism, which is more frequent in the English corpus, it is located in the middle part of the text (move 3), which somehow softens the impact of the negative comments.

As regards the consideration of the texts at the micro-level, the analysis showed that English and Spanish book review writers use the same evaluation-loaded rhetorical strategies or discourse categories, though the frequency of use of those items sometimes varies between the two languages, as illustrated in Figure 1.

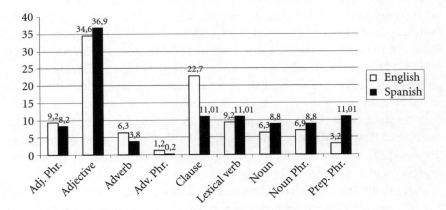

Figure 1. Frequency of use in percentages of the different evaluative items in the English and Spanish corpora

English and the Spanish book reviewers seem to share a common preference of use of the different grammatical categories to express evaluation, and
adjectives and lexical verbs are highly used in the two writing cultures. However, there are differences in the use of some evaluation-loaded grammatical
categories such as the clause, whose frequency is much greater in English than
in Spanish, and the prepositional phrase, which is noticeably more preferred in
the Spanish corpus.

Conclusions

In terms of the rhetorical moves schematic structure that book reviewers employ in the two corpora, English and Spanish present quite similar characteristics. The analysis of the texts following Motta-Roth's (1998) move analysis led
to the detection in the two corpora of four different options in move 4 (*Providing closing evaluation of the book*). *Option C* (*Recommending the book despite
indicated shortcomings*) arose as especially relevant in the present study because
it implied some sort of disqualification of the book under review; in fact, this
was the only means by which English and Spanish book review writers seemed
to adopt a condemnatory position towards the book being reviewed.

From a more evaluation-focused viewpoint, the English and the Spanish
corpora shared the characteristic that instances of evaluation were to be found
in any part of the texts, though moves 3 (*Highlighting parts of the book*) and 4
(*Providing colosing evaluation of the book*) were the most highly evaluative. Another common feature between the two languages was the general tendency to
evaluate other authors' works positively, instead of adopting a negative stance.
However, the analysis revealed that English book reviewers seem to be much
more likely to make negative remarks than Spanish reviewers. Finally, the two
groups of reviewers used exactly the same grammatical categories with similar
frequencies of use in the expression of evaluation except for some slight differences, such as the high use of the clause in the English corpus against the
high use of the prepositional phrase in the Spanish corpus. Especially noteworthy was the frequent intervention of adversative and concessive metatext in the
expression of evaluation in the corpus.

The study has provided interesting findings in relation to English and
Spanish book reviewers' behavioural patterns by focusing on evaluation and
its structural function in text. It has also made a contribution to the refine-
ment of the book review genre. However, further research should approach
more deeply the study of the role of evaluation as a text-organising device in

book reviews, and attempt to identify recurrent strategies of evaluation, such as the combination of praise and criticism, and their role in the book review genre.

Notes

1. Which she defines as "words and phrases that express attitudes toward knowledge", following Chafe (1986).

2. Thompson & Hunston distinguish basically among the good-bad, the certainty, the expectedness and the importance parameters. According to them, the good-bad parameter is the central one to evaluation, though "...evaluation is essentially one phenomenon rather than several..." (2000:25).

3. This is an idea that the two authors attribute to Sinclair (1987).

4. "The *Lead* (L) that initiates and selects a topic and a modality, the *Follow* (F) that continues with the topic, and the *Valuate* (V) that has the structural function of closing the segment and the discourse function of giving an opinion" (Bolívar 2001:137).

5. See below for details of the Move Analysis.

6. Though Motta-Roth (1998) did allow for the possibility of finding 'sub-function 10B' with the opposite meaning, she did not state that possibility as a distinct option explicitly. In the present study it was necessary to give option C a separate status.

7. Adversative and concessive metatext, though not evaluative in itself, intervenes in a strikingly high number of evaluation strategies in the corpus of the present study.

References

Barton, E. (1993). Evidentials, argumentation, and epistemological stance. *College English*, 55 (7), 745–769.

Belcher, D. (1995). Writing critically across the curriculum. In D. Belcher & G. Braine (Eds.), *Academic Writing in a Second Language: Essays on Research and Pedagogy* (pp. 135–155). Norwood, NJ: Ablex Publishing Corporation.

Besnier, N. (1993). Reported speech and affect on Nukulaelae Atoll. In J. Hill & J. Irvine (Eds.), 161–181.

Bolívar, A. (2001). The negotiation of evaluation in written text. In M. Scott & G. Thompson (Eds.), *Patterns of Text. In Honour of Michael Hoey*. Amsterdam & Philadelphia: John Benjamins.

Burgess, S. (2002). Packed houses and intimate gatherings: Audience and rhetorical structure. In J. Flowerdew (Ed.), *Academic Discourse* (pp. 196–215). Harlow: Longman.

Chafe, W. L. (1986). Evidentiality in English conversation and academic writing. In W. L. Chafe & J. Nichols (Eds.), *Evidentiality: The Linguistic Coding of Epistemology* (pp. 261–272). Norwood, NJ: Ablex.

Conrad, S. & Biber, D. (2000). Adverbial marking of stance in speech and writing. In Hunston & Thompson (Eds.), 56–73.

De Carvalho, G. (2001). Rhetorical patterns of academic book reviews written in Portuguese and in English. In Iglesias L. Rábade & S. M. Doval Suárez (Eds.), *Studies in Contrastive Linguistics* (pp. 261–268). Proceedings of the 2nd International Contrastive Linguistics Conference. Santiago de Compostela, October 2001.

Fredrickson, K. & Swales, J. M. (1994). Competition and discourse community: Introductions from Nysvenska Studier. In B.-L. Gunnarsson, P. Linell, & B. Nordberg (Eds.), *Text and Talk in Professional Contexts* (pp. 9–22). Uppsala, Sweden: ASLA.

Halliday, M. A. K. (1994). *An Introduction to Functional Grammar* (2nd ed.). London: Edward Arnold.

Hunston, S. & Thompson, G. (Eds.). (2000). *Evaluation in Text*. Oxford: Oxford University Press.

Hyland, K. (2000). *Disciplinary Discourses. Social Interactions in Academic Writing*. Harlow: Pearson Education.

Lyons, J. (1977). *Semantics*. Cambridge: Cambridge University Press.

Martin, J. R. (2000). Beyond exchange: Appraisal systems in English. In Hunston & Thompson (Eds.), 142–175.

Motta-Roth, D. (1998). Discourse analysis and academic book reviews: A study of text and disciplinary cultures. In I. Fortanet, S. Posteguillo, J. C. Palmer, & J. F. Coll (Eds.), *Genre Studies in English for Academic Purposes* (pp. 29–58). Castelló: Universitat Jaume I.

Sinclair, J. M. (1987). Mirror for a text. Mirror for a Text. *Journal of English and Foreign Languages, 1*. Hyderabad.

Stubbs, M. (2003). Review of Swales, J. M. & Feak, C. B. (2000). *English in Today's Research World: A Writing Guide*. Ann Arbor: University of Michigan Press. *English for Specific Purposes, 22* (4), 419–421.

Swales, J. (1990). *Genre Analysis*. Cambridge: Cambridge University Press.

Thompson, G. & Hunston, S. (2000). Evaluation: An introduction. In Hunston & Thompson (Eds.), 1–27.

From corpus to register

The construction of evaluation and argumentation in linguistics textbooks

Maria Freddi
Università di Bologna, Italy

The present paper argues that there exists a partial overlapping between expressions of evaluation and argumentation in academic discourse, and subsequently tests the hypothesis of a LEXICO-GRAMMAR OF ARGUMENTATION. This is found to be close to the LOCAL GRAMMAR OF EVALUATION posited by Hunston and Sinclair (2000). The hypothesis is tested against corpus data, namely the introductory chapters of 10 linguistics textbooks. Using descriptive statistics as a tool for analysing data, the findings show that evaluative/argumentative patterns emerge systematically from the analysis of selected concordances. In particular, some of these patterns prove to be style-specific, that is, typical of the style of each writer represented in the corpus.

Introduction

One of the background assumptions of this investigation into ways of construing evaluation in academic discourse can be summed up in Stubbs' statement that "words are used in predictable combinations, which often have characteristic evaluative meanings" (2001:4).

In order to provide a definition of evaluation, one can draw from different approaches. Although evaluation is a much-overused term to account for a wide range of linguistic resources, there is also agreement as to its core defining traits: writer's attitude, stance, opinion and attitudinal lexis, appraisal, connotation (and connotative meaning), affect, judgement, appreciation are all terms used to indicate the semantics of evaluation.

Indeed, different scholars elaborate on different classifications, with a certain amount of overlapping among them. However, there seems to be general agreement as to the recognition that evaluation is a fuzzy phenomenon, whose linguistic realizations typically are not discrete units, but rather show a wave-like pattern (Hunston 1994; Hunston & Thompson 2000; Martin & Rose 2003; Ravelli 2000). In other words, given a certain evaluative meaning, e.g. a value-judgment, or an attitude, the linguistic resources that can be used to construe it affect each other with a cumulative effect, such that a text is often interspersed with evaluation and it is difficult for the analyst to identify grammatical boundaries and distinct units of analysis.

The wave metaphor, as opposed to the particle metaphor, which linguists borrow from physics (particularly Halliday 1982, 1994), is used to help understand this prosodic feature of evaluation, characteristic of "continuous forms of expression, often with indeterminate boundaries" (Halliday 1994: 35). According to Halliday, prosody is characteristic of the clause when thought of as exchange, that is, its interactional dimension.[1] Hunston and Thompson (2000: 74) note that evaluation is parasitic on other resources, and it is somewhat dispersed across a range of structural options shared with non-evaluative functions. Ravelli (2000) shows how these meanings established in a text are scattered throughout it, without necessarily being associated or attached to a particular grammatical structure. Hunston and Sinclair (2000) argue that this is so because we abandon more grammaticalised systems and enter the realm of lexis.

This prosodic contour, which has traditionally been studied in the field of intonation, but which applies here to semantics, raises the question of the indeterminacy of categorisation and brings us back to Stubbs' initial quote on the evaluative potential of collocation. This phenomenon has been named *semantic prosody* and its implications have been identified and stressed both by Sinclair (1991, 1996) and Louw (1993). In Louw's terms, semantic prosody is the "consistent aura of meaning with which a form is imbued by its collocates" (Louw 1993: 157). In other words, it is the load of positive or negative evaluative orientation that a word triggers in its context, i.e. by virtue of its collocates.[2] More recently, Tognini Bonelli (2001: 111) and again Stubbs (2001: 65) have used the expression *discourse prosody* to emphasise the function fulfilled by such merging of an item with its environment at a discourse-cohesive level. Conversely, within the systemic-functional framework, although Martin agrees that evaluation is prosodically realised (Martin 2000, 2003), he proposes a classification of the repertoire of grammatical devices used by speakers to construe and negotiate emotions, value judgments about people and things, and personal and moral evaluations (Martin & Rose 2003: 22). Indeed, the modelling of the system of APPRAISAL by Martin (2000, 2003), Martin and Rose (2003) and White (2000) recognises a systematic relation between these meanings (attitudes, emotions, moral judgments, etc.) and their realisations in the grammar of English.

However, as I indicate above, other approaches, notably Hunston and Thompson (2000), although taking a broadly functional perspective, maintain that it is difficult to model a close system of grammar for a description of evaluation.

Even though I share the view that, but for the system of modality, which is more grammaticalised, i.e. "more integrated into the structure of the clause with its own dedicated structure" (Hunston & Thompson 2000: 3), evaluation can be explored mainly in lexical terms, I also believe, together with Hunston and Sinclair (2000), that one can amass enough evidence to show that there are recurrent patterns that can be systematically associated with it.[3] And if there are recurrent behaviours, then generalisability is possible. After all, one of corpus linguistics' tenets is that repeated linguistic behaviour, frequency, is meaningful, and if meaningful, it is predictable or probable.[4] Besides, in the history of language change, patterns that are frequently used in discourse become conventionalised as grammar.

Evaluation and argumentation

The interpersonal, i.e. participant-oriented, function of evaluation allows me to link it with argumentation and to put forward the claim that there is a dialectic relationship between the two. In fact, if we consider the interactive level of discourse (again Hunston & Thompson 2000; but also Hyland 2000 and Bondi 2002) and if we assume a common ground between writer and reader (Bondi 2002: 261), evaluation has to be seen as dialogic and dialectic. Evaluation is an argumentative strategy: it is construed against a reference scale which is always culturally conditioned, e.g. a set of shared norms or beliefs. Indeed, evaluation is not interesting unless there is a counterpart to it. Evaluation aims at persuading the interlocutor (who in some cases can coincide with the speaker or writer himself); it is a way for the writer to lock the reader in. Evaluation implies tension: there are studies that show that evaluative patterns are more frequent where there is more conflict (for instance, Hunston 1993b, 1994, this volume).

This is true also of registers typical of scientific communication, which have often been considered to be objective and impersonal, but where instead there is a great deal of subjective, evaluative interventions aiming at persuasion of the scientific community.[5] Textbook writing is no less argumentative and evaluative than other registers of academic discourse (Bondi 1999; Freddi 2005; Hyland 2000; Love 2002). In particular, Love (2002) has focused on the expression of negative and positive evaluation in a renowned sociology textbook as a means for developing argumentation. Love investigates the role of an author's cutting edge ideas and biases. By noticing that, in many social sciences, students might be exposed to competing theories and alternative interpretations, she poses the following question crucial to her investigation: "will a writer's cutting edge ideas influence the approach to initiating novices into the discipline? Or, is the discipline presented in an uncontroversial, unproblematic manner?" and concludes that indeed student-readers are not just introduced to the fundamentals of the discipline of sociology, but also to the writer's particular theoretical position within it, thus being initiated into the disciplinary debate.

The close relation between evaluation and argumentation is also implicitly affirmed by Martin when he illustrates the particular sub-system of ENGAGEMENT. This is seen as the positioning of one opinion in relation to another (Martin 2003: 174) and is realised in the grammar by projection (quoting and reporting) and acknowledgment of a possibility (concession), thus showing both an inter-subjective and argumentative function.

In their 2000 volume on evaluation, Hunston and Thompson identify three functions that evaluation is used to perform: (a) to express the speaker/writer's opinion, and in doing so to reflect the value system of that person and their community; (b) to construct and maintain relations between the speaker/writer and the hearer/reader; and (c) to organise the discourse.[6]

Amongst the array of evaluative resources which are identified and discussed in the literature, the main types can be summarised as follows: MECHANISMS of ATTRIBUTION and REPORTING (*it has been___ that, the + NG + that* ∧ Projection), usually associated with VOICES or PARTICIPANT ROLES (the personal pronouns *I, we* and *you,* but also other sources) and with MOVES (*if we* ∧ Exemplification); then MODALITY and HEDGING (*will almost certainly...*), RETROSPECTIVE and PROSPECTIVE EVALUATION of information linked to METADISCOURSIVE expressions (*this can be referred to as,* or, *As I have noted before...*), and, last but not least, ATTITUDINAL lexis. Let me briefly comment on each.

Mechanisms of attribution and reporting

The role of reporting verbs as a means to express the author's stance has been widely investigated (Bondi 1999; Freddi 2005; Hunston 1993b, 1994, 1995, in press; Hyland 2000, 2002c; Thompson & Ye 1991). Reporting verbs are considered to be evaluative in that they function as a way to incorporate voices in a text[7] and to signal the writer's own distancing from (or closeness to) those voices. In academic genres, such a strategy is used to build consensus within the academic community (Hunston in press). Love, in her 2002 study of a sociology textbook, mentions the usage of reporting verbs among the forms of authorial negative evaluation: *claimed* is the commonest reporting verb, which, she shows, signifies author disagreement. Conversely, she notes, reporting verbs are abandoned when the evaluation construed is positive; otherwise *argue* is chosen as a reporting verb which acknowledges the plausibility of the reported proposition.

Voices or participant roles

Much has been written on the argumentative function of interpersonal pronouns and Subject participants *I/we/you* (Bondi 1999; Tang 1999) and on other interpersonal features used to maintain writer-reader relations. In particular, Hyland (2002a, b) analyses directives and questions, respectively, while Ravelli (2000) considers those Moods involving more interpersonal engagement, typically, Imperatives and Interrogatives used to engage the reader's attention.

Moves

Another way to look at the status of an utterance within a text and the knowledge it presents is to identify it as a specific move within the unfolding of argumentation. Bondi (1999, 2001, 2002) analyses those moves corresponding more directly to the enquiry procedures typical of scientific investigation. Among the argumentative moves that are common in textbooks, and, within these, in the introductory chapters, we find Concession (Freddi 2005 and Thompson 2001[8]), or argumentative prolepsis; in other words, the inclusion by the author of an Objection in order to immediately refute it. The force of this rhetorical move resides in the fact that the adversary Claims and Arguments are voiced by the author himself, so that the whole argumentation so developed tends to prove irrefutable: the reader is inclined to think that the author has contemplated all possible objections.

Argumentative prolepsis is usually realised in the framework of Concession, that is, by expressions such as *of course...but*, or, *indeed... however.*[9]

Modality and hedging

Modality has been variously defined as the strength or detachment of a writer's opinion, or the intermediate space between the negative and the positive poles, the degrees or nuances between a yes and a no, dos and don'ts (Halliday 1994: 88).

Hyland (1998) has shown that hedging is a fundamental characteristic of academic discourse. More recently, Martin (2003: 175) has effectively described hedging as another way to expand the play of intervening voices (also White 2003).

Retrospective and prospective evaluation – Metadiscourse

I am here referring specifically to Hunston (1994) who considers the steps that are signalled by explicit metadiscursive expressions as crucial to textual progression. She observes that evaluation has an important organising role in discourse, in that it indicates points in the text that help the reader orient themselves through the unfolding of argumentation. Such points are marked by relevance markers, or metadiscourse, that have an anaphoric or cataphoric element. This places the preceding or subsequent text within a category of significance (the phenomenon is exemplified in the Results and Discussion section).

Categories of importance or significance (also Lemke 1998) are another form of positive evaluation that leads us to the next feature, attitudinal lexis.

Attitudinal lexis

This has been most thoroughly investigated by Martin (2000) and by the contributors of the aforementioned (2003) monographic issue of *Text* on evaluation. As far as attitudinal lexis in academic discourse is concerned, relevant work includes that of Hunston mentioned earlier, and Lemke (1998), but there is certainly room for further work focusing on the role of emotions in scientific writing.

Having identified some of the areas dealt with in the literature, I can now move on to discuss the insights gained by analysing my corpus data.

Data and methodology

In another paper (Freddi 2005) I advanced the hypothesis of a "lexico-grammar of argumentation" based on frequency counts in a small corpus of introductory chapters to linguistics textbooks, on keywords identification (Scott 1997, 2001a, b) and analysis of concordances. The idea was that one could identify a set of structures realising ways of building up an argument about linguistics, which is something close to Hunston and Sinclair's notion of a "local grammar of evaluation":

> i.e. the belief that it is possible to identify patterns whose primary purpose is to evaluate, thus starting from the expression, the wording in Hallidayan terms, then ending up with a more systematic picture of a local grammar accounting for phenomena which do not exhibit a behaviour generalisable enough to fit into a general description of grammar.   (Hunston & Sinclair 2000: 75–76)

In order to test the hypothesis of a lexico-grammar of argumentation against corpus data,[10] I am here suggesting that various types of comparisons be drawn. For example, a first step would be to consider the different textbooks writers included in the corpus with each individual compared to another in turn. Then, the linguistic features pertaining to each individual textbook writer can be further considered and compared with the rest of the corpus, which can be thus thought of as representative of the population of textbook writers-linguists.[11] It should be noted that I am starting from the assumption that a local grammar intersects with both registerial[12] and stylistic variation.

In my analysis, therefore, I have first compared the frequency lists pertaining to each textbook with the one derived from the totality of the other textbooks, that is the rest of the corpus, (henceforth referred as *CORPUS*). Second, I have analysed the concordance lines of some of the words whose frequency was found to be more significant in each of the textbooks, with a view to identifying patterns of argumentation/evaluation in which they might occur.

Following Oakes (1998: 28–29), who measures similarity between different text corpora, in order to interpret which variation in the frequencies is likely to be significant (vs. random), I have applied a statistical test of significance, namely the chi-square test. The chi-square test allows "an estimation of whether the frequencies in a table differ significantly from each other. It allows the comparison of frequencies found experimentally with those expected on the basis of some theoretical model" (Oakes 1998: 24).[13]

For this purpose, I have set up a Microsoft Excel worksheet to calculate the distance between the frequencies found experimentally in each writer and

Table 1. 25 most frequent words in Brown and *CORPUS*

BRO =	15,307		*CORPUS* =	161,300	
WORD	Freq.	%	WORD	Freq.	%
THE	1,070	6.99%	THE	9,728	6.03%
OF	763	4.98%	OF	7,984	4.95%
TO	524	3.42%	TO	4,636	2.87%
AND	507	3.31%	AND	4,422	2.74%
A	406	2.65%	IN	4,300	2.67%
IN	385	2.52%	A	3,856	2.39%
IS	380	2.48%	IS	3,582	2.22%
WE	284	1.86%	LANGUAGE	2,364	1.47%
THAT	272	1.78%	THAT	2,132	1.32%
BE	265	1.73%	IT	1,972	1.22%
LANGUAGE	214	1.40%	AS	1,962	1.22%
IT	205	1.34%	BE	1,763	1.09%
THIS	181	1.18%	ARE	1,553	0.96%
WILL	167	1.09%	THIS	1,376	0.85%
AS	166	1.08%	OR	1,255	0.78%
CAN	164	1.07%	FOR	1,195	0.74%
ARE	162	1.06%	WE	1,180	0.73%
FOR	117	0.76%	WHICH	1,122	0.70%
AN	102	0.67%	NOT	1,049	0.65%
OR	102	0.67%	WITH	977	0.61%
ON	100	0.65%	BY	857	0.53%
WITH	95	0.62%	HAVE	836	0.52%
NOT	92	0.60%	BUT	813	0.50%
HAVE	91	0.59%	ON	759	0.47%
USE	86	0.56%	THEY	737	0.46%

those expected when compared to the *CORPUS*. An example of the data is shown in Table 1, where the frequency of occurrence based on the textbook by Brown is given together with the frequency based on the overall *CORPUS*.

Of the various comparisons between each individual textbook and the *CORPUS*, I will discuss here only three cases, namely the ones which consider the textbooks by Brown (hereafter BRO), Crystal (CRY), and Widdowson (WID) in order to illustrate the methodology employed and some of the findings. The results obtained are discussed in the next section.

Table 2. Chi-square of word frequencies in BRO/*CORPUS*: First 25 words

BRO WORD	O1	O2	E1	E2	CHI Sq. Test (O1-E1)^2/E1	CHI Sq. Test (O2-E2)^2/E2
WILL	167	468	55	580	227.8	21.6
WE	284	1,180	127	1,337	194.5	18.5
TIGER	26	26	5	47	102.5	9.7
CAN	164	733	78	819	95.7	9.1
MODEL	39	70	9	100	92.4	8.8
KNOWLEDGE	69	196	23	242	92.3	8.8
KEPT	26	31	5	52	89.8	8.5
COMPETENCE	46	108	13	141	79.9	7.6
TELEPHONE	21	23	4	40	77.5	7.4
MARZIPAN	17	17	3	31	67.0	6.4
SENTENCES	63	209	24	248	65.9	6.3
HUGE	18	20	3	35	65.7	6.2
TEXT	25	43	6	62	61.9	5.9
COMMUNICATIVE	27	50	7	70	61.9	5.9
DIAL	15	15	3	27	59.1	5.6
SENTENCE	53	170	19	204	58.7	5.6
DESCRIPTION	42	123	14	151	53.6	5.1
SINCE	36	95	11	120	53.5	5.1
CONTEXT	31	74	9	96	52.7	5.0
CONSIDER	30	72	9	93	50.6	4.8
RECOGNIZE	21	39	5	55	48.0	4.6
SEMANTIC	25	56	7	74	46.0	4.4
BE	265	1,763	176	1,852	45.3	4.3
REAL	22	46	6	62	44.0	4.2
MEANINGS	33	95	11	117	43.3	4.1

Results and discussion

The chi-square statistics for BRO/*CORPUS* are shown in Table 2, with all the words ranked according to their chi-square value.

Words that have a higher value are those whose distance from the expected value based on probabilities in *CORPUS* is higher and more significant: if we cross-check the sum of the first 5 items in the last two columns (780.6) with the critical value of chi-square on 4 degrees of freedom at 99% significance level, the calculated sum (780.6) must be greater than or equal to the critical value (13.3) in order for it to be significant.[14]

Interestingly, *WILL* and *WE*, having the highest and second highest chi-square, are words that function at the interpersonal level of discourse: a modal verb and a 1st person pronoun, respectively. An examination of the concordances might reveal patterns that reflect evaluative argumentative strategies of the author under consideration.

Indeed, analysis of the concordance data shows that *we* and *will* co-occur in 48 out of the 167 occurrences of *will*; moreover, most of the time *we* is followed by a modal verb and functions not only as reader-inclusive *we*, or, generic/impersonal *we*, but also as a royal *we* (*pluralis maiestatis*) for the author's voice, and it is actually often difficult to tell whether the former or the latter use is the case. This is particularly true of those instances in which *we will* signals the mapping of the textual development, e.g. *We will consider each briefly...* or *Embedding is a more difficult case, which we will illustrate with a well-known example,* or *We will look at such matters in more detail in the next section*; as well as when *we will* seems to correspond to a more didactic *let us* form which always includes 'you', and tracks the line of reasoning, e.g. *we will assume/suppose that*, as is visible in the concordance lines below. The reader-inclusive or exclusive meaning seems to depend also on the process involved. The processes that follow the modal are highlighted in bold.

```
together in English. To start the discussion we will assume that two kinds of
eed any others that may seem to be relevant, we will assume that it is possib
ing. In the chapters that immediately follow we will assume a division of des
on to such a vocabulary, and in what follows we will be trying to externalize
ned with some of the explanatory claims, and we will be in a better position t
  o consider data of this kind here, instead we will briefly discuss some ways i
r with articles and adjectives to form units we will call noun phrases, and that
'decontextualization' and 'standardization'. We will consider each briefly. Regu
  any other way. In this and the next section we will consider some ways in which
ill have a set of rules, the nature of which we will examine in Chapters 4 and 5
```

It can further be noticed that *will* is often accompanied by a modal adjunct, such as *probably, almost certainly, surely, generally, obviously, readily*, etc., or else it occurs in a hypothetical environment, i.e. *if....* The typical context for the modality so expressed seems to be the speculative one, where the epistemic evaluation is part of the process of hypothesis formation, as shown by the following example: *The anomaly will also persist if these sentences are used in particular contexts....*

Furthermore, the structure whereby the modal *CAN* is followed by the passive form of a cognitive process, as in *x can be regarded as, referred to as, understood/seen as, illustrated, used to*, etc. is used by the author to relate a concept he is trying to clarify to some other relevant category or evidence so as to build up a better understanding of it. This pattern exemplifies the prospective evaluation introduced before in the Evaluation and Argumentation section.

Table 3. Chi-square of word frequencies of CRY/*CORPUS*: First 25 words

CRY WORD	O1	O2	E1	E2	CHI Sq. Test $(O1-E1)^2/E1$	CHI Sq. Test $(O2-E2)^2/E2$
A	1,269	3,856	1,019	4,106	61.4	15.2
WOULD	186	380	113	453	48.0	11.9
TO	1,450	4,636	1,210	4,876	47.6	11.8
THIS	508	1,376	375	1,509	47.5	11.8
THEORY	104	168	54	218	46.1	11.4
WHICH	425	1,122	308	1,239	44.8	11.1
STUDY	148	299	89	358	39.3	9.8
IT	664	1,972	524	2,112	37.4	9.3
MANY	145	302	89	358	35.5	8.8
FOR	427	1,195	322	1,300	33.9	8.4
WAS	181	422	120	483	31.2	7.7
APPROACH	55	79	27	107	30.2	7.5
HAD	77	137	43	171	27.9	6.9
THERE	218	551	153	616	27.7	6.9
IF	169	405	114	460	26.4	6.5
HUMAN	26	313	67	272	25.4	6.3
I	177	437	122	492	24.7	6.1
ABOUT	175	435	121	489	23.8	5.9
PEOPLE	110	243	70	283	22.6	5.6
POINT	90	190	56	224	21.2	5.3
KIND	74	148	44	178	20.2	5.0
WERE	104	234	67	271	20.2	5.0
OF	2,233	7,984	2,031	8,186	20.0	5.0
SEE	75	153	45	183	19.4	4.8
PROBLEMS	40	62	20	82	19.2	4.8

Even words such as *TIGER, TELEPHONE, MARZIPAN* and *DIAL* can, however indirectly, tell us something of the rhetorical strategies of Brown, who, in fact, uses a brief extract from Iris Murdoch to illustrate some of his points. Similarly, one could add that words such as *SEMANTIC* and *MEANINGS* reveal the semiotic approach of the author who sets out by stating that *Language is the most sophisticated and versatile means available to human beings for the communication of meanings.* However, issues concerning the subject matter and the ideational level of discourse go beyond the scope of this paper.

If we consider another author, Crystal, and the evidence in his textbook (CRY) as compared with the *CORPUS*, we get the ranking given in Table 3.

Some observations can be made on the usage of *WOULD, THIS, THEORY, IT* and *I. WOULD, THIS* and *IT* can be discussed together, at least to a certain extent, for they generate a common pattern. The most common co-text for *WOULD* is the following:

It as anticipatory Subject + *would be* (or any other relational process instead of *to be*) + evaluative/attitudinal Adjective + *to* infinitive clause (embedded clause functioning as Subject).[15]

The same usage is also identified by Hunston and Sinclair (2000: 84) among the patterns of evaluation. They notice how the Adjective expresses the evaluative category, and the clause (either finite or non-finite, i.e. a *that*- clause, *wh*-clause, *to*- clause, or an *-ing* clause), the thing evaluated.

Consider the following citations from the concordance with the evaluative adjective in bold:

```
have consistently heard - the sheep! But it would be wrong to ridicule, for Psam
oint than who, which is more colloquial. It would be as inappropriate to introd
ig paragraph are of this general nature. It would be misleading and naive to be
 part of the country they come from. And it would be very unlikely that anyone
s of drawing together remedial material. It would be premature to expect too mu
rquired for the study of language, then, it would be necessary to point to such
pex, and involve so many variables, that it would be impossible to reach any ge
ind have four hundred pages or more! And it would be naive of an author to expec
use criticisms of subjectivity, and that it would be difficult to defend themse
the way in which the voice cords worked, it would be important to make it absolu
powers of mentalistic generative theory, it would become necessary for them to r
; the second might not (cf. p. 80). Then it would certainly be true to say that
 all in this way is a matter of dispute. It would certainly be unfair to deny a
 much more attractive ring about it! But it would have been dishonest to call i
e, in a project about number in English, it would obviously be necessary to de
these problems face the younger manager. It would presumably be ideal if one cou
```

Sometimes we find the variant *This would be* followed by the same pattern (e.g. *confusing, highly misleading*).

Another regularity that can be noted is *This is* with *this* fulfilling both the co-referential function, by associating with the entire preceding clause, and at the same time evaluating its importance prospectively (for example, *And this is true to a very considerable extent still*, or, *This is a deceptively simple statement*, etc.).

THIS is also associated with more idiosyncratic uses like, for example, the expression *of this kind*, which, however, are less interesting for our investigation.

Those instances of *WOULD* where the modal does not occur in the pattern identified above can be seen as a way of hedging a statement, as in *They are part of a sound-system, and would be called 'phonemes' by most linguists*.

A consideration of the most frequent collocates of *THEORY* gives *a theory, linguistic theory* and *theory is*. This is so because of Crystal's idiosyncratic

Table 4. Chi-square of word frequencies of WID/*CORPUS*: First 25 words

WID WORD	O1	O2	E1	E2	CHI Sq. Test (O1-E1)^2/E1	CHI Sq. Test (O2-E2)^2/E2
OXFORD	21	25	3	43	106.8	7.5
MIGHT	51	204	17	238	69.8	4.9
DIFFERENT	73	385	30	428	61.0	4.3
PAT	11	12	2	21	59.5	4.2
SAME	52	232	19	265	59.4	4.2
COMBINE	16	29	3	42	57.4	4.0
RIDE	9	9	1	17	51.6	3.6
REALITY	17	40	4	53	46.8	3.3
HUMAN	58	313	24	347	46.3	3.3
BIKES	8	8	1	15	45.9	3.2
PARAMETERS	8	8	1	15	45.9	3.2
DESIGN	11	18	2	27	43.3	3.1
SPECIES	17	45	4	58	40.9	2.9
ACTUALITY	7	7	1	13	40.1	2.8
HANG	7	7	1	13	40.1	2.8
OGRE	7	7	1	13	40.1	2.8
LANGUE	14	32	3	43	39.8	2.8
SEQUENCE	14	32	3	43	39.8	2.8
IDEALIZATION	9	13	1	21	39.4	2.8
IS	359	3,582	259	3,682	38.4	2.7
WEAR	7	8	1	14	36.6	2.6
IT	216	1,972	144	2,044	36.1	2.5
THEY	99	737	55	781	35.2	2.5
ACTUAL	22	80	7	95	34.8	2.5
CAPABILITY	6	6	1	11	34.4	2.4

preference for *linguistic theory* rather than simply *linguistics*. Also, before describing what language theory is in particular, he defines what we mean by theory, in general.

The usage of the 1st person singular pronoun is particularly typical of Crystal's popular style: the author deliberately chooses the Subject pronoun for a more personal involvement in the scientific enquiry process. This specific preference is also associated with one for the present in present aspect of the verb, anchoring the prose to the *hic et nunc* which coincides with the very moment of reading for the potential reader, thus with a flavour typical of spoken discourse, e.g. *I am not saying that such speculations. . .*, *What I am arguing is that. . ..* When the verb following *I* is just a simple present, the sharing of a common reasoning ground and moment with the readership is meant to be nonetheless full: *I do not mean to imply...*, *I have more on this point below, I hope you do not mind...*, *Here I would simply emphasize*, and the like.

Finally, I will consider the comparison between Widdowson's textbook and the *CORPUS*, shown in Table 4; one can see that the words *MIGHT*, *IT* and *IS* are worth commenting on briefly.

It is interesting to notice that it is yet another modal expression that has the second highest chi-value: Widdowson uses *MIGHT* when introducing moves such as Concession, e.g. *It might be argued/ thought that*, or *one might claim*, *the question might arise, speakers might well find the difference difficult to perceive*. When *might* co-occurs with the subject pronoun *we*, as, for example, in *We might want to shift our attention to the level of words*, and *We might count 'wasted' and 'waste' as tokens of the same type*, its meaning is analogous to *we will* observed in BRO.

As for *IS*, together with the already seen *it is* followed by Adj. (*easy, convenient, important*, etc.) and embedded clause, there is also another pattern, namely, pseudo-cleft clauses, such as *What is distinctive about language in general is...*, *What is central in language is...*, *What is different and controversial about... is...*, which are used to attribute evaluation (see also Hunston & Sinclair 2000: 89).

Conclusion

After reviewing some of the linguistic phenomena identified in the literature as expressing evaluations, I have attempted to show that in academic writing various forms of evaluation function as argumentative strategy, and have consequently tested the hypothesis of a lexico-grammar of argumentation against corpus evidence.

For this purpose, I have moved from observation and interpretation of word frequency to an analysis of the patterning revealed by concordance data. In particular, I compared word frequency found in three textbooks, namely, BRO, CRY and WID with those in *CORPUS*. To estimate the significance of the variation in the frequencies, the chi-square statistical measure, as presented by Oakes (1998), was used. This analysis of specific concordances has allowed patterns of evaluation to emerge, which reflect the argumentative style of each author considered and, in certain cases, are probed by more than one author.

Uses that have no significant frequency, thus which do not matter quantitatively, obviously crop up only when we leave aside the concordance and read the text as a whole. So, for example, when reading AKMA for attitudinal lexis, we can spot the following expressions: *growing and exciting area of study, important impact, key components, emerging field, fascinated with complex manageable questions, reasonable results,* etc. To that extent, I agree with Tognini Bonelli (2001) on the different type of insights that a corpus and a text can provide the analyst with. A probabilistic approach, however, such as the one adopted here, allows us to dispense with a grammar of 'all or none' rules for a description of manners of expression, that is, of style.

Notes

1. This view is opposed to the one seeing the clause as message, i.e. focusing on its textual organisation, which favours culminative patterns, with peaks of prominence, e.g. the thematic structure; and the clause as representation, i.e. its experiential function, with its discrete segmental organisation, e.g. the components of the transitivity system. See also Halliday (1996/2002:399–400) on indeterminacy in the grammar.

2. See Channel (2000) for an application of the notion.

3. Although with differing implications, both SFL and corpus linguistics (Halliday's 1994 'lexico-grammar' and Sinclair's 1991 'collocation' and 'colligation') conceive of lexis and grammar as inseparable.

4. See, for example, Partington (1998) and Stubbs (1993, 2001).

5. Among the numerous studies on the role of persuasion and the rhetoric of scientific registers, see Bondi (1999); Hunston (1993a, 1994, 2000); Hyland (2000, 2002a, b, c).

6. This third sense seems to me to refer to what Hyland has formalised as 'metadiscourse', that is, the writer's explicit evaluation and signalling of his/her own text structure and organisation, which also hints at the reflexive nature of much academic discourse (Bondi 1999), i.e. the folding of a text onto itself. For reasons of space, I will not deal with the relation between evaluation and metadiscourse here.

7. See in particular Hyland (2000:107–108) who, drawing on Fairclough's notions of 'interdiscursivity' and 'intertextuality', stresses the dialogicity realised in textbooks by means of incorporation of original sources, so that other texts are manifestly present in textbooks.

8. Thompson (2001) also focuses on these interactional/argumentative choices in the introductory sections.

9. Love (2002) observes how in Giddens' textbook, the countering of each claim is achieved with an adversative move, while concessions to possible plausibility are heavily modalised.

10. See Corpus for full citations and Appendix for a synoptic view of the textbooks and their relative length. For the sampling criteria followed in designing the corpus, see Freddi (2005).

11. I will not, however, deal here with the major theoretical problem of representativeness and specialised corpora.

12. According to Hunston and Sinclair (2000), local grammars are linked to the notion of 'sub-language', i.e. a variety with its own integrity, used continuously on appropriate occa-

sions, a complete language event. If seen in these terms, local grammars are not far from Halliday's register-specific grammars, or, how he puts it, "the redressing of probabilities in the grammar" (Halliday 1991, 1992, 1993). Following Stubbs (2001:215) once again, I quote, "There are strong probabilistic relations between lexico-syntax [lexico-grammar], semantics (different preferred collocations), pragmatics (expression of speaker attitude), and distribution across text-types (formal vs. informal)." If it is true that, for Hunston and Sinclair, it is more a matter of phenomena that leak and are not easily accounted for by a more generalised grammar, while Halliday talks about a redistribution of probabilities in the grammar, it seems to me that for all three scholars, the approach is probabilistic rather than absolute (see also Oakes 1998:77 on this), and therefore comparable, at least in this respect.

13. In Scott's interpretation, you can rank words according to their chi-square value of significance. Such value corresponds to the degree of 'keyness' of each word in a text (Scott 1997, 2001a, b), so that those words with a higher keyness are considered to be typical of that text, that is 'keywords'. I have attempted to problematise the application of Scott's *Keywords Tool* in Freddi (2005). For an analysis of keywords in academic writing, see also Tribble (2000, 2002).

14. I will not deal here with the criticism expressed by Kilgarriff (1996) and others (for instance, Stubbs 1995) on use of the chi-square test for testing the significance of difference of frequencies. See also Freddi (2005) for an attempt to tackle the problem.

15. See also Halliday (1994:98) for an illustration of this grammatical structure, *It was fortunate for me* [[*that...*]], or, *It is impossible* [[*to protect...*]], etc., which shows how modal meanings and attitudinal lexis share a common territory.

References

Baker, M., Francis, G., & Tognini Bonelli, E. (Eds.). (1993). *Text and Technology. Studies in Honour of John Sinclair*. Amsterdam & Philadelphia: John Benjamins.

Bondi, M. (1999). *English Across Genres. Language Variation in the Discourse of Economics*. Modena: Il Fiorino.

Bondi, M. (2001). Small corpora and language variation. In Ghadessy et al. (Eds.), 135–174.

Bondi, M. (2002). Attitude and episteme in academic discourse: Adverbials of stance across genres and moves. *Textus, XV* (2), 249–264.

Channel, J. (2000). Corpus-based analysis of evaluative lexis. In Hunston & Thompson (Eds.), 38–55.

Flowerdew, J. (Ed.). (2002). *Academic Discourse*. London: Longman.

Freddi, M. (2005). Arguing linguistics: Corpus investigation of one functional variety of academic discourse. *Journal of English for Academic Purposes, 4* (1), 5–26.

Ghadessy, M., Henry, A., & Roseberry, R. L. (Eds.). (2001). *Small Corpus Studies and ELT: Theory and practice*. Amsterdam & Philadelphia: John Benjamins.

Halliday, M. A. K. (1991). Corpus studies and probabilistic grammar. In K. Aijmer & B. Altenberg (Eds.), *English Corpus Linguistics. Studies in Honour of Jan Svartvik* (pp. 30–43). London: Longman.

Halliday, M. A. K. (1982). How is a text like a clause? In S. Allen (Ed.), *Text Processing: Proceedings of Nobel Symposium 51* (pp. 209–239). Stockholm: Almquist & Wiksell International.

Halliday, M. A. K. (1992). Language as system and language as instance: The corpus as a theoretical construct. In J. Svartvik (Ed.), *Directions in Corpus Linguistics* (pp. 61–77). Berlin: De Gruyter.

Halliday, M. A. K. (1993). Quantitative studies and probabilities in grammar. In M. Hoey (Ed.), *Data, Description and Discourse. Papers on the English Language in Honour of John McH Sinclair on his sixtieth birthday* (pp. 1–25). London: Harper Collins.

Halliday, M. A. K. (1994). *An Introduction to Functional Grammar* (2nd ed.). London: Arnold.

Halliday, M. A. K. (1996/2002). *On Grammar and Grammatics*. In J. J. Webster (Ed.), *On Grammar, Vol. 1 in the Collected Works of M. A. K. Halliday* (pp. 384–417). London: Continuum.

Hunston, S. (1993a). Evaluation and ideology in scientific writing. In M. Ghadessy (Ed.), *Register Analysis: Theory and Practice* (pp. 57–73). London: Pinter.

Hunston, S. (1993b). Professional conflict. Disagreement in academic discourse. In Baker et al. (Eds.), 115–136.

Hunston, S. (1994). Evaluation and organisation in a sample of written academic discourse. In M. Coulthard (Ed.), *Advances in Written Text Analysis* (pp. 191–218). London: Routledge.

Hunston, S. (1995). A corpus study of English verbs of attribution. *Functions of Language, 2* (2), 133–158.

Hunston, S. (2000). Evaluation and the planes of discourse: Status and value in persuasive texts. In Hunston & Thompson (Eds.), 176–207.

Hunston, S. (in press). It has rightly been pointed out... Attribution, consensus and conflict in academic discourse. In M. Bondi, L. Gavioli, & M. Silver (Eds.), *Proceedings of the Conference on 'Academic Discourse: Genre and small corpora'*. Roma: Officina.

Hunston, S. & Sinclair, J. (2000). A local grammar of evaluation. In Hunston & Thompson (Eds.), 74–101.

Hunston, S. & Thompson, G. (Eds.). (2000). *Evaluation in Text. Authorial Stance and the Construction of Discourse*. Oxford: Oxford University Press.

Hyland, K. (1998). *Hedging in Scientific Discourse*. Amsterdam & Philadelphia: John Benjamins.

Hyland, K. (1999). Talking to students: Metadiscourse in introductory coursebooks. *English for Specific Purposes, 18* (1), 3–26.

Hyland, K. (2000). *Disciplinary Discourses. Social Interactions in Academic Writing*. London: Longman.

Hyland, K. (2002a). Directives: Argument and engagement in academic writing. *Applied Linguistics, 23* (2), 215–239.

Hyland, K. (2002b). What do they mean? Questions in academic writing. *Text, 22* (4), 529–557.

Hyland, K. (2002c). Activity and evaluation: Reporting practices in academic writing. In Flowerdew (Ed.), 115–130.

Kilgarriff, A. (1996). Comparing word frequencies across corpora: Why chi-square doesn't work, and an improved Lob-Brown comparison. In *ALLC-ACH'96: Conference Abstracts, Posters and Demonstrations* (pp. 169–172).

Lemke, J. (1998). Resources for attitudinal meaning. *Functions of Language, 5*, 33–56.

Love, A. (2002). Introductory concepts and 'cutting edge' theories: Can the genre of the textbook accommodate both? In Flowerdew (Ed.), 76–91.

Louw, B. (1993). Irony in the text or insincerity in the writer? The diagnostic potential of semantic prosodies. In Baker et al. (Eds.), 157–176.

Martin, J. R. (2000). Beyond exchange: APPRAISAL Systems in English. In Hunston & Thompson (Eds.), 142–175.

Martin, J. R. (2003). Introduction. *Text, 23* (2), (Special Issue on Evaluation) 171–181.

Martin, J. R. & Rose, D. (2003). *Working with Discourse. Meaning beyond the Clause.* London: Continuum.

Oakes, M. (1998). *Statistics for Corpus Linguistics.* Edinburgh: Edinburgh University Press.

Partington, A. (1998). *Patterns and Meanings.* Amsterdam & Philadelphia: John Benjamins.

Ravelli, L. (2000). Getting started with functional analysis of texts. In L. Unsworth (Ed.), *Researching Language in Schools and Communities* (pp. 27–64). London: Cassel.

Scott, M. (1997). PC analysis of key words and key key words. *System, 25* (2), 233–245.

Scott, M. (2001a). Comparing corpora and identifying key words, collocations, and frequency distributions through the Wordsmith Tools Suite of computer programs. In Ghadessy et al. (Eds.), 47–67.

Scott, M. (2001b). Mapping key words to *Problem* and *Solution.* In M. Scott & G. Thompson (Eds.), *Patterns of Text. In Honour of Michael Hoey* (pp. 109–127). Amsterdam & Philadelphia: John Benjamins.

Sinclair, J. (1991). *Corpus, Concordance, Collocation.* Oxford: Oxford University Press.

Sinclair J. (1996). The search for units of meaning. *Textus, 9*, 75–106.

Stubbs, M. (1993). British traditions in text analysis: From Firth to Sinclair. In Baker, Francis, & Tognini Bonelli (Eds.), 1–33.

Stubbs, M. (1995). Collocations and semantic profiles: On the cause of the trouble with quantitative studies. *Functions of Language, 2* (1), 23–55.

Stubbs, M. (2001). *Words and Phrases. Corpus Studies of Lexical Semantics.* Oxford: Blackwell.

Tang, R. (1999). The 'I' Identity: Exploring writer identity in student academic writing through the first person pronoun. *English for Specific Purposes, 18*, 23–39.

Thompson, G. (2001). Interaction in academic writing: Learning to argue with the reader. *Applied Linguistics, 22* (1), 58–78.

Thompson, G. & Ye, Y. (1991). Evaluation in the reporting verbs used in academic papers. *Applied Linguistics, 12* (4), 365–382.

Tognini Bonelli, E. (2001). *Corpus Linguistics at Work.* Amsterdam & Philadelphia: John Benjamins.

Tribble, C. (2000). Genres, keywords, teaching: Towards a pedagogic account of the language of project proposals. In L. Burnard & T. McEnery (Eds.), *Rethinking Pedagogy from a Corpus Perspective* (pp. 75–90). Frankfurt: Peter Lang.

Tribble, C. (2002). Corpora and corpus analysis: New windows on academic writing. In Flowerdew (Ed.), 131–149.

White, P. (2000). Dialogue and inter-subjectivity: Reinterpreting the semantics of modality and hedging. In M. Coulthard, J. Cotterill, & F. Rock (Eds.), *Working with Dialogue* (pp. 67–80). Tuebingen: Niemeyer.

White, P. (2003). Beyond modality and hedging: A dialogic view of the language of intersubjective stance. *Text, 23* (2), (Special Issue on Evaluation) 259–284.

Corpus

Aitchinson, J. (1995). *Linguistics. An Introduction.* London: Hodder & Stoughton.

Akmajian, A., Demers, R. A., Farmer, A. K., & Harnish, R. M. (1995). *Linguistics: An Introduction to Language and Communication* (4th ed.). Cambridge MA: MIT Press.

Brown, K. (1984). *Linguistics Today.* London: Fontana.

Crystal, D. (1990). *Linguistics* (2nd ed.). London: Penguin.

Lyons, J. (1981). *Language and Linguistics.* Cambridge: Cambridge University Press.

Radford, A., Atkinson, M., Britain, D., Clahsen, H., & Spencer, A. (1999). *Linguistics: An Introduction.* Cambridge: Cambridge University Press.

Robins, R. H. (1989). *General Linguistics. An Introductory Survey* (4th ed.). London: Longmans.

Wallwork, J. F. (1985). *Language and Linguistics* (2nd ed.). London: Heinemann.

Widdowson, H. G. (1996). *Linguistics.* Oxford: Oxford University Press.

Yule, G. (1996). *The Study of Language* (2nd ed.). Cambridge: Cambridge University Press.

Appendix

Author	Abbreviation	No. of words of introductory chapters	% of *CORPUS*
Aitchinson	AIT	9,978	6.2%
Akmajian	AKMA	2,028	1.3%
Brown	BRO	15,307	9.5%
Crystal	CRY	46,063	28.6%
Lyons	LYO	23,044	14.3%
Radford	RAD	7,592	4.7%
Robins	ROB	25,064	15.5%
Wallwark	WAL	8,775	5.4%
Widdowson	WID	12,359	7.7%
Yule	YUL	11,090	6.9%
TOTAL	*CORPUS*	**161,300**	**100%**

On the boundaries between evaluation and metadiscourse

Annelie Ädel
Göteborg University, Sweden

This paper argues for a distinction between evaluation and metadiscourse, which is illustrated with examples from corpora of argumentative essays in English. While 'evaluation' is often used as a cover term for a wide variety of discourse moves, 'metadiscourse' specifically foregrounds relations between the writer and the target reader. The paper argues that 'evaluation' could be kept for the relations between the participants and the subject-matter.

It is often the case that 'metadiscourse' and 'evaluation' are treated as one uniform phenomenon. More specifically, in most studies of metadiscourse, evaluation is considered part of metadiscourse (see e.g. Hyland 1998; Markkanen et al. 1993; Vande Kopple 1988). The claim to be made in this paper is that metadiscourse and evaluation are conceptually different and should be treated as two distinct categories. I will begin with basic definitions of the two categories, then give some historical background. Finally, I will present a model that allows us to draw a theoretical distinction between metadiscourse and evaluation.

My ideas about these phenomena were developed in the context of my doctoral work on the use of metadiscourse in argumentative texts (Ädel 2003), for which I used two corpora of essays written by university students, both native and non-native speakers of English. They are the SWICLE (The Swedish component of the International Corpus of Learner English) and the LOCNESS (The Louvain Corpus of Native English Essays) (see Granger 1993, 1998), the latter divided into two subcorpora of American English (AmE) and British English (BrE). All examples given in the following have been taken from these corpora, except for those in Table 1, which come from the literature on metadiscourse.[1]

'Metadiscourse' is defined in Ädel (2003) as reflexive linguistic expressions referring to the evolving text *per se* or its linguistic form, including references to the writer persona and the imagined reader *qua* writer and reader of the current text.[2] Examples are given in (1), in which the main metadiscursive units are marked with italics.

(1) a. The solutions *mentioned in this essay* dealt mainly with cultural and social understanding, which led on to creating a better working climate for both Swedes and immigrants.   (SWICLE)

 b. *As I stated above*, I believe that these have always been men of low moral standards.   (SWICLE)

 c. *Finally I would like to discuss the topic* which has to do with nature. Dogs love to follow you on your walks in the forest, and this is also a good way of spending your spare time.   (SWICLE)

 d. Has the modern world made us forget to have dreams? As we step forward in time everything gets more and more advanced. *By this I principally mean* the science, technology and industrialization matters.   (SWICLE)

 e. You are supposed to feel at home in the resident halls. How are you supposed to feel at home when you can't do the same things you were doing at home? *I understand you may be thinking*, what about the person you share a room with?   (AmE)

 f. *What do we mean by* imagination then? Roget's Thesaurus' subtitles are: "vision, thought, idea, imagination, and falsehood".   (SWICLE)

 g. Science technology and industrialization are often, *as we have seen*, the stimuli and the means to the fulfillment of many of our dreams and imaginations.   (SWICLE)

The term 'evaluation', on the other hand, refers to linguistic material that expresses the speaker's attitude towards what is said. It is more or less equivalent to 'stance', defined by Biber et al. (1999:966) as expressing "personal feelings, attitudes, value judgments, or assessments" added to any communication of propositional content. Examples are given in (2). The italicised parts are the ones we will focus on here; there may, however, be additional examples of markers of evaluation in the co-texts.

(2) a. If my mother really wants to escape the Christmas stress I think she has to go to that little hotel in the country where people wait on her and she just relaxes. *Personally I love* Christmas!   (SWICLE)

b. I think we all want our children and grandchildren to have the same right as we to clean air, clean water and green forests. *I also think it is of great importance* to look after animals' interests.   (SWICLE)

c. It is amazing to read how a whole group of people were stopped from buying what they wanted. The indians were not allowed to buy liqour for about one hundred years *if I remember it right.*   (SWICLE)

d. [...] have chosen because it interests you so much. You feel that you want to learn more about that particular subject and *perhaps you want to* meet people with the same interest. You also learn to discuss and understand how [...]   (SWICLE)

e. [...] there should be strict rules regarding abortions. *We all know* the consequences of sex, especially unprotected sex and if a person decides to play the game they should be held accountable for the results of their horseplay.   (AmE)

Metadiscourse is a complex and difficult research area; at the heart of the complexity lie issues of delimitation. As Schiffrin (1980:201) puts it, "[t]he wide range of phenomena that can be identified as meta-linguistic and the vagueness surrounding the boundaries between meta-lingual and other functions of language complicate the task of finding a set of empirical linguistic indicators for [such phenomena]". Ädel (2003) argues that research on metadiscourse needs to achieve greater theoretical rigour and work on delimiting the category more clearly.

Researchers into metadiscourse have most commonly adopted a Hallidayan approach,[3] which I will refer to as the 'SFG-inspired' model.[4] In this model, metadiscourse is defined as linguistic items which explicitly serve the *interpersonal* and/or *textual* functions. Textual and interpersonal material stand in contrast to the *ideational* (or 'propositional') material of a text.

The interpersonal-textual duality, to put it in SFG-oriented terms, is a matter of debate among researchers into metadiscourse. Mauranen (1993) has identified two strands of research into metadiscourse: one preferring a broad definition (the so-called 'integrative approach'), and the other a narrow definition (the so-called 'non-integrative approach').[5] In fact, this distinction boils down to whether or not evaluation is included in the concept of metadiscourse. Table 1 sums up the two approaches. The shaded brackets gives examples of studies within each approach.

The non-integrative model restricts metadiscourse to refer to linguistic elements "whose function in the first place is to describe the text in which they are located" (Markkanen et al. 1993:142), while interpersonal elements are largely

Table 1. The integrative and non-integrative approaches to metadiscourse

The **INTEGRATIVE** approach, e.g. Vande Kopple (1985, 1988), Markkanen et al. (1993), Hyland (1998)		
Function	INTERPERSONAL	TEXTUAL
Description	Linguistic elements that display the writer's attitude to what is said in the text	Linguistic elements that show how the text is organised or that make references to the text itself
Examples	*certainly; surprisingly; perhaps; might; you may not agree that*	*in the present work; secondly; X will be discussed later; as noted earlier; in conclusion*

	The **NON-INTEGRATIVE** approach, e.g. Mauranen (1993), Bäcklund (1998)

excluded.[6] In the integrative model, on the other hand, both functions are included. This leads to the concept of metadiscourse being too all-inclusive, in my view. For example, the integrativists Markkanen et al. (1993:143) themselves point out that metadiscourse "covers such a wide area of language use that it requires subclassification; saying that some item in a text is metadiscourse does not say much".

Some historical background will help us to understand the motivation for treating the two phenomena of metadiscourse and evaluation as one. Before the 1990s, the primary focus of text research seems to have been on aspects of the subject matter itself. In one of the early linguistic articles on metadiscourse published in the late 1980s, Vande Kopple (1988:233) begins by claiming that "[m]uch of the recent work on the nature of informative texts and on the processes that readers apply to them proceeds as if there is only one kind of meaning in such texts, the referential, ideational, or propositional".

By the early 1990s, linguists had begun to react against the strong emphasis on propositional or 'subject matter' meaning. This led to the creation of a dichotomy between 'subject matter' and 'non-subject matter' (i.e. everything else) in a text; the latter was labelled 'metadiscourse'. This development led to new research perspectives on written text, among which studies of metadiscourse and evaluation have gained prominence.

This development can be seen as part of a more general movement towards rethinking the notion of language as a purely referential system of transferring information that is either true or false about things in the real world. We can trace it back to the origin of functional approaches to language. For example, the observation that language is used not only to convey referential information but also to create and sustain expressive meanings goes back to Malinowski in the 1930s. Roman Jakobson also deserves mention for his theorising about the basic functions of language. Other important approaches that focus on the structural organisation of the content of texts are Prague School functional grammar and Hallidayan systemic functional grammar.

It seems that, in drawing a gross distinction between propositional content and other aspects of a text, researchers ended up labelling a large, heterogeneous agglomeration of linguistic phenomena 'metadiscourse'. A decade or so ago, it was probably necessary to stress this opposition in order to shift the focus of research. Today, however, we are in a better position to do more fine-grained analyses of these phenomena.

Ädel's (2003) model of metadiscourse offers an alternative way of viewing these phenomena. I will briefly outline it in the following, focussing specifically on how it relates to evaluation. I believe that not only does this alternative functional model work well for studies of metadiscourse, but it can also be extended to inform studies of evaluation. In fact, the model proves to be a useful way of drawing a distinction between metadiscourse and evaluation.

This model is considerably more restricted than the integrative approach. It is similar to the non-integrative approach in that it excludes evaluation from the domain of metadiscourse, and instead focuses on the reflexive properties of metadiscourse. However, it is different from the non-integrative approach in that it takes as a starting point Roman Jakobson's (see e.g. 1995) *metalinguistic, directive* and *expressive* functions of language. These suit the present definition of metadiscourse (which, in addition to the text itself, includes the writer and imagined reader) better than the SFG-inspired model. For arguments in favour of the alternative Jakobsonian model, see Ädel (2003: 66–67).

Only four of the original six Jakobsonian functions, those shown in Table 2, will be relevant to the current discussion. The *phatic* and *poetic* functions have not been listed.

Table 2. The four Jakobsonian functions used in the model to draw a distinction between metadiscourse and evaluation

	Function	Speech event component	Refers to...
(a)	*metalinguistic*	text/code	the text or language itself
(b)	*expressive*	writer	the writer persona
(c)	*directive*	reader	the imagined reader
(d)	*referential*	world/'context'	entities in the 'real world'

Metadiscourse is defined here in terms of three of Jakobson's functions of language. One or more of the first three functions, (a)–(c), are dominant, with the metalinguistic function indispensable, situating the category in the world of discourse.

Unlike metadiscourse, evaluation is not reflexive language; it does not involve the metalinguistic function. In evaluation, functions (b)–(d) of Table 2 are involved, with the expressive function now the indispensable one. The referential function, representing the 'real world', is also important, situating the category in the 'real world'. In evaluation, the writer and the reader are not primarily present *qua* 'writer persona' and 'imagined reader' of the current text, but rather as experiencers in the 'real world', about which they possess feelings and opinions. Expressions of stance are used to show whether the writer agrees or disagrees with ideas or viewpoints that are discussed as the topic of the discourse. They display the writer's standpoint with regard to some statement or assessment that the text (or a portion of the text) revolves around.

Figure 1 shows the partial overlap between metadiscourse and evaluation. The discourse participants – the writer and the reader – are both central components. However, metadiscourse ties the writer and reader to the current text or world of discourse, while evaluation ties them to the 'real world'.

If the writer and/or reader are visible in metadiscursive expressions, they are present (acting) in the world of discourse, i.e. as writer personas and imagined reader personas. By contrast, when the writer and reader are visible in evaluation, they are acting within the 'real world', towards which they express their attitudes. The world of discourse, of course, is in some sense part of the 'real world', too, but enjoys a special status within it. For straightforward examples of both kinds, see (1) and (2) above.

The great majority of examples in the material studied are straightforward. However, it is well known that multifunctionality is a fact of language. A writer

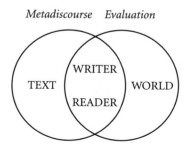

Figure 1. The speech event components involved in metadiscourse and evaluation

can also express her attitudes within the world of discourse, for instance towards the text itself or the reader(ship), as in *By doing so I hope it will become clear to the reader why it is impossible to pick neither integration nor assimilation as some sort of patent-solution* (SWICLE). Using politeness markers such as *I hope* when referring to the reader is one way in which metadiscourse and evaluation can overlap.

Let us now extend the models of metadiscourse and evaluation and split up Figure 1, to allow finer distinctions to be drawn. For example, we can draw distinctions within the categories, based on the configuration of the components. Figure 2 shows the four configurations (a)–(d) of components that constitute metadiscourse. As we have seen, the text component is the hub, or the indispensable function, in this constellation.

This figure presents four subtypes of metadiscourse. If only the text is foregrounded, without reference to the writer or reader, we can call it *text-oriented metadiscourse* (2a). If it is primarily the text and the writer who are involved, it is called *writer-oriented* (2b). If it is primarily the text and the reader who are involved, it is called *reader-oriented* (2c). If all three are involved, we call it *participant-oriented* (2d).

We can also find similar configurations for evaluation. Three subcategories of evaluation are illustrated in Figure 3.

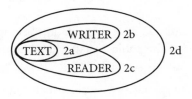

Figure 2. Configurations of metadiscourse

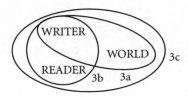

Figure 3. Configurations of evaluation

If the writer and the world are involved, we can call it *writer-oriented evaluation* (3a). If the writer and the reader are involved, it can be called *reader-oriented* (3b). If all three are involved, it can be called *participant-oriented* (3c).

There is a discrepancy between the extensions of the two models. Unlike component 2a in Figure 2, focus on the writer alone – the hub – does not seem possible in evaluation (Figure 3) since the writer always has to be situated somewhere – whether in the world of discourse or in the 'real world'. This leaves us with three, rather than four, different configurations for evaluation. A configuration involving solely the reader and the world components does not seem possible either, since it is the indispensable *writer*'s opinion and attitudes that we are dealing with in cases of evaluation.

Table 3 below exemplifies the subcategories. Examples given in (1) and (2) have been keyed to the subcategories illustrated in Figures 2 and 3. The final column, 'subcategory', gives the codes of the various subcategories. Recall that metadiscursive expressions are necessarily text-oriented (2a), but can also be writer-oriented (2b), or reader-oriented (2c). If both participants are referred to, the term participant-oriented (2d) can be used. Expressions of evaluation are of necessity writer-oriented (3a), but they can also be reader-oriented (3b), or both, which we can refer to as participant-oriented evaluation (3c). Examples of metadiscourse have been marked in grey.

I have found that, while there are some cases of overlap of metadiscourse and evaluation, the majority of examples do seem to fall clearly into one category or the other.

In conclusion, metadiscourse and evaluation belong together in the sense that they foreground *not* the subject matter, but rather (a) the structure of

Table 3. Examples keyed to the subcategories of metadiscourse and evaluation

Examples (extracts from (1) and (2) above)	Text	Writer	Reader	World	Sub-category
In this essay...	√				2a
As I stated above,...	√	√			2b
By this I principally mean...	√	√			2b
You may be thinking that...	√		√		2c
What do we mean by x?	√	√	√		2d
Personally I love Christmas!		√		√	3a
I think it is of great importance...		√		√	3a
Perhaps you want to meet people with the same...			√	√	3b
We all know the consequences of sex...		√	√	√	3c

the discourse (in the case of metadiscourse), (b) the interaction between the writer persona and imagined reader (in the case of metadiscourse), and (c) the attitudes of the writer and imagined reader to the subject matter (in the case of evaluation). When text linguists began to focus on such phenomena in texts, they drew a coarse-grained distinction between 'subject matter' and 'non-subject matter', and often treated metadiscourse and evaluation as the same thing. Following Mauranen (1993), we can call this the integrative approach to metadiscourse. Like Mauranen, I argue that the concept of metadiscourse becomes too broad in an integrative approach; if our definitions lead us too far out of the realm of explicit reflexive language, and too far into linguistic expressions of speaker attitude, we lose in stringency and focus.

I have introduced an alternative model of metadiscourse, which is considerably more restricted than this integrative approach. It is similar to the non-integrative approach in that it excludes stance from the domain of metadiscourse, and instead focuses on its reflexive properties. However, it is different from the non-integrative approach in that it takes as a starting point Jakobson's *metalinguistic*, *directive* and *expressive* functions of language, which results in a more accurate model of metadiscourse. Using a model of Jakobsonian functions, I hope to have shown that metadiscourse and evaluation are conceptually different and, therefore, should be treated as two distinct categories in our analyses of text.

Notes

1. All extracts from the corpora are presented without correction of grammatical or typographical errors or misspellings.

2. Although there are several objections to raise regarding the appropriateness of the term *metadiscourse* (or *metatext*, see e.g. Mauranen 1993:145), it is, by now, an established term, and there is as yet no truly satisfying alternative term. Analogous word formations, such as 'metafiction', speak in favour of using the term 'metadiscourse'. Metafiction (or 'self-reflexive fiction') can be described as fiction about fiction, which "includes within itself a commentary on its own narrative and/or linguistic identity" (Hutcheon 1984).

3. Note, however, that Halliday himself does not discuss or define metadiscourse in terms of his framework.

4. 'SFG' stands for Systemic-Functional Grammar, which is also referred to as Systemic-Functional Linguistics (SFL). SFL can be described as "a theory of language centred around the notion of language function. While SFL accounts for the syntactic structure of language, it places the function of language as central (what language does, and how it does it), in preference to more structural approaches, which place the elements of language and

their combinations as central. SFL starts at social context, and looks at how language both acts upon, and is constrained by, this social context" (http://www.wagsoft.com/Systemics/Definition/definition.html).

5. Instead of 'metadiscourse', the term 'metatext' is commonly used by non-integrativists.

6. Whether this is true in practice is debatable, however, since the subcategory 'addressing the reader' is included both in Mauranen (1993) and in other research based on it (e.g. Bäcklund 1998).

References

Ädel, A. (2003). The use of metadiscourse in argumentative texts by advanced learners and native speakers of English. Unpublished Ph.D. dissertation, Göteborg University, Sweden.

Bäcklund, I. (1998). *Metatext in Professional Writing: A Contrastive Study of English, German and Swedish*. (Texts in European Writing Communities 3.) Uppsala: Uppsala University.

Biber, D., Johansson, S., Leech, G., Conrad, S., & Finegan, E. (1999). *The Longman Grammar of Spoken and Written English*. London: Longman.

Granger, S. (1993). The International Corpus of Learner English. In J. Aarts, P. de Haan, & N. Oostdijk (Eds.), *English Language Corpora: Design, Analysis and Exploitation*. Amsterdam: Rodopi.

Granger, S. (Ed.). (1998). *Learner English on Computer*. London & New York: Longman.

Jakobson, R. (1995). *On Language*. Ed. by L. R. Waugh & M. Monville-Burston. Cambridge: Harvard University Press.

Hutcheon, L. (1984). *Narcissistic Narrative: The Metafictional Paradox* (2nd ed.). New York & London: Methuen.

Hyland, K. (1998). Persuasion and context: The pragmatics of academic discourse. *Journal of Pragmatics, 30*, 437–455.

Markkanen, R., Steffensen, M. & Crismore, A. (1993). Quantitative contrastive study of metadiscourse: Problems in design and analysis of data. *Papers and Studies in Contrastive Linguistics, 28*, 137–152.

Mauranen, A. (1993). *Cultural Differences in Academic Rhetoric: A Textlinguistic Study*. Frankfurt am Main: Peter Lang.

Schiffrin, D. (1980). Metatalk: Organizational and evaluative brackets in discourse. *Sociological Inquiry: Language and Social Interaction, 50*, 199–236.

Vande Kopple, W. J. (1985). Some exploratory discourse on metadiscourse. *College Composition and Communication, 26*, 82–93.

Vande Kopple, W. J. (1988). Metadiscourse and the recall of modality markers. *Visible Language, XXII*, 233–272.

Language as a string of beads
Discourse and the M-word

© John Sinclair
The Tuscan Word Centre, Italy

Human language can refer to itself, and users frequently make it do so, thus giving rise to the term *metalanguage* and other similar constructs with *meta-*. The term *metadiscourse*, however, is misleading because discourse is perfectly linear and the encapsulation of words and phrases about the language, or the cohesive connections from one part of a text to another, are all performed on a single level. Since *metadiscourse* is much used in the literature this would be a rather pedantic observation except that recent research suggests that the hierarchy which it implies is distracting attention from the mechanism whereby a linear text is made available to be interpreted by a hierarchical grammar.

Misleading terminology can interfere with your thinking; this is a reasonable deduction from the Sapir/Whorf hypothesis (Sapir 1958 (1929); Whorf 1956 (1940)), and although few scholars now believe in that hypothesis in its entirety, most will nevertheless probably agree with this deduction. My short contribution to this book is the record of an intervention that I made at the Pontignano seminar where I found myself once again objecting to the use of the term 'metadiscourse' for passages in a discourse where the topic is the discourse itself.[1] After giving a standard exposition of my concern about such usage, I became aware that there was another reason for objecting to the widespread use of this term, more fundamental than merely bickering about terminology. Perhaps its use has masked some important patterns in the sequential structure of written and spoken discourse, and if only for safety's sake I would urge that we reconsider the appropriateness of this term.

One of the characteristic features of human language is the ability of users to talk about language in the same way as they can talk about anything else. Language – talk and writing – is part of the world around us, and therefore frequently is itself talked about in conversation or in documents. We talk about language as we talk about politics or fruit or the weather, using the same structures and the appropriate vocabulary.

This feature has been remarked on by several linguists over the years. Hockett (1960) called it *reflexivity* and included it in his list of the defining characteristics of human language, to distinguish our unique communication potential as a species from competing claims from supporters of the likes of honey bees, ticks and chimpanzees. Lyons (1977) developed the theme. A dog cannot bark about barking, but a person can sing about singing (Gene Kelly, for example, in the famous musical *Singin' in the rain*[2]).

In this paper I will use the neutral term *self-reference* when discussing this concept.

The vocabulary that we use for discussing language has been called the 'metalanguage' – the familiar terminology of *noun, verb* etc. and all the arcane terms of modern linguistics. Metalanguage contrasts with *object language*, which is the language that is being talked about. The prefix *meta* indicates 'more abstract' or 'on a higher level', though in Greek it mainly has to do with change and sharing and following. Aristotle, according to Onions (1966) called his *Metaphysics* by that name because it was seen as following in order the treatises on the natural sciences; "although Gr. *metá* does not normally imply "beyond" or "transcending" it came to be so interpreted in this word" (op.cit.: 572–573).

As we shall see, there is an irony in the etymology of *meta*, the enhancement of its meaning from indicating linear sequence to suggesting a more abstract level of organisation, that points up my main argument.

So an apple is something in the world, and the word *apple* is also something in the world. The word *word*, on the other hand, is in the metalanguage, which exists on a higher or more abstract level than the physical world. Of course, it is also a word, and neither the word *word* nor the word *apple* will ever be tasty to bite into. A purist could indeed say that my citation of "the word *apple*" placed *apple* temporarily in the metalanguage since I was writing about it, citing it rather than just using it. But in citing it I am using it ...... there is no way out of this labyrinth, once entered.

We do not need to enter, because this use of *meta-* is not one that bothers me much. It sounds a bit pompous and important, as if those of us who can handle meta-this and meta-that are particularly clever. There is no need to call this area of usage anything except the technical language of linguistics. It is pretty obvious when people are talking about language and when they are talking about apples, so we hardly need the artillery of philosophy to guide us.

At some point, I presume, the word *metadiscourse* was coined by analogy, though I have not tracked down its origin. This is a dangerous term, and I believe that it distorts the model of language that linguists have.

First let me make clear the distinction between *metalanguage* and *metadiscourse*. Here is a quotation from a recorded conversation:

> Do you have to get onto a boat or are there bridges across?

Imagine two situations in which this sentence occurs. One is in a language class, where the teacher is explaining different types of question and uses this as an example of an alternative question. The teacher might play it on a tape machine and then say:

> That is an interesting question.

The question has been cited and the teacher will no doubt proceed to explain why it is interesting. No-one makes the slightest effort to answer the question because they all appreciate that it is not addressed to them.

The other situation is if the conversation from which the recording was taken continues with another speaker saying:

> That is an interesting question.

In this case there is a discernible effect on the discourse, because in spoken discourse an utterance can *challenge* the *illocutionary force* of its predecessor (Sinclair & Brazil 1982) by talking about it, as this response does, instead of attending to its prospections. The asking of a question is a pre-emptive act that preclassifies all possible next utterances – essentially according to how close they are to an adequate answer to the question.

For an ongoing discourse to refer to itself is a normal, natural and frequent tactic in speech and writing. In writing, one use of it is in *encapsulation*, which is probably the commonest way in which coherence is maintained (Sinclair 1993). In conversation it is quite normal for every third or so utterance to be an act of self-reference (Sinclair & Brazil, op.cit.). Organising acts in discourse, explaining the structure of a complex document or intimating a new topic in a conversation are acts of self-reference. In terms of what they are about, they are about the discourse itself, but in terms of what they are as linguistic events, they are successive moves in a linear string of moves.

Linearity is a major issue here. While linguists, if they give the matter any thought, subscribe to the notion that both the written and the spoken forms of the language are essentially linear, they do not dwell on this fundamental property of language; since the main work of the said linguists is to erect elaborate non-linear structures above and below and around the texts to demonstrate how they make meaning, it is not surprising that this property is left largely in the background. A grammar is an attempt to explain how a set of intricate networks is somehow squashed into a structure with the properties of a row of beads. The interest lies not in the row of beads but in the magic landscapes and faery palaces of the grammar.

In terms of linearity, of actual physical succession, no utterance is meta-anything. They are just all strung along in a row. This is the level, just above the dreaded 'performance', where there is no room for metadiscourse. Some moves *increment* the conversation (Brazil 1995), others help to manage the interaction, and are sensitive to the way in which an increment may be received and understood; others are in between, and there are many isolated acts of cohesion, of course, only some of which would be considered self-referential outside the grammar of the clause. The idea that some of these transcend the others has no value at this level.

Until recently I was grudgingly willing to accept that at a higher level of analysis some hierarchical model that placed the self-references 'above' the increments became justified, though I have never felt any benefit from it. But ongoing research suggests quite the opposite – that the rough alternation of increments and self-references is best seen as strictly linear and that even discontinuity is too abstract for the first steps in analysis.

The ongoing research that has sharpened the issue is a kind of shallow parsing that begins by assigning provisional boundaries to the linear stream of text.[3] The assumption behind it is that a person with command of a language possesses a basic analytical skill which allows them to see a text as divided into small portions, each of which is a coherent segment that can be recognised as all or part of a structural unit of the language. While individual analysts may differ in detail, this is not important, because there is a lot of flexibility in the relationship between the text, the boundaries and the analysis.

This skill of boundary assignment seems to be relevant to both the spoken and written forms of the language, and it is particularly interesting when applied to transcripts of impromptu spoken recordings. As well as operating satisfactorily despite the information loss in transcripts, the analytical method can cope with degenerate signals, poor recordings and badly written or damaged documents. It is, in other words, robust.

This provisional boundary assignment can be studied under experimental conditions, although some artificiality has to be accepted in the procedures. At an early stage in the research it became obvious that speakers recognised a distinction between units that were *topical increments*, using Brazil's term, and those that were discourse-oriented, and would be called "metadiscourse" in current parlance. This is not a new observation, of course (Sinclair & Brazil, op.cit.), but I had not realised how central it was in the process of interpretation that I was trying to model. As participants in a conversation produce a stream of speech, perhaps fast and overlapping each other, each participant expressing a complex and unique point of view, they are all simultaneously sorting the segments into the two types differentiated above before proceeding to work out what each of them means.[4]

There is one more point to conclude my case, and I can only briefly refer to it here, and ask the reader to take a lot for granted. It will be dealt with at length in a forthcoming publication.[5] At its simplest the hypothesis is that the onset of a textual unit of meaning is often signalled, but the termination of such a unit is rarely if ever marked by any special words or phrases. Especially in speech, participants often recognise the ending of a unit only by the appearance of words and phrases which are incompatible with the structural prospections of the previous unit, and therefore must be part of a new one.

The expectation of a participant in a discourse is thus that their initial structural experience of the discourse is likely to be an alternation of topical increments and self-reference segments which have a role in discourse-management. This expectation is a vital part of the set towards the discourse, and the alternation is a most valuable guide to the termination of textual units.

The self-reference segments are easily recognisable; there is reason to believe that they constitute a definable set of items (with some internal variations). If so, in practical terms they provide a most valuable foil to the open-ended increments, which have inherent options of elaboration and continuation which, coupled with the lack of termination markers, could make discourse very unwieldy indeed. But the very frequent deployment of self-reference in conversation improves the coherence of the text not only in the function that each of the segments has, but in the identification of their occurrence in the linear stream of speech.

I hope that it is now clear that my reservations about using the term 'metadiscourse' are well-founded, and perhaps the term has obscured our access to the kind of structural points that are made here. Much of the descriptive distortion is a consequence of our lack of attention generally to the implications of linearity, and one of the changes in priority that I expect in the coming years is a greater respect for the actual sequence of events in texts.

Notes

1. The ensuing lively argument led to an unspoken taboo being placed on the utterance of this term, and everyone referred to "the *M*-word" for the remainder of the seminar.

2. The first four lines are: *I'm singin' in the rain/Just singin' in the rain/What a glorious feeling/I'm happy again.*

3. This is a piece of work I am doing with Prof. Anna Mauranen of Helsinki University, Finland. It is called Linear Unit Grammar (LUG).

4. As in any attempt to elaborate a procedure in human behaviour, I do not want to be taken literally when saying, for example, that one stage comes before another – even if a case can be made for the logical necessity of this. What actually happens is probably a much more partial, risk-littered, fly-by-the-seat-of-our-pants kind of affair, especially in the real time of conversation. The researcher, who cannot replicate the conditions of conversation, has to accept poor second best and apologise for smoothing over and tidying up the near-chaos of real-time interpretation.

5. Unfortunately this paper is intended for a festschrift, and so I cannot supply a bibliographical reference before publication.

References

Brazil, D. (1995). *A Grammar of Speech*. Oxford: Oxford University Press.

Hockett, C. (1960). Logical considerations in the study of animal communication. In W. Lanyon & W. Tavolga (Eds.), *Animal Sounds and Communication* (pp. 392–430). Washington, DC: American Institute of Biological Sciences.

Lyons, J. (1977). *Semantics*. Vols. 1 & 2. Cambridge: Cambridge University Press.

Onions, C. (1966). *The Oxford Dictionary of English Etymology*. Oxford: Clarendon Press.

Sapir, E. (1929). The status of linguistics as a science. In E. Sapir (1958), *Culture, Language and Personality* (Ed. D. G. Mandelbaum). Berkeley, CA: University of California Press.

Sinclair, J. (1993). Written discourse structure. In J. M. Sinclair, M. Hoey, & G. Fox (Eds.), *Techniques of Description: Spoken and Written Discourse* (pp. 6–31). London & New York: Routledge. Also in J. Sinclair (2004), 82–101.

Sinclair, J. (2004). *Trust the Text: Language, Corpus and Discourse*. London & New York: Routledge.

Sinclair, J. & Brazil, D. (1982). *Teacher Talk*. Oxford: Oxford University Press.

Whorf, B. (1940). Science and linguistics. *Technology Review, 42* (6), 229–231, 247–248. Also in B. L. Whorf (1956), *Language, Thought and Reality* (Ed. J. B. Carroll). Cambridge, MA: MIT Press.

Academic vocabulary in academic discourse

The phraseological behaviour of EVALUATION in Economics research articles

David Oakey
University of Birmingham

This paper describes an attempt to apply the results of recent vocabulary research to a particular problem experienced by non-native English speaking students of Economics at a university in Britain. These students were perceived to have difficulty reading research journal articles because of the large amount of unfamiliar lexis contained in the discourse. Several computer applications were used to examine the vocabulary in one journal article in relation to recent research into academic vocabulary, and to investigate the relationship between the meaning of individual words in the article and the meaning of the article as a whole. These findings led to an investigation in a larger corpus of Economics research articles of the frequent phraseologies of the various forms of EVALUATION, which resulted in a revision of the original diagnosis. The study concludes that the atomistic approach to meaning taken by vocabulary researchers obscures some lexico-grammatical aspects of academic discourse, and that students' difficulties in reading arose less often from encounters with unfamiliar words, but more often from unfamiliar combinations of familiar words. The pedagogical implications of the study are that phraseological information needs presenting alongside more traditional vocabulary items.

Academic vocabulary

For nearly a century, an important strand in English language teaching research has focused on vocabulary. During this time the word, a string of characters bounded by two spaces, has had prime status as the unit of meaning, research, and pedagogy. In the first half of the twentieth century this was primarily because the language system was seen to consist of "words entering into grammatical constructions" (Jeffery in West 1953:v). The aim of English language learning materials developers was to identify "the minimum number of words that could operate together in constructions capable of entering into the greatest variety of contexts" (ibid.). The *General Service List of English Words* (GSL) (West 1936, 1957) provided a list of the 2000 most useful (according to the prevailing definition of "useful") and frequent English words and their common inflections and derived forms.

In the second half of the twentieth century, the introduction of computers into language research aided the investigation of large amounts of language data in different ways. Computer software allowed the manipulation of great quantities of electronic textual data and the analysis – or presentation for human analysis – of strings of characters between two spaces. Electronic text corpora could be annotated in some way to reflect prevailing theoretical assumptions about grammar, and then computer analysis could provide more information about the behaviour of particular grammatical structures. The first tagged corpus, the BROWN corpus (Francis & Kučera 1964), was compiled in the 1960s and was hand-tagged a decade later with part-of-speech-information. The introduction of computers into vocabulary research reinforced the separation of vocabulary from the grammatical system. The unit of analysis remained the individual word, as this was the form most easily identified by computer software. In the field of lexicography a different approach was taken, as will be seen below.

The twin goals of vocabulary studies with respect to language learning have been related to assessment and diagnosis. Vocabulary is a convenient, measurable sign of how much of a language a learner knows, the rule of thumb being the more words known, the more language a learner can understand and produce. Secondly, identifying salient words in a particular language register assists in the preparation of learning materials for students who are expected to be able to work with the language in that register. In the 1970s various studies into the vocabulary used in academic contexts were carried out, and their results were brought together in the University Word List (Xue & Nation 1984). This contained 808 words which are frequent in academic texts but which are not on West's GSL.

More recent vocabulary research in English for Specific Purposes has also focused on the vocabulary frequently used in academic discourse (e.g. Thurston & Candlin 1998). This *academic vocabulary* is considered not specific enough in meaning to belong to the terminology of a specific discipline, but at the same time to be rather more formal than 'general' English.[1] The application of computer processing to a corpus of academic texts recently produced an important new vocabulary learning resource, the Academic Word List (AWL) (Coxhead 1998). This lists the most frequent academic vocabulary which occurs across academic disciplines in Humanities, Law, Science, and Commerce. It consists of 570 word "families" chosen principally on the basis of the coverage of academic texts which these words provide. The AWL has become a benchmark for designers of materials for teaching academic English (e.g. Campbell & Thompson 2003; Cobb 2002; Haywood 2003; Nelson 2003).

Two problems: Coverage and the word family

A key criterion for the usefulness of a word list to learners is *coverage*. The more texts a word list covers, the fewer unknown words will be encountered by a learner who knows the words on that word list. For example if a learner of English who has learned the 2000 words on the GSL also learns the members of the 570 word families from the AWL, the coverage of academic text increases from 78.1%, where roughly one word in five is unknown to the learner, to 86.6%, where merely one word in ten is unknown (Nation 2001: 17). Learners are intended to add layers of meaning to the meaning they originally associated with a word when they first learned it, according to the context in which they find the word in subsequent encounters with it. Nation (2001: 27) specifies the various features of use which must be part of a learner's knowledge of a word, see Table 1 below.

It seems, however, that the learner's improved recognition of individual words in the AWL, which is assisted by the coverage provided by the list, is implicitly equated with improved understanding of meaning. As noted above, words in the AWL "make the difference between 80% coverage (one unknown word in every five running words) and 90% coverage (one unknown word in every ten running words)" (Coxhead & Nation 2001: 252). But while the words on the two lists may match 90% of the *words* which occur in academic dis-

Table 1. What is involved in knowing a word in terms of use (Nation 2001: 27)

grammatical	R	In what patterns does the word occur?
functions	P	In what patterns must we use this word?
collocations	R	What words or types of words occur with this one?
constraints on use	R	Where, when, and how often would we expect to meet this word?
register, frequency....	P	Where, when, and how often can we use this word?

R = receptive, P = productive

course, it does not necessarily follow that learners who know the words on those lists will understand 90% of the *texts* they encounter in that register. The meaning of a text is more than the meanings of its component parts or meaningful units, and so, as Sinclair puts it, "its particular meaning is not adequately accounted for by any organised concatenation of the fixed meanings of each unit" (Sinclair 1998:5). Thus an atomistic approach to vocabulary will not in itself prepare learners to use these items in texts.

Although the unit of coverage is the single orthographic word, corpus linguistic research originating in lexicography has for several years suggested that the relationship between meaning and the single orthographic word is not simply one-to-one. The notion of the open choice and idiom principles (Sinclair 1991) views texts as "a large number of semi-preconstructed phrases that constitute single choices, even though they might appear to be analysable into segments" (ibid. 1991:110). Thus while a text can be broken up into its constituent words, lists such as the AWL may break up more meaningful word combinations.

In the field of computational linguistics, it has been pointed out how Zipf used his *k* constant to predict how often the most frequent word in any word frequency list should occur. He found that the most frequent word, i.e. *the*, should only occur 0.000025 times in any list, and to Zipf this was "a very absurd statement no matter how a word is defined" (Zipf 1965 [1935]:43 in Danielsson 2001:55). However Danielsson suggests that "these irregularities at the top end of the frequency list can be explained by the fact that single word units are inadequate as units of analysis in language" (Danielsson 2000:55). Finally, a recent study of the idiom and open choice principles in written and spoken texts appeared to support Sinclair's hypothesis. It found that "the production of a text involves frequent alternation between prefab and non-prefabricated strings" (Erman & Warren 2000:51), and that, in a text of around 100 words, on average only 45 single-word choices would be made.

The second problem with word lists is the grouping of individual words into families. This is related to the vexed lexicographical problem of headwords or lemmas, where difficult choices need to be made over whether derivations and inflections of root or stem forms are distinct enough in meaning to be given a separate entry in the dictionary. Words in the AWL are grouped into families because "lexical items that may be morphologically distinct from one another are, in fact, strongly enough related that they should be considered to represent a single lexical item" (Coxhead 2000:217). Coxhead defines *word family* as a stem plus all closely related affixed forms. The word *evaluation*, for

Table 2. Members of the evaluation word family[2] (Coxhead 1998:17)

evaluate
evaluated
evaluates
evaluating
evaluation
evaluations
evaluative
re-evaluate
re-evaluated
re-evaluates
re-evaluating
re-evaluation

example, is the most frequently occurring member of the word family in sublist 2 of the AWL (Coxhead 1998:17), as illustrated in Table 2.

It is claimed that once the base form of a word is learned, other related forms should pose few problems for learners: "comprehending regularly inflected or derived members of a family does not require much more effort by learners if they know the base word and if they have control over basic word building processes" (Coxhead 2000:218). For example, "the learning burden of *mends* if the learner already knows *mend* is negligible" (Nation 2001:8).

Since computers were introduced into lexicographical studies, however, the soundness of traditional word classes has been questioned by analyses of language data. It is debatable, for example, whether similar word forms should be grouped into lemmas merely because they look like each other and contain almost the same characters in the same order. Sinclair contends that "there is a good case for arguing that each distinct form is potentially a unique lexical unit, and that forms should only be conflated into lemmas when their *environments* show a certain amount and type of similarity" (1991:8, my italics). It is not unreasonable to suggest that, if some members of a word family display strong patterning and regularity of combination alongside their more open choice uses, these patterns might also be considered as multi-word members of the word family – their phraseological cousins, as it were. This paper thus investigates one word family from the AWL to see whether any of the phraseological environments of its members might merit their inclusion as separate items in the same word family.

Evaluations – a lexical item?

This study of *evaluation* in academic discourse arose from a perceived reading problem in my class of 50 postgraduate students of Economics at the University of Birmingham. These students are already expected to be able to use English for the academic purposes of reading textbooks and journal articles, and attending lectures, and are soon to be writing module assignments. They were asked to read a previously-unseen journal article about the economics of tipping (Lynn & McCall 2000). The first sentence of the abstract, the part of the research article most likely to be encountered first, caused immediate difficulty:

(1)   The relationship between tip size and evaluations of the service was assessed in a meta-analysis of seven published and six unpublished studies involving 2547 dining parties at 20 different restaurants.

Readability tests using a variety of measures, outlined in Table 3, confirmed that this was a difficult text, suitable for readers at postgraduate level requiring more than 12 years study.

Research on the difficulties of academic reading in disciplines such as Genetics, Biology, Political Science, and History has identified heavy noun phrase subjects such as "the relationship between tip size and evaluations of the service" to be problematic (Cohen et al. 1988:158). It seemed useful to check whether there were other problems to do with the individual words. The vocabulary in the Lynn and McCall abstract was easily checked against various word lists using Vocabulary Profiler software (Cobb 2005) as can be seen in Table 4 below.

The abstract certainly seems to be covered as predicted by the AWL. Only around 10% of words in the abstract were on neither the GSL or AWL, thus it does not contain many more infrequent words than expected. Use of the *WordSmith* Keywords tool (Scott 1999) gave an indication of the key words in the article, those which explicitly signalled or located its aboutness (Philips 1989; Scott 2000). The Keywords tool compared the frequency list from the

Table 3. Readability results summary value

Readibility Measure	Result
Gunning Fog Index	17.00 (post-graduate level)
Flesch Reading Ease	13.95% (100% is easiest)
Flesch-Kincaid Grade	12.00 (years of schooling required)

Table 4. Vocabulary profile of the abstract of Lynn and McCall (2000) using Cobb (2005)

	Frequency	Percentage
K1 Words (1 to 1000)	102	67.11%
K2 Words (1001 to 2000)	14	9.21%
AWL Words (academic)	21	13.82%
Off-List Words	15	9.87%

article with a word frequency list from a much larger collection of texts, in this case from the 90 million words from the written part of the British National Corpus. The most "key" word in Lynn and McCall (2000) was *evaluations*.

The interesting feature of *evaluations* in this article is that it is never, on its own, used as a single lexical item. A concordance of the 47 occurrences of the word shows the regularity in the left hand environment of *evaluations*. The lines in Table 5 are sorted alphabetically by the first three words to the left of the node, but much regularity can be seen up to and beyond six words. *Evaluations* is almost always part of a compound noun, such as *service evaluations*, very often in a binomial pair, as in *tip size and evaluations of the service* and usually as part of a postmodifying prepositional phrase, such as *the correlation between tip sizes and evaluations of the service*.

Analysis of *evaluations* using the Academic Word List and the Wordsmith Keywords tool shows, therefore, that it is a member of an important word family in academic English, and that it is important for understanding what the Lynn and McCall article is about. However, it is apparent that *evaluations* as a single orthographic word is rarely used in isolation, but is instead repeatedly found in longer patterns. If this word is rarely used on its own then its utility in a list on its own is doubtful. In general, items in a word list, although presented as members of the same word family, may have widely different phraseologies, and a learner who attempts to learn family members in isolation may find that such words have little in common other than their spelling. It may be worthwhile to consider adding the frequent phraseological tendencies of *evaluations* to the entry on the word list. It is of course necessary to learn more about the behaviour in this area of academic discourse of the word family to which *evaluations* belongs, EVALUATION. To this end, a collection of 1,360 research articles from 7 Economics journals was analysed (see Table 6), and the resulting frequent patterns are shown in the next section.

Table 5. Regular patterning of *evaluations* in Lynn and McCall (2000)

```
1  ecifically, customers' moods should affect evaluations of foo
2  n of the relationship between tip size and evaluations of the
3      The relationship between tip size and evaluations of the
4  positive relationship between tip size and evaluations of the
5  : 1) the correlation between tip sizes and evaluations of the
6  ationship between restaurant tip sizes and evaluations of the
7  s will be related to a variety of customer evaluations.
8  ood; 2) the correlation between customers' evaluations of the
9  erver performance, and/or solicit explicit evaluations of
10  trolling for patronage frequency and food evaluations. These
11  e relationship between tip sizes and food evaluations should
12  subject, an average of the different food evaluations was
13  s after statistically controlling for food evaluations; 4)
14  t after statistically controlling for food evaluations, r =
15  sed in tests of the effects involving food evaluations. For
16  and the correlation of tip size with food evaluations; 5)
17  ip between patronage frequency and service evaluations was
18  on between patronage frequency and service evaluations. Meta-
19   effect of patronage frequency and service evaluations on tip
20  on between patronage frequency and service evaluations; 7) th
21   relationship between tip size and service evaluations was st
22   relationship between tip size and service evaluations was we
23   relationship between tip size and service evaluations. Howev
24   relationship between tip size and service evaluations more t
25   correlation between tip sizes and service evaluations after
26  correlations between tip sizes and service evaluations that s
27  relationship between tip sizes and service evaluations remain
28  relationship between tip sizes and service evaluations and th
29  able to that between tip sizes and service evaluations.        T
30   correlation between tip sizes and service evaluations after
31  elationships between tip sizes and service evaluations (Lynn
32   correlation between tip sizes and service evaluations is tha
33  he correlation between tipping and service evaluations. These
34  r' patronage frequency on tips and service evaluations rather
35  ariable's effects on both tips and service evaluations. One l
36  r bill-adjusted residual tips) and service evaluations. Tests
37  and positive relationship between service evaluations and ti
38   in tests of the effects involving service evaluations. Simil
39  the effects of customers' moods on service evaluations and ti
40  < .0004, and marginally related to service evaluations, r = 0
41  ipping relationship is specific to service evaluations and th
42  n the correlation of tip size with service evaluations and th
43  mers' evaluations of the service and their evaluations of the
44   then tips should be positively related to evaluations of the
45  tip size. Mood effects are not specific to evaluations of ser
46  ice evaluations. Similarly, in cases where evaluations of mul
47  e obtained from this study. In cases where evaluations of mul
```

Table 6. A corpus of Economics research articles

Journal	Articles	Words (approx)
Journal of Economic Perspectives	170	1,015,722
Agricultural Economics	241	1,231,289
Economic Theory	379	2,321,754
Journal of Economic Theory	123	949,892
Journal of Socioeconomics	180	996,944
Journal of Economic Literature	72	1,079,756
Economic Journal	195	1,426,779
Total	1360	9,022,137

Frequent phraseological environments of *EVALUATION*

Evaluation

A common occurrence of *evaluation* in journal articles is in the initial position of the title of individual papers and of other works cited. The most common patterns are:

(2) Evaluation of X
     An evaluation of X
     An economic/econometric evaluation of X
     X: a _____ evaluation

While *evaluation* is used in paper titles with either a zero or a definite article, *the evaluation of* is used less often, and rarely in initial position. It is more often used after a preceding noun phrase:

(3) Uncertainty and the Evaluation of Public Investment Decisions.

or after a preposition:

(4) A Decision Theoretic Approach to the Evaluation of Training Programs

Such findings relate to the teaching of definite, indefinite and zero articles, which are notoriously difficult to teach on their own. The benefits of drawing attention to their use with certain nouns in different contexts like this has been well illustrated by Johns (1998).

Another common use of evaluation is as part of a binomial pair, such as *the X and evaluation of Y*:

(5)   Improved understanding of the audit process is likely to provide guidance in a number of policy areas, including the comparison and evaluation of alternative tax administration systems and the development of better audit selection methods.

Finally the majority of occurrences of *evaluation* occur in compounds such as *economic evaluation*, and *experimental evaluation*.

Evaluate

Two thirds of the occurrences of *evaluate* are in the infinitive with *to*. The commonest occurrence is with various analysis tools which are the object of *use*, in both active and passive voices:

(6)   use X
      use X analysis to evaluate Y
      use the X approach

(7)   This paper uses laboratory methods to evaluate whether price-fixing conspiracies break down in the presence of opportunities to offer secret discounts.

More lexical variation is apparent when *use* is in the passive voice:

(8)   model
      objectives
      functions
      ratio   is/are (then) used to evaluate Y
      assumption
      measures
      test
      approach

(9)   A research-induced technical change is modelled as a shift of the commodity supply function, and Marshallian producer and consumer surplus measures are used to evaluate the welfare consequences of the given supply shift.

The other frequent pattern associated with *evaluate* concerns the purposes of the journal article:

(10)   the goal
       the objective   of X is to evaluate Y
       the purpose
       our intention

(11)   The purpose of this paper is to evaluate options for reducing the external
       costs associated with the spread of serrated tussock.

The most frequent objects of *evaluate* relate to some kind of consequences:

(12)   benefits
       to evaluate the effect   of Y
                   impact(s)
                   risk(iness)

Evaluates

The most frequent subjects of *evaluates* were both human and metaphorical:

(13)   buyer
           player
           person
           decision maker   evaluates Y
       the individual
           study
           paper

When *evaluates* has a human agency it has a slightly different sense than with
a metaphorical use, as the human agency is largely hypothetical and relates to
how an economic agent is predicted to behave by a particular theory:

(14)   Examples of monotonic rules include those in which the agent evaluates
       each strategy according to the minimum payoff, the maximum payoff, or
       the average payoff that the strategy has received in the past.

Evaluated

This form shows more variation and fewer obvious repeated patterns:

(15)   BE evaluated at the rate of Y
       BE evaluated using Y

Evaluating

Again, this form was commonly used in initial position in paper titles:

(16) Evaluating the Accuracy of Sampling-Based Approaches to the Calculation of Posterior Moments in Bayesian Statistics

but also displayed a variety of phraseological environments:

(17) criteria/basis for evaluating Y
      criterion/consideration in evaluating Y

(18) When evaluating Y

(19) All agents are expected utility maximizers when evaluating lotteries over bundles.

and various *approaches to evaluating* things:

(20) The addition of appropriately designed and measured psychological constructs may conceptually improve the traditional neoclassical economic approach to evaluating choice behavior by allowing the consideration of well established determinants of behavior such as attitudes.

Evaluations

Despite its very regular environment in the Lynn and McCall article, *evaluations* displayed less regularity in the larger corpus. Just over half of the occurrences were followed by *of*:

(21) X evaluations of Y

A way to draw students' attention to the long noun groups causing the reading problem for my Economics students came from the practising the various ways in which lexical and grammatical word forms combine into larger meaningful units. Students were given the twenty most frequent words in the article and asked to combine as many of them as possible in order to produce a noun group with a more precise meaning. They could use each word only once, with the exception of *of* and *the*. This was a controlled way of building up longer phraseological environments which commonly occur with evaluations in Lynn and McCall (2000).

(22)   service evaluations
       evaluations of the service
       the relationship between tipping and service evaluations
       the relationship between tipping and evaluations of the service
       studies of the relationship between tip sizes and evaluations of the service

The last of these is similar to the original problematic sentence in the article abstract.

Conclusions

The unitary nature of the AWL reflects its origin in the field of vocabulary testing. Individual words are suitable testing units, but such tests can only assess a learner's memorisation and recognition of single orthographic words. It follows from this that coverage (by the words in a wordlist) of a collection of texts is not the same as understanding of words encountered by a learner in the texts. This study has illustrated the different forms of computer analysis which language teachers can use to examine the behaviour of vocabulary which students are likely to encounter. It suggests the way teachers can identify the more common phraseological tendencies of particular words which can then be presented alongside individual word family members. The single orthographic word will necessarily remain the primary unit of computer analysis for the time being. It does not follow, however, that it will always be the primary unit of meaning. It does not therefore need to be the primary unit of vocabulary teaching.

Notes

1. The distinction between *words* and *terms* (Curado Fuentes 2001; Pearson 1998) is not so clear-cut. Tognini Bonelli (2002) has shown how the semantic prosody of a word is influenced by its co-text and can give a "general" word a terminological meaning, e.g. the use of *peg* in *The Economist*.

2. There seems little reason why *re-evaluations* and *re-evaluative* should not also be included.

References

Biber, D., Johansson, S., Leech, G., Conrad, S., & Finegan, E. (Eds.). (1999). *Longman Grammar of Spoken and Written English*. London: Longman.

Campbell, C. & Thompson, P. (2003). Developing a 'Vocabulary for EAP' course. Paper Presented at *Vocabulary and EAP*, CELTE, University of Warwick, February 15th 2003.

Cobb, T. (2005). *Web Vocabprofile* (http://www.lextutor.ca/vp/, an adaptation of Heatley & Nation's (1994) *Range*).

Cohen, A., Glasman, H., Rosenbaum-Cohen, P. R., Ferrera, J., & Fine, J. (1988). Reading English for specialized purposes: Discourse analysis and the use of student informants. In P. L. Carrell, J. Devine, & D. E. Eskey (Eds.), *Interactive Approaches to Second Language Reading* (pp. 152–167). Cambridge: Cambridge University Press.

Cortes, V. (2002). Lexical bundles in freshman composition. In R. Randi Reppen, S. Fitzmaurice, & D. Biber (Eds.), *Using Corpora to Explore Linguistic Variation* (pp. 131–145). Amsterdam & Philadelphia: John Benjamins.

Coxhead, A. (1998). *An Academic Word List*. (English Language Institute Occasional Publication Number 18.) Wellington: Victoria University of Wellington.

Coxhead, A. (2000). A new academic word list. *TESOL Quarterly, 34* (2), 213–238.

Coxhead, A. & Nation, I. S. P. (2001). The specialised vocabulary of English for Academic Purposes. In J. Flowerdew & M. Peacock (Eds.), *Research Perspectives on English for Academic Purposes* (pp. 252–267). Cambridge: Cambridge University Press.

Curado Fuentes, A. (2001). Lexical behaviour in academic and technical corpora: Implications for ESP development. *Language Learning and Technology, 5* (3), 106–129. http://llt.msu.edu/vol5num3/curado/default.html

Danielsson, P. (2001). *The Automatic Identification of Meaningful Units in Language*. Unpublished Ph.D. thesis, University of Göteborg, Göteborg.

Erman, B. & Warren, B. (2000). The idiom principle and the open choice principle. *Text, 20* (1), 29–62.

Francis, W. & Kučera, H. (1964, revised 1971, revised and amplified 1979). *Manual of Information to Accompany A Standard Corpus of Present-Day Edited American English, for use with Digital Computers*. Providence, RI: Brown University, Department of Linguistics.

Haywood, S. (2003). Making effective use of the AWL. Paper presented at *Vocabulary and EAP*, CELTE, University of Warwick, 15 February 2003.

Heatley, A. & Nation, P. (1994). *Range*. Victoria University of Wellington, NZ. (computer program, available at http://www.vuw.ac.nz/lals/)

Johns, T. F. (1998). *The or no the?* (Kibbitzer No. 48.) In http://www.eisu.bham.ac.uk/Webmaterials/kibbitzers/kibbitzer48.htm

Lynn, M. & McCall, M. (2000). Gratitude and gratuity: A meta-analysis of research on the service-tipping relationship. *Journal of Socio-Economics, 29*, 203–214.

Nation, I. S. P (2001). *Learning Vocabulary in Another Language*. Cambridge: Cambridge University Press.

Nelson, M. (2003). *Mike Nelson's Business English Lexis Site*: http://users.utu.fi/micnel/business_english_lexis_site.htm

Pearson, J. (1998). *Terms in Context*. Amsterdam & Philadelphia: John Benjamins.

Phillips, M. (1989). *Lexical Structure of Text.* (Discourse Analysis Monographs 12.) Birmingham: ELR, University of Birmingham.

Scott, M. (1999). *WordSmith Tools 3.0.* Oxford: Oxford University Press. http://www.lexically.net/wordsmith/index.html

Scott, M. (2000). Focusing on the text and its key words. In L. Burnard & T. McEnery (Eds.), *Rethinking Language Pedagogy from a Corpus Perspective* (pp. 103–122). Frankfurt am Main: Peter Lang.

Sinclair, J. M. (1991). *Corpus, Concordance, Collocation.* Oxford: Oxford University Press.

Sinclair, J. M. (1998). The lexical item. In E. Weigand (Ed.), *Contrastive Lexical Semantics* (pp. 1–24). Amsterdam & Philadelphia: John Benjamins.

Thurston, J. & Candlin, C. N. (1998) Concordancing and the teaching of the vocabulary of academic English. *English For Specific Purposes, 17* (3), 267–280.

Tognini Bonelli, E. (2002). Between phraseology and terminology in the language of economics. In S. Nuccorini (Ed.), *Phrases and Phraseology – Data and Descriptions* (pp. 65–83). Bern: Peter Lang.

West, M. (1953). *A General Service List of English Words.* London: Longman, Green & Co.

Xue, G. Y. & Nation, I. S. P. (1984). A university word list. *Language Learning and Communication, 3,* 215–229.

Evaluation and its discontents

Wolfgang Teubert
University of Birmingham, UK

This paper rounds off this volume with a wide-ranging argument about the contrasts between language as a mental phenomenon and language as a social phenomenon. It is argued that corpus linguistics cannot investigate the relations between speakers and hearers, but only relations between texts; there is no privileged access to discourse-external reality. Thus, the role of corpus study should be to analyse intertextual features, attribution etc., and this, it is argued, will lead to penetrating results.

The remit of corpus linguistics

All human activities can be studied either as mental phenomena or as social phenomena. I can analyse a ballet from the point of view of the individual dancers and the decisions they constantly take. But I can also analyse it as social interaction, as a sequence of events and the reactions they cause, without probing into the dancers' minds as to what makes them do whatever they are doing.

Corpus linguistics looks at language as a social phenomenon. What it is interested in are not the mental processes connected with the generation and the interpretation of texts; rather it is the distribution of content among the members of a group. Corpus linguistics thus is empirical. It deals with linguistic phenomena that can be observed outside of the minds of speakers or hearers. Texts are the data that corpus linguistics draws upon. All the texts that have been spoken and listened to by the members of a given community represent the discourse of this community.

The existence of language presupposes humans, not humans as monadic entities, though, but humans as members of a community. Nobody learns a language in isolation. Usually children learn to speak a language through interaction with the people they relate to. These are often adults. Adults, however, tend to overestimate their importance. Equally relevant is the peer group. It is through the interaction with their peer group that children learn regional accents and dialects even if their parents always speak the standard variety of a language. Children growing up in isolation remain mute. If they grow up in a group of other children of similar age, yet without adults they relate to, they tend to invent their own language. Thus, our language faculty can be turned on only within a community. That tells us something about the role language plays. We can see it as a social lubricant. It enables us to live with each other, sometimes even in peace, and do things together. Discourse analysis and integrational linguistics focus on the social aspect of language. Corpus linguistics, however, deals only with the discourse, and not with what brings this discourse about and what effects it may have on some discourse-external reality. It is only interested in the effects the negotiations among the members of the discourse community have on the discourse itself.

Corpus linguists thus explore the relationship one text has with the other texts that constitute the discourse (or the discourse segment under investigation). If they, on the basis of their reading of a text, develop hypotheses about the social reality in which this set of texts is situated and about the relationships between the people involved, they are no better qualified than any other member of the discourse community. Corpus linguistics does not deal with social realities. Another limitation is important. Corpus linguistics does not deal with the non-verbal contexts in which utterances occur. It focuses always on written texts or transcripts of spoken texts; that is to say, stored texts. What effect these texts have on relations between people and on the social reality is not included in their remit.

Why has corpus linguistics, in principle, nothing to say about the social reality in which texts are situated? Why does it not talk about the intentions of the authors of texts and how these intentions are reflected in the their texts? For the corpus linguist, *auctor semper est incertus*. Little is known, for instance, about the authors of the gospels. We cannot be sure about their intentions, not even whether they are not just figments of Christian tradition. Their personae are constructs of the discourse. As Derrida pointed out, this is, in principle, true for all authors of written texts (Derrida 1988: 19ff.). Neither should we call the readers the readers of these texts participants in a social interaction. Written texts have an audience, namely the people that read these texts. This audience can be confined to one person (as is normally the case for private letters), or they have, in the case of published texts, a much wider audience, which is hard to pin down as we can never be quite sure who is actually reading them. Again, corpus linguists cannot study the effects a text has on its audience.

Only if the reaction to a text is another text can they analyse the relationship between the two. We can say therefore that corpus linguistics does not deal directly with relationships between members of the discourse community but with references made at an intertextual level.

Let me now consider evaluation studies. Many evaluation studies cover a great deal more ground than just the expression of social relations. They investigate speakers' opinions concerning the goodness and desirability of objects, people and events talked about in the discourse, and they probe speakers' attitudes concerning the relevance, certainty and expectedness of these discourse objects. When they analyse the linguistic expression of social relations, they appear to be less concerned with the overt features expressing social meaning in spoken language than with those more elusive ways of constructing and maintaining social relations between the speakers and their audiences. Could and should the scholar who chooses to work from a corpus try to make a contribution to the study of evaluation?

In the following sections, I will set out to explore the limits of corpus work in the study of evaluation, first making a comparison between transcribed discourse and the script of a play. I will go on to discuss how the expression of an opinion can be linked to lexical choice, and then consider a much more general issue: the relationship of a text (segment) to reality. When we are expressing an opinion or an assessment, are we then commenting on something that is a real-world event, or are we commenting on what has been said before? My claim will be that our knowledge of real-world events is bound to be a first-person experience. The only way to introduce it into the discourse is to turn it into testimony, into a text. As I have mentioned above, corpus linguistics does not allow us to analyse how what is being said affects the relations between the members of the discourse community. The question is, if it cannot analyse how what is being said is related to reality, then what is its role in the study of evaluation?

To answer this question we have to consider that each text is related to the other texts of the discourse. An investigation of these relationships can improve our reading of a text. By reacting to other texts, texts take a stance. The attitudes and beliefs they express are ensconced in the phrases that they import from previous texts. If we know the contexts in which these phrases are embedded in other texts, we will better understand the evaluative function of these phrases in the text we are analysing. This is the limit of corpus linguistics' contribution to the field of evaluation.

The discourse as a play: Arguments against cognitive interpretations

Corpus linguistics, as I have mentioned above, studies language as discourse. I understand the discourse as the totality of all texts that the members of a discourse community have contributed or are contributing to it. Corpus linguistics describes language as content by identifying the units of meaning into which the content of a text can be broken down. A unit of meaning can be a single word. More often it is a phrase, a more or less fixed expression. Units of meaning are textual elements embedded in their context. This (narrow) context accounts for the way a unit of meaning is being used within the discourse, or within the corpus as a subset of the discourse. Whenever the meaning of such a unit is in question, we will find, in the narrow context, paraphrases, explanations and even definitions which tell us what it means.

The narrow context is however often not sufficient to tell us what a text is about. What we say, we often say in reaction to what has been said before. It will be full of sometimes explicit but often also implicit, covert references to what we have heard. When we talk, we cannot but use the phrases, the expressions that have been used in other texts. This is why we also have to analyse the wider context of the key phrases of a text, i.e. the set of texts in which these phrases typically occur. I maintain that this wider context can tell us more about the beliefs and attitudes expressed in our text than the text itself.

Thompson and Hunston (2000) define evaluation as the function of language "to construct and maintain relations between speaker or writer and hearer or reader". Yet what do corpus linguists really know about what drives the members of a discourse community? What people feel, what they believe and how they are disposed is what is commonly called first-person experiences to which third persons (with the questionable exception of cognitive linguists) do not have access. Whenever we talk about other people's opinions, attitudes and beliefs, we do not refer to their first-person experiences but to their testimony. As a corpus linguist, I can base my investigation on nothing but texts: the texts I investigate, the previous texts to which these texts are reactions, and the subsequent texts which show reactions to them.

A corpus linguist, therefore, is very much like someone who reads a play. All we know about the characters of a play, their attitudes and their opinions is what we find in the lines the author assigns to his characters. It is nothing but the text of the play that constructs them. The text of a play, while embedded in the discourse at large, can be seen as a (fictitious) discourse in its own right. It is the play's lines (and not the author's introduction or stage directions) that create the social reality. In a play, there are no first-person experiences to which we can relate the lines a character has. Actors may have first-person experiences; the characters they play do not.

The script of a play is not the same thing as a transcript of a naturally-occurring discourse: a play has an author. Because we know (or think we know) that there is an author, we tend to believe that there is an intention behind what we are told and what we are not told. Obviously it is part of human nature to try to make sense of what is being communicated to us. However, from the evidence to which the corpus linguist has access, the discourse organises it-self, without the speakers' intentions. It would still be the same discourse if it had been produced by a gigantic but nonetheless unintentional computer programme.

Cognitive linguists see it as their task to find out how what is being said is related to the mental representations of the speaker, how it can be identified with their first-person intentionality. Corpus linguists content themselves with probing into the meaning of a text or a text segment. For them, the "relations between speaker or writer and hearer or reader" (Thompson & Hunston 2000) must be evidenced in the text, or, if that is inconclusive, in the wider context. All we know about the speakers (or hearers) of the texts we analyse as corpus linguists is what is said in the lines they have in the discourse (or in our corpus). We will never know more about Eliza Dolittle's feelings for Professor Higgins than what can be found in the lines he has in Shaw's *Pygmalion*.

I think that Thompson and Hunston would agree. When they say that the first evaluative function of language is to "express the speaker's or writer's opinion, and in doing so reflect the value system of that person and their community" (2000:6) , they are not endorsing a programme of psychological and/or mental enquiry into first-person experiences. For them, and for corpus linguists in general, the speakers' opinions are something that can only be in-vestigated in their contributions to the discourse. Likewise, the value systems of the communities in which they live can only be found in the discourses of these communities. Whether people really act according to these values can be of no concern to the corpus linguist.

Deontic meanings and the speakers' opinions: Arguments against a 'real world' interpretation

Opinion can be expressed by grammatical choice and by lexical choice. It can, in the words of Thompson and Hunston (2000:24), be classified along four parameters: good-bad (goodness), certainty, expectedness, and importance.

Invoking Halliday, Thompson and Hunston group the first two of these parameters (goodness and certainty) together as being primarily "real-world oriented", and the other two (expectedness and importance) as having an "added text-oriented function; they can serve to guide readers or listeners towards the intended coherence of what they are reading or hearing".

In this section, I will focus on the parameter of goodness. Is the choice of a word implying goodness the expression of an opinion about the real world? In what sense do words implying goodness really express opinions?

Thompson and Hunston (2000: 6ff.) give the example of the noun *workaholic* for expressing an opinion through lexical choice. The full sentence they quote is *My husband runs his own business and is a workaholic*. For Thompson and Hunston this noun expresses the speaker's opinion 'She disapproves of her husband's reluctance to take a holiday', and they maintain that this opinion is grounded on communal 'ideological assumptions' such as "that taking holidays is normal behaviour whereas continuous work is not". I thoroughly agree with this analysis. Most (but not all) people think workaholics are in need of treatment. This is shown by the paraphrases we find in Google (searching for "*a workaholic is*" [409 hits]), among them:

> What Is A Workaholic? – Peter Griffiths Daily Herald Column 1992
> **A workaholic is** a person who gradually becomes emotionally crippled, arid and addicted to control power in a compulsive drive to gain approval and success.
> www.lib.sk.ca/booksinfo/DailyHerald/DH1992/DH920919.html

> Even The Bishop Takes Time To Relax And Recreate
> ... workaholic. **A workaholic is** one who cannot take time off from his work and is always obsessed by having to do something.
> www.catholicstarherald.org/archive/dimarzio/2001/bp082401.html

The noun *workaholic* certainly has what Fritz Hermanns calls a deontic meaning. The term *deontic*, he says, "denotes that (part of the) meaning of words and fixed expressions which defines our attitude and our ways to deal with what is meant by a given word or expression" (Hermanns 1989: 74). His key example is the German word *Ungeziefer* 'weed, vermin', where part of its meaning is that it is something we should try to get rid of. While the adjective *deontic* refers, *sensu strictu*, only to ethical values, I will also use it to denote desirability or undesirability, i.e. emotional values. A *treat* is something to be desired, and unless the speaker marks the fact that they renounce this part of the meaning ("You have had enough treats already."), we have to assume that the speaker is in favour of whatever they call a *treat*. When I describe someone as *cute*, I am saying that I find her pretty or attractive. I would hardly be understood if I said "She is cute but neither pretty nor attractive." Unless it is spelt out explicitly in the context ("They may all find her cute, but she fails to attract me."), it will be assumed that a speaker who calls someone *cute* finds them attractive and pretty or handsome. The deontic meaning of *cute* is thus that the speaker says that they find a certain person or anthropomorphic object on whom they employ this epithet desirable. Similarly, if someone does not agree with the commonly held view that workaholics display dysfunctional behaviour, they have to argue their case. Otherwise they are understood to be subscribing to that view. What Hermanns calls deontic meaning is, in effect, a shared attitude, an ideological assumption held by the discourse community. Unless we explicitly disagree with such attitudes, we endorse them.

Should we agree with Halliday that expressions of shared attitudes have a 'real world' orientation? At first glance, this assertion appears to make sense. There are some people who are, unlike the rest, constantly busy. To call them *workaholics* is to add the slant that this behaviour is unhealthy and needs to be corrected. *Weeds* are just like any other plants but common sense has it that we must get rid of them from our gardens. *Cute* boys or girls don't really differ from those who are not; it is only our subjective bias that makes them look different.

It is not reality that tells us what can be cute and what cannot. There are *cute* teddy bears, there are *cute* lion cubs, there are *cute* boys and perhaps even *cute* little old grannies. There may also be *cute* bonsais, *cute* books, *cute* behaviour, and even a *cute* bark. It seems that objects, states and events that can be called *cute* share little other than the attraction they exert on the speaker. This seems to puzzle many language users. It is therefore not surprising that Google has 509 hits for the question "What is cute?". It shows that we are programmed to think that if there is a word it must refer to something rather tangible out there in the 'real world'. These are some of the Google results:

> You said I am cute. What is cute???
>
> Asians identify more easily with the characters in Japanese soap operas, and in cartoons, because these better fit Asian notions of what is cute than the Western versions of these genres.
>
> Is it good and happy to be cute?
>
> Americans have no idea what is cute.
>
> I'm pretty muscular from working out a lot and most girls say that they think I'm really cute (by the way, what is cute supposed to mean?)

What is cute? The technical definition encompasses revealing distinctions that tend to be elided in normal conversation, where cute is cute and everyone knows what this means. Cute by the book derives etymologically from 'acute,' and its establishing usage dates to circa 1731.

Such examples show that it is the discourse community that negotiates the meaning of words, particularly of words that refer to shared attitudes. My fellow speakers decide, at the end of the day, whether they let me get away with calling the Montblanc *a cute little mountain*. If they think it funny they may even start calling it *cute* themselves. It would not affect the mountain, though. Reality has nothing to do with it. This is, *mutatis mutandis*, also the case for *workaholic*. It is not just that reality cannot guide us as to what is an excessive amount of anything. It cannot even tell us what work is, as opposed to other kinds of occupying oneself. Again it is the discourse community that first establishes what we call *work*, and then negotiates the point at which a *worker* becomes a *workaholic*. Expressions for shared attitudes do not tell us anything about the 'real world' out there.

So far I have purposefully avoided the question of whether shared attitudes are opinions. Thompson and Hunston (2000) do not stipulate, I think, that a word like *workaholic* is generally the expression of an opinion. If a wife calls her husband a *workaholic*, we can interpret this statement as her opinion. But what exactly makes it an opinion? Is it an opinion if the poor husband is not 'objectively' working too hard? Is it the relationship with the 'real world' that makes a statement an opinion?

What we call an *opinion* is a statement which is controversial. In a discourse in which everyone refers to a husband as a *workaholic*, we would be inclined to take those statements as statements of a fact. If everyone agrees that this person is workaholic, then it becomes a shared attitude. For all normal purposes, the husband's quality of being a workaholic would then be as 'real' as the quality of this fruit as an orange.

But this changes once there is disagreement. If there is someone else who calls the husband *a diligent, hardworking man with a strong sense of obligation towards his family*, and perhaps also someone who says he is *a man working harder than most other men in his situation*, then we would call the wife's injunction an opinion. As it turns out, the question whether a statement is an opinion or the expression of a shared attitude can be settled without ever referring to the 'real world'. All it takes is to look at the other relevant texts of the discourse. And this is where corpus linguistics can help.

We express an opinion if we expressly do not share the attitude that other members of the discourse community have. If someone has their own opinion on something, we take this to mean that this person does not accept somebody else's or the mainstream view of the discourse object in question. Therefore we can only be sure that someone is expressing an opinion if we know what other members of the discourse community have said. There is a husband as a discourse object, and the members of the discourse community are saying different things about him. Opinions are about discourse objects, not about objects of the real world.

Do corpus linguists need reality?

The common view held by many linguists is however that it matters that there is a real world which is the object of our discourse. It matters because in order to assess statements (or, in the case of cognitive linguists, our individual mental representations), we have to compare them to reality. For these statements and representations can be true or false, or they can be biased or slanted, and in order to detect their truth or bias or spin, we must find out the true state of affairs.

However, as Nelson Goodman pointed out many years ago, it is the people, the members of the discourse community who create reality. There is not one world; there are many, many worlds, and what may be true in one world may not be true in another world. "[T]ruth", he says, "cannot be defined or tested by agreement with 'the world'; for not only do truths differ for different worlds but the nature of agreement between a version and a world apart from it is notoriously nebulous" (Goodman 1978: 17). Yet if there is no real-world object, can we have an opinion about it? Take work, for instance. We are told that there are people who work and others who do not, and we perceive people as working or not working. But is 'work' an ontological category, a category such as 'lemon' or 'orange', that would also be true if nobody ever talked about work? Is 'work' something that really occurs in the world out there?

Without language, there can be no lies. And lies are misrepresentations of reality. To find out what it takes for any statement to be true has been the programme of analytic philosophy for the last hundred years. But what do the relevant concepts in this discussion really mean? What do dictionaries tell us about *fact*, *truth* and *reality*? The New Oxford Dictionary of English (NODE), for instance, has this to say (here, and in subsequent quotes, I leave out technical details, examples and further senses):

fact: a thing that is indisputably the case; the truth about events as opposed to the interpretation

truth: the quality or state of being true; that which is true or in accordance with fact or with reality; a fact or belief that is accepted as true

reality: the world or state of things as they actually exist, as opposed to an idealistic or notional state of them

There is a surprising amount of circularity here. Fact is what is the truth, and truth is what is in accordance with fact or reality, and reality is the state of things as they actually exist. This all points to something which is outside of the reach of corpus linguists. For them, however, a unicorn is as real as a rhinoceros, as both are perfectly legitimate discourse objects. Is there a way to reconcile these two opposing views? Fortunately, the NODE, displaying its excellence, makes some allowance for us corpus linguists. A *fact* is also something "that is indisputably the case", referring to a possible dispute that may have taken place or could take place at any time in the discourse. *Truth* is also a belief that is accepted as true, by at least one member of the discourse community, regardless of 'what actually exists'.

Thus I am not contradicting the received wisdom of lexicographers when I claim that, in the context of this enquiry, a fact is what the large majority of members of the discourse community hold to be inalterably true so that any resumed negotiations among members of the discourse community would lead to the same results. It is in this sense only that we can say facts are 'open to verification'. If there is a dispute about weapons of mass destruction in Iraq, it means that the existence of them is not verified. This is therefore a discourse matter. Once the discourse shows no more disagreement concerning these weapons, their existence is as good as verified. Similarly, we accept as verified that there are no unicorns. But how do we know? Just because they have eluded us so far, it does not mean there are no unicorns. We accept there are no unicorns because their non-existence is undisputed.

The discourse contains nothing but testimony. It is each hearer's personal decision to accept one testimony as a fact, and to reject another testimony as untrustworthy. It is not the text (segment) that refers to the (or one specific) real world; it is the speaker/hearer who, through their first-person experiences, consciously (i.e. by a mental act, not by a mental process) links a text segment to what it is about.

Let me concede for the moment the existence of some discourse-external reality. Still, whenever we exchange our views about this world, we exchange only testimonies of what we think to be the case, not our first-person experiences themselves. Even if we watch together a video with a soundtrack, each of us can enter our first-person experiences, i.e. our sensory perceptions, into the discourse only as third-person textual representations. You tell me you see the police invading private premises, and I retort that I see the police being asked to enter. Is it really open to verification which version is true? Let us take Hunston's example (2000: 188):

> Energy World was recently invaded by police without warning at seven one morning. Exits were sealed, and all the computer files were commandeered; Mr Barnett's private quarters were ransacked.

Hunston points out that a more factual way to present this story would be to replace *invade* by *enter*, *seal* by *close*, *commandeer* by *take away*, and *ransack* by *search*. That might indeed be the way the story would be related in a police report. But why should we call it more factual? This does not mean, however, that *ransack* does not have a deontic meaning. We all share the view that *ransacking* is something that nice people do not do. But it also means that we agree to call a place ransacked only if it looks, after the act, rather disorganised, with many things scattered around and some things broken or demolished. If we say a place has been searched, we are commonly understood to mean that the place would not look as if it had been ransacked. Indeed we could say that *search*, in our case, would be a euphemism, an opinion, at least if there is someone else who calls the place *ransacked*.

Equally the statement that Mr Barnett's private quarters were ransacked becomes an opinion only if another member of the discourse community expresses doubt as to the factuality of the event or as to the legitimacy of the use of the word *ransacked*. "That is your opinion", someone might say. "As I see it, the police were only helping Mr Barnett to look for things, because he couldn't remember whether he had them."

As soon as first-person experiences are introduced into the discourse, they become hearsay, or testimony, for whoever hears them. But the only way we can perceive reality is as first-person experiences. It is only the mind of the speaker and the hearer that is able to relate hearsay or testimony to reality. The mind, however, is outside the remit of corpus linguists. Their object is the discourse.

In this perspective, what is commonly called a fact needs to be redefined. A fact is what people hold to be true and what is not disputed by other members of the discourse community. As Friedrich Nietzsche once said, "There are no facts; there are only interpretations". Whenever a member of the discourse community disputes a statement that was thought to be factual, it becomes the expression of an opinion or an assessment. The linguist is not better qualified than anyone else to decide whether a discourse object is 'true' or not. It is up to the members of the discourse community to negotiate the factuality of a statement. Corpus linguists are entirely at their mercy.

Intertextual references

There are some important differences between speech and writing. In the case of a conversation we normally know who the participants are. Normally every one of them can react to what has been said before. It was only with the arrival of writing that people began asking what a text meant. In a conversation, we normally do not ask the previous speaker what their text meant, but what they meant. All speakers of a conversation are there for direct questioning. The content of oral utterances includes the verbal and the non-verbal setting in which it occurs.

However, in most forms of written language, it is no use trying to identify the 'participants'. Many written texts are not addressed to a fixed set of readers. Being published, they become public in a way an informal conversation normally is not. Published texts are addressed to whoever takes an interest in reading them. Whoever might be the author(s) of a (frequently unsigned) newspaper editorial does not consider their readers the participants of a joint interaction. The most they can expect as a reaction are 'letters to the editor', purportedly written by their readers. This is, at the most, interaction by proxy – with texts, not people, as participants.

Written texts establish a relationship with previous texts by referring to them in various ways: by quoting them directly or implicitly, by alluding to them, or by asserting or rejecting the claims made in them. Yet, unlike in a conversation, subsequent speakers in an exchange of written texts do not have to know each other personally. A new text can quote a text whose author is dead or whose author is otherwise unbeknownst to the professed author of the new text. I do not know if this would also be Hunston's position. Her focus is different. She calls the references to previous texts attribution; and for her this phenomenon plays a key role in evaluation. Drawing on Sinclair (1981), she discusses attribution in contrast with averral: "If a piece of language is averred, the writer him or herself speaks." But "[i]f a piece of language – spoken, written or thought – is attributed, it is presented as deriving from someone other than the author." The difference for her is that "a writer assumes responsibility for what is averred, but delegates responsibility for what is attributed to the attributee" (Hunston 2000: 178). What Hunston is interested in is the status of what we are talking about. Status, for her, is largely concerned with certainty: "[f]or example, a 'fact' is more certain than an 'assessment' [i.e. an opinion], and an averred assessment is treated by the text as more certain than an attributed assessment" (Hunston 2000: 202).

What we may ask ourselves is whether we really use the instrument of quotation or attribution primarily to distance ourselves from what is being said. Although the delegation of responsibility for what is being said ("It has been suggested that there are no unicorns, but why should we believe it?") to someone else may express distance, there can be many other reasons why a text refers to another, previous text. One could think of at least three important parameters that play a role in a speaker's decision to quote a previous text. One is *agreement*. We often quote a text we agree with, yet sometimes we also quote a text we disagree with. Then there is the *importance of the quoted source*. If we quote a recognised authority, it will lend credibility to our text. While we normally tend to quote important people, dead or alive, a Prime Minister may sometimes find it appropriate to quote their driver. The third and most important parameter perhaps is *benefit*. If our adversaries were to benefit from being quoted by us, why should we mention them? The following listing reasons why we may decide to quote is far from exhaustive:

1. Referring to someone's 'personal communication' shows how close one is to important people.
2. If you quote them, they might quote you.
3. Quoting authorities supports one's own claims.
4. Quoting the Bible can obviate contradiction.
5. Quoting people further up the hierarchy can improve one's career outlook.
6. Quoting members of the suspected readership can induce them to engage in an interaction with the speaker.

There may also be good reasons why we should avoid quoting people we disagree with:

1. Quoting adversaries will improve their standing in the Science Citation Index.
2. Quoting alternative opinions will render one's own stance as relative.

On the other hand, there may also be reasons why it can make sense to quote one's adversaries:

1. Quoting adversaries can show the weakness of their argumentation.
2. Quoting common enemies can win points with one's readership.

3. Quoting adversaries can show that one is not partisan but views things from a superior vantage point.

Indeed, referring to other people's texts is the only way to establish, maintain or modify our relations with other members of the discourse community. Compared to bonding in a casual conversation, this amounts to very little. But it is something on which corpus linguists can work.

I would like to illustrate this with an example taken from the letters section of the *London Review of Books* (LRB). Here we find nice examples of texts that are simultaneously addressed to different audiences. They are normally read by the person to whose article they refer. They are also read by a large portion of the usual readership of the LRB. And they are written to shine a bright light on the letter-writer in the circle of his or her friends and colleagues. They present the signatory as knowing something more or knowing it better than the author to whom they ostentatiously refer. So while these letters habitually contain some kind of an attack on the quoted article, they often also quote other sources in order to substantiate their attack. Let us take this example (LRB 3 April 2003):

> Perry Anderson attacks the Nuclear Non-Proliferation Treaty because it restricts nuclear weapons to an elite club (LRB 6 March). This makes about as much sense as the common American notion that because criminals carry guns, the rest of us should be allowed to have them too. In defence of his claim, Anderson cites Kenneth Waltz' 'The Spread of Nuclear Weapons: More May Be Better', claiming it has 'never been refuted'. In fact, the most recent version of Waltz' essay appears in *The Spread of Nuclear Weapons: A Debate*, where the Stanford political scientist Scott Sagan subjects it to a powerful critique. Sagan shows that during the Cold War we got lucky . . . and asks whether impoverished, unstable Third World states will handle nuclear safety even as well as the US and USSR.

Leaving aside the *auctor semper incertus* axiom for the moment, we find that the writer of the letter, Matthew Rendall, refers to a text by Kenneth Waltz which has been cited by Perry Anderson's text (to which this letter ostensibly refers) in order to support his key argument. Rendell tries to undermine the force of Waltz's (and, thus, indirectly, of Anderson's) claim by invoking Scott Sagan as someone who, as the letter has it, invalidates this argument. This attribution serves to present the letter writer's assessment as more 'factual' than the Anderson/Waltz claim: what is *shown* is how things are 'in reality'. What Anderson really said was: "The nuclear oligopoly of the five victor powers of

1945 is equally indefensible. Kenneth Waltz ... long ago published a calm and detailed essay, which has never been refuted, 'The Spread ...'". The book to which Rendall refers is not so *recent* as we may think; it was first published in 1995, and its two authors are Kenneth Waltz (called by Anderson the "doyen of international relations theory, an impeccably respectable source") and Scott Sagan. So if the very senior Kenneth Waltz agrees to co-author a book with Scott Sagan, Sagan may criticise him here and there, but will not thoroughly refute him.

An indication of the social relevance of this letter is that the Public Affairs Office of the University of Nottingham refers to it in their Press Releases: "*London Review of Books* 3, 4: Dr. Matthew Rendall of Politics writes a letter on war and intervention."

There are other interesting aspects. We find Anderson's LRB article on at least eight webpages, one with the date of 27 February 2003 (more than a month before its publication in the LRB), and also translated into German, Turkish and Spanish. The early dates, as far as they are available, suggest that Perry Anderson probably submitted the article to the various webpages himself.

All I can surmise about the relationships between Matthew Rendall, Perry Anderson, Kenneth Waltz and Scott Sagan is what I have gleaned from Google. Google also tells us something about the relationship between frequency of occurrence and importance. Kenneth Waltz (the 'doyen' from Berkeley) has 3,300 hits in Google, while the more media-minded Perry Anderson (UCLA) scores 7,880 hits (we may discount one or two thousand because there seem to be some less prominent namesakes). The more junior Scott Sagan from Stanford scores only 890 hits, while Nottingham lecturer Matthew Rendall has to be content with 82 hits. Rendall may have come across Scott Sagan in the American academic journal *Security Studies*, to which both have contributed, on different topics. Rendall's research focus is Russia in the early 19th century. His degrees are from Yale and Columbia, and the grants he has received are from Columbia University and from the Harriman Institute. Perhaps one of the reasons for this letter is to make Perry Anderson and Scott Sagan aware of Matthew Rendall. All these Google findings and any deliberations based on them are nonetheless strictly speaking outside of the remit of corpus linguistics. Corpus linguistics deals with texts, not with authors. If one text quotes another text this establishes first of all a relationship with the two texts. It does not necessarily engage the authors of the two texts in a relationship. The quote by itself cannot be seen as social meaning.

Without any textual evidence of reactions, corpus linguists cannot know if the readership of a text was impressed. What might go on in the hearers' heads can be of no concern to them. All they can observe is that a text is sending out certain signals to those who read it. But does that already constitute the creation of a relationship? A character in a play, e.g. Antony in *Julius Caesar*, might be shown as addressing a large audience. As long as the play does not provide us with any textual feedback we cannot form any assumptions about the kind and quality of such a relationship.

In the end, corpus linguistics has nothing to say about the social reality in which written texts are situated, apart from what can be gleaned from other texts. But it is uniquely qualified to analyse the relevance of what is said in one text in the context of other texts. A great deal of what is being said in any given text has been said before. We must bear in mind, though, that by no means do all texts leave traces in subsequent texts. The relevance of a text, or a text segment, is largely independent of the size of the audience. A casual remark in a letter to a friend might be quoted by that friend in another text that catches the attention of many more readers, and sooner or later it might end up in *Bartletts Familiar Quotations*, and we will find traces of it in countless other texts, while fortunately most of what is printed in millions of copies in the *Sun* is forgotten the next day. Identifying traces in texts should become the core business of corpus linguists, for it will show how a given text is positioned in relationship to all the previous texts that are part of the discourse. The relevance of a text in relationship to the discourse as a whole can only be analysed in terms of their intertextual features.

Searching for ideological fingerprints

So far, corpus linguistics does not have the means to search for the origins of phrases or text chunks in more than a random way. There is still no monitor corpus to tell us to which texts a new text refers, which it quotes, whether confirming or rejecting what has been said there. In the absence of such a monitor corpus, Google can be quite useful. The discourse parameter of relevance can tell us much more than when exactly a phrase occurred for the first time. It tells us also about the ideology a given text subscribes to. Let us take the British Eurosceptic movement. A highly influential and therefore relevant text has been Margaret Thatcher's speech given in Bruges in 1988. Among the key phrases we find "a European superstate exercising a new dominance from Brussels", "some sort of identikit European personality", "decisions taken by an appointed bureaucracy", and "collectivism and corporatism at the European level". All these phrases may have been used before. But now they are habitually attributed to the Bruges speech. All of them are still being repeated in endless permutations. Today, to take just one example, Google lists 2,000 occurrences of *identikit + europe*, all of them, of course, critical of European integration. Traces like these let us make assumptions about the attitudes and beliefs a text subscribes to. They do not tell us whether the speaker actually has these attitudes and beliefs; only that the speaker represents himself as someone having them. Identifying such traces places the text in a relationship with other texts. Google lists 52,000 hits for *abortion + "right to choose"* and 11,400 hits for *abortion + "unborn babies"*. The mutually incompatible collocations *right to choose* and *unborn babies* tell us about the ideology a text subscribes to. (How these positions differ can be gleaned from the 1,700 webpages in which *"right to choose"* and *"unborn babies"* co-occur.) It is neither possible nor necessary to find out in which text these phrases were first used. They have now become the fingerprints of certain beliefs and attitudes. Whenever we find them in a text we can read them as indicators of a given underlying ideology.

Coming back to Matthew Rendall's letter, I will look at some phrases that signal how it wants to be read. Perry Anderson's "nuclear oligopoly" is represented in the letter as "the elite club". Google gives us 765 hits for *nuclear + elite club*. The collocation *elite club* is more charged with emotion than *oligopoly*. Membership of an elite is often equated with arrogance. This is exemplified by the following citation, taken from an article by David Krieger titled "Politics rooted in arrogance are certain to fail":

> It is a policy of nuclear apartheid in which select states are bestowed (or bestow upon themselves) nuclear privilege while others are attacked for seeking to enter the elite club of nuclear powers. (www.wagingpeace.org)

Oligopoly is much more like a technical term. Most of the paraphrases we find in Google for *oligopoly* are similar to this one: "An oligopoly is a market form in which a market is dominated by a small number of sellers." Rendall's letter, which is in defence of the nuclear oligopoly, thus makes Anderson's text sound more emotional than it is, and even attempts to link it to the ideology of communist diehards: "Can it be allowed that a couple of countries which have set up an elite club should order all the rest about?" asks the Blacktown Branch of the Communist Party of Australia (www.agitprop.org.au). Rendall's letter also suggests that to call the nuclear oligopoly *indefensible* is comparable to subscribing to the often quoted quip ascribed to the American actor James Earl Jones "Because criminals carry guns, we decent law-abiding citizens should also have guns.", repeated on 72 webpages, most of them close to the much criticised right-wing American gun-lobby. The real danger, as Rendall's letter sees it, comes from Third World states. Google lists 54 hits for *impoverished* + *unstable* + *"third world states"*. For the variant in which *countries* replaces *states* there are even more: 658 hits. If we add the item *dangers* to the query, we still have, for this variant, 132 hits. Google is not a monitor corpus; it does not tell us in which text the idea that Third World countries are dangerous because they are impoverished and unstable originated. Google can show us, though, which texts bear the same ideological fingerprint. On the webpage of America's Defense Monitor, a Professor Helms informs us that "[t]he international arms trade ... mak[es] it very, very easy for politicians or groups in these often unstable Third World countries to get access to the most modern weapons" (www.cdi.org). In the webpage of the Virginia Veterans of Foreign Wars, we are told that "despite the growing threat of unstable Third World countries armed with nuclear, chemical or biological warheads for ballistic missiles" the current U.S. defence programme is not giving missile defence enough weight (www.vfw.virginia.com). Another phrase is the collocation *nuclear safety* in the context of the *US*. Google lists ca. 3,000 hits for the query *"united states"* + *promotes* + *"nuclear safety"*, and while there are numerous dissident webpages, the orthodox perspective is expressed in quotes like this: "The [National Nuclear Security Administration] promotes international nuclear safety and supports programs to ensure the security of nuclear weapons materials in Russia and other countries" (www.nnsa.doe.gov). Rendall's letter thus presents itself as the voice of reason as opposed to Anderson's text rife with extremist and dangerous emotions.

Enlarging the context: New corpora for intertextuality

In this article I have argued that corpus linguistics cannot investigate the relations between speakers and hearers, but only relations between texts. I have further argued that whatever corpus linguistics may have to contribute to the issue of the expression of shared attitudes or opinions, it has no privileged access to discourse-external reality. What corpus linguistics can be expected to account for is the relationship a text has to the other texts constituting the discourse. It is the analysis of intertextual features, of what Hunston, citing John Sinclair, calls *attribution* for which corpus linguistics is best qualified (Hunston 2000: 178 et passim).

A thorough analysis of these features will reveal the attitudes, beliefs and opinions as expressed in a text. In cases where the discourse community as a whole, or relevant members of it, hold different views, opinion can be seen as someone's personal view of or concerning a discourse object. Opinions thus contest the testimony given by others; they do not refer to real-world events. As long as everyone agrees that the police ransacked Mr Barnett's private quarters, the discourse community will accept the act of *ransacking* as a fact. Once the diverging view that the police were only *searching* his quarters is entered into the discourse, both views will be discussed as opinions. This is why it is necessary to analyse all the other relevant texts of the discourse if we want to identify the beliefs, attitudes and opinions of a given text.

The agenda of evaluation thus forces us to reconsider the issue of the corpus. Complementary to the traditional corpus as a random selection of texts representing a certain sub-discourse, we would also need corpora of texts that relate to each other in a pre-defined way. Only within these corpora can we identify the intertextual references that reveal the ideology of a text. Just as we will not learn about the meaning of lexical items as long as we look at single words in isolation, we will not find out about the relations between texts as long as we look at single texts in isolation. Texts repeat and refer to what has been said before; and what is new will only emerge if we are able to distinguish it from the traces that connect it with previous texts.

These new corpora might be quite small, but they will have an explicit diachronic dimension. They start with a text chosen by the researcher and then feature other texts which contain reactions to this first text, and then texts reacting to these texts, thus establishing a chronological order between all the texts of such a special corpus. We have to remember, though, that such a corpus is embedded in the discourse as a whole, and that there are always references to and from other texts which are not a part of such a special corpus. Therefore we have to look also at the wider context defined by the intertextual features, and finally at the discourse as a whole.

The small special corpora that we need for investigating evaluation are monitor corpora *in nuce*. The larger we make them the more complex is the evolving picture of the relations that obtain between the texts of the discourse. This new generation of corpora will let us analyse not only the stance expressed in a given text; it will also show how the expression of ideas, attitudes and beliefs of individuals, social groups and the discourse community as a whole undergo continuous change over time. Taking corpus linguistics to these new shores will make corpus linguistics a powerful ally for critical discourse analysis, and indeed all kinds of discourse-oriented social studies.

Acknowledgments

I would like to thank Geoff Barnbrook and Michaela Mahlberg for their valuable comments, and, in particular, Elena Tognini Bonelli for the many improvements which this article owes to her.

References

Derrida, J. (1988). *Limited, Inc.* Evanston: Northwestern University Press.
Goodman, N. (1978). *Ways of Worldmaking.* Indianapolis: Hackett.
Hermanns, F. (1989). Deontische Tautologien: Ein linguistischer Beitrag zur Interpretation des Godesberger Programms (1959) der Sozialdemokratischen Partei Deutschlands. In J. Klein (Ed.), *Politische Semantik.* Opladen: Westdeutscher Verlag.
Hunston, S. (2000). Evaluation and the planes of discourse: Status and values in persuasive texts. In Hunston & Thompson (Eds.), 176–207.
Hunston, S. & Thompson, G. (Eds.). *Evaluation in Text: Authorial Stance and the Construction of Discourse.* Oxford: Oxford University Press.
London Review of Books.
The New Oxford Dictionary of English (NODE) (1998). Oxford: Oxford University Press.
Sinclair, J. M. (1981). Planes of discourse. In S. N. A. Ritzvi (Ed.), *The Two-Fold Voice: Essays in Honour of Ramesh Mohan* (pp. 70–89). Salzburg: University of Salzburg.
Teubert, W. (1996). The concept of work in Europe. In A. Musolff, C. Schäffner, & M. Townson (Eds.), *Conceiving of Europe: Diversity in Unity* (pp. 129–146). Aldersot: Dartmouth.
Thompson, G. (1996). *Introducing Functional Grammar.* London: Edward Arnold.
Thompson, G. & Hunston, S. (2000). Evaluation: An introduction. In Hunston & Thompson (Eds.), 1–27.

Notes on contributors

Annelie Ädel earned her Ph.D. in English Linguistics from Göteborg University, Sweden, in 2003. Her doctoral dissertation dealt with the reflexive function of language and its realisations in written text. Her research interests include text and corpus linguistics, discourse analysis, translation studies, contrastive linguistics and EFL. She has presented her work at conferences in Europe and the US, and has held a position for two years as a visiting scholar at Boston University.

Karin Aijmer is Professor of English at Göteborg University. Among her publications are *Conversational Routines in English: Convention and Creativity* (1996) and *English Discourse Particles: Evidence from a Corpus* (2002). She is the co-editor of *English Corpus Linguistics. Studies in Honour of Jan Svartvik* (1991). Her research interests include text and discourse, spoken English, corpus linguistics, cross-cultural linguistics, and learner English.

Julia Bamford is Associate Professor in the Faculty of Economics at the University of Rome 'La Sapienza' where she is also Head of the Language Centre. Her research interests and publications have been in the field of conversation analysis, repetition and reformulation and language testing. More recently she has looked at academic discourse, both written and spoken, with a special emphasis on academic lectures, of which she has compiled a small, specialised corpus. The latter has been examined from a pragmatic and discursive point of view with emphasis on evaluation, metadiscourse, the achievement of intersubjectivity, deixis and the relation between the visual and the verbal.

Maria Freddi is currently a research assistant at the University of Bologna, where she teaches in the English Language Studies programme of the Faculty of Modern Languages and Literature. She obtained her doctorate with a dissertation on Science and Argumentation. Her publications and research interests focus on the areas of ESP and academic discourse, corpus linguistics, and systemic-functional grammar applied to the teaching of English.

Susan Hunston is Professor of English Language at the University of Birmingham. She specialises in discourse analysis and corpus linguistics and teaches on courses in these subjects at undergraduate and postgraduate level. She is author of *Corpora in Applied Linguistics* (CUP, 2002), co-editor of *Evaluation in Text: Authorial Stance and the Construction of Discourse* (OUP, 2000) and co-author of *Pattern Grammar: A Corpus-driven Approach to the Lexical Grammar of English*. She is particularly interested in the expression of stance or evaluation in all kinds of discourse, but especially in academic prose, and in the use of corpora to describe the lexical grammar of English.

Sylvain Loiseau is a Ph.D. student at the Department of Linguistics, University of Paris X Nanterre, France. His current areas of research include philosophical discourse, discourse analysis and corpus linguistics, and his work aims at combining quantitative and qualitative approaches from a semantic point of view.

David Oakey is a lecturer in English language at the University of Birmingham, UK. He has taught at schools and universities in Japan, Korea, Turkey, and the UK. In 1998 he was awarded an MEd in TESOL by the University of Leeds and in the same year took up a post at the University of Hull, moving to Birmingham in 2001. His research interests include the use of computers to investigate phraseological aspects of written academic English, the relationship between phraseology and metaphor, and the use of the internet for teaching English for Academic Purposes.

Akiko Okamura teaches English at Takasaki City University of Economics, Japan. She was a lecturer in Japanese at University of Newcastle upon Tyne, UK where she obtained her Ph.D. on the roles of culture, science and sub-culture in scientific research articles. Her main interests are in interlanguage pragmatics and use of address forms in cross-cultural communication.

Céline Poudat is a Ph.D. student at the Department of Linguistics, University of Orléans, France. Her current research interests include genre analysis, corpus linguistics, contrastive analysis, quantitative methods and linguistic discourse.

Ute Römer holds a Ph.D. in English linguistics from the University of Hanover, Germany, where she works as a research/teaching assistant in the English Department. She has just published a monograph on the use of progressives in spoken English and 'school' English, *Progressives, Patterns, Pedagogy. A Corpus-driven Approach to Progressive Forms, Functions, Contexts and Didactics* (John Benjamins, 2005) and has written articles on corpus analysis and its applications in linguistics, language teaching, and literary studies. Her most recent research project aims at a systematic investigation of expressions of evaluative meaning in written academic discourse.

John Sinclair was Professor of Modern English Language at the University of Birmingham for most of his career. His education and early work was at the University of Edinburgh, where he began his interest in corpus linguistics, stylistics, grammar and discourse analysis. He now lives in Italy, where he is President of The Tuscan Word Centre. He holds an Honorary Doctorate in Philosophy from the University of Gothenburg, and an Honorary Professorships in the Universities of Jiao Tong, Shangai and Glasgow. He is an Honorary Life Member of the Linguistics Association of Great Britain and a member of the Academia Europæa. He is the Founding Editor-in-Chief of the Cobuild series of language reference materials.

Lorena Suaréz-Tejerina is a Ph.D. candidate at the University of León, Spain, currently holding a grant from the Spanish Ministery of Education and Science. Her fields of study are contrastive rhetoric and discourse analysis. She has done research as a visiting scholar at the Universities of Lancaster, Birmingham, Ann Arbor and IUPUI (Indiana), and has presented several papers related to her Ph.D. thesis, *Modes of Evaluation and Rhetorical Patterns: A Contrastive Study of English and Spanish Book Reviews*. She also teaches English as a second language at the Nursing School of the University of León.

Wolfgang Teubert obtained his D.Phil. from Heidelberg University. For many years he has been senior research fellow at the Institut für Deutsche Sprache in Mannheim, responsible for numerous European projects in the field of multilingual resources and technology. Since 2000, he has been Chair for Corpus Linguistics at the University of Birmingham. His articles deal with theoretical aspects of corpus linguistics, critical discourse analysis, and the hermeutical approach to language studies. He is co-author (together with M. A. K. Halliday, Colin Yallop and Anna Cermakova) of *Lexicology and Corpus Linguistics* (Continuum, 2004), and is also the editor of the *International Journal of Corpus Linguistics*.

Paul Thompson is a lecturer in Applied Linguistics at the University of Reading. His research interests are advanced academic discourse, applications of corpus linguistics and the uses of technology in language teaching. In collaboration with Hilary Nesi, he has developed corpora of spoken and written academic English (the BASE and BAWE corpora) and with Alison Sealey he has researched the potential for using corpora with British primary school children for an evidence-based approach to learning about language.

Index

In the series *Studies in Corpus Linguistics (SCL)* the following titles have been published thus far or are scheduled for publication:

22 SCOTT, Mike and Christopher TRIBBLE: Textual Patterns. Key words and corpus analysis in language education. *Expected April 2006*

21 GAVIOLI, Laura: Exploring Corpora for ESP Learning. xi, 173 pp. + index. *Expected December 2005*

20 MAHLBERG, Michaela: English General Nouns. A corpus theoretical approach. xiii, 199 pp. + index. *Expected December 2005*

19 TOGNINI-BONELLI, Elena and Gabriella DEL LUNGO CAMICIOTTI (eds.): Strategies in Academic Discourse. 2005. xi, 212 pp.

18 RÖMER, Ute: Progressives, Patterns, Pedagogy. A corpus-driven approach to English progressive forms, functions, contexts and didactics. 2005. xiv + 328 pp.

17 ASTON, Guy, Silvia BERNARDINI and Dominic STEWART (eds.): Corpora and Language Learners. 2004. vi, 312 pp.

16 CONNOR, Ulla and Thomas A. UPTON (eds.): Discourse in the Professions. Perspectives from corpus linguistics. 2004. vi, 334 pp.

15 CRESTI, Emanuela and Massimo MONEGLIA (eds.): C-ORAL-ROM. Integrated Reference Corpora for Spoken Romance Languages. 2005. xviii, 304 pp. (incl. DVD).

14 NESSELHAUF, Nadja: Collocations in a Learner Corpus. 2005. xii, 332 pp.

13 LINDQUIST, Hans and Christian MAIR (eds.): Corpus Approaches to Grammaticalization in English. 2004. xiv, 265 pp.

12 SINCLAIR, John McH. (ed.): How to Use Corpora in Language Teaching. 2004. viii, 308 pp.

11 BARNBROOK, Geoff: Defining Language. A local grammar of definition sentences. 2002. xvi, 281 pp.

10 AIJMER, Karin: English Discourse Particles. Evidence from a corpus. 2002. xvi, 299 pp.

9   REPPEN, Randi, Susan M. FITZMAURICE and Douglas BIBER (eds.): Using Corpora to Explore Linguistic Variation. 2002. xii, 275 pp.

8   STENSTRÖM, Anna-Brita, Gisle ANDERSEN and Ingrid Kristine HASUND: Trends in Teenage Talk. Corpus compilation, analysis and findings. 2002. xii, 229 pp.

7   ALTENBERG, Bengt and Sylviane GRANGER (eds.): Lexis in Contrast. Corpus-based approaches. 2002. x, 339 pp.

6   TOGNINI-BONELLI, Elena: Corpus Linguistics at Work. 2001. xii, 224 pp.

5   GHADESSY, Mohsen, Alex HENRY and Robert L. ROSEBERRY (eds.): Small Corpus Studies and ELT. Theory and practice. 2001. xxiv, 420 pp.

4   HUNSTON, Susan and Gill FRANCIS: Pattern Grammar. A corpus-driven approach to the lexical grammar of English. 2000. xiv, 288 pp.

3   BOTLEY, Simon Philip and Tony McENERY (eds.): Corpus-based and Computational Approaches to Discourse Anaphora. 2000. vi, 258 pp.

2   PARTINGTON, Alan: Patterns and Meanings. Using corpora for English language research and teaching. 1998. x, 158 pp.

1   PEARSON, Jennifer: Terms in Context. 1998. xii, 246 pp.